# Journalism: Theory and Practice

# Journalism: Theory and Practice

Kai Hughes

New York

Published by NY Research Press
118-35 Queens Blvd., Suite 400,
Forest Hills, NY 11375, USA
www.nyresearchpress.com

Journalism: Theory and Practice
Kai Hughes

International Standard Book Number: 978-1-63238-828-5 (Hardback)

This book contains information obtained from authentic and highly regarded sources. All chapters are published with permission under the Creative Commons Attribution Share Alike License or equivalent. A wide variety of references are listed. Permissions and sources are indicated; for detailed attributions, please refer to the permissions page. Reasonable efforts have been made to publish reliable data and information, but the authors, editors and publisher cannot assume any responsibility for the validity of all materials or the consequences of their use.

**Trademark Notice:** Registered trademark of products or corporate names are used only for explanation and identification without intent to infringe.

**Cataloging-in-Publication Data**

Journalism : theory and practice / Kai Hughes.
    p. cm.
Includes bibliographical references and index.
ISBN 978-1-63238-828-5
1. Journalism. 2. Journalism--Methodology. 3. Press. I. Hughes, Kai.
PN4731 .J68 2020
070.4--dc23

# Contents

# Preface

The production and distribution of reports on recent events is known as journalism. A few forms of journalism are access journalism, advocacy journalism, broadcast journalism and citizen journalism. Journalistic media include print, television, internet and radio. Journalism can be produced by media organizations or individuals. There are no universal codes of conduct for the journalists, but there are common core elements present in all codes. These elements include remaining objective, being honest and providing the truth. This book is compiled in such a manner, that it will provide in-depth knowledge about the theory and practice of journalism. Its objective is to give a general view of the different areas of this field. Coherent flow of topics, student-friendly language and extensive use of examples make this book an invaluable source of knowledge.

A foreword of all chapters of the book is provided below:

**Chapter 1** - The production as well as distribution of information about recent events is known as journalism. Some of the different types of journalism are photo journalism, convergence journalism, citizen journalism and yellow journalism. The chapter closely examines these diverse types of journalism to provide an extensive understanding of the subject.; **Chapter 2** - The information regarding current events is known as news. The two major types of news are hard news and soft news. This chapter has been carefully written to provide an easy understanding of the varied facets of news such as its elements, its audience and its commercialization.; **Chapter 3** - There are a number of different elements which are used to write news reports such as the 5 Ws, the lede and the nut graf. The chapter closely examines the concepts which are used for writing different types of news such as feature writing, opinion piece and editorials in order to provide an extensive understanding of the subject.; **Chapter 4** - The process of selecting and preparing images, writings and sounds in order to efficiently convey information is known as editing. The diverse aspects of news editing such as principles of editing and the importance of editing have been thoroughly discussed in this chapter.; **Chapter 5** - The process of discovering and selecting the relevant facts as well as weaving them into a comprehensible story is known as news reporting. Some of the different kinds of news reporting are sports reporting, political reporting, crime reporting, investigative reporting and education reporting. The topics elaborated in this chapter will help in gaining a better perspective about the types of news reporting.; **Chapter 6** - The work which is done in a systematic manner for increasing the quantum of knowledge on different topics is known as news research. Some of the key components of news research are determining the focus of the story and verifying the details. The chapter closely examines these major aspects of news research to provide an extensive understanding of the subject.; **Chapter 7** - The process of asking questions and receiving answers is known as interviewing. There are numerous types of interviews such as hard news interview, informational interview, adversarial interview and personal interview. All the diverse principles of these types of interviews have been carefully analyzed in this chapter.; **Chapter 8** - The distribution of video and audio content to a widely dispersed audience through any of the mediums of mass communication is known as broadcasting. Content can be broadcasted over a variety of mediums such as TV, radio and internet. The topics elaborated in this chapter will help in gaining a better perspective about these diverse types of broadcasting.; **Chapter 9** - The ethics of journalism are a bunch of code of ethics which have common elements such as truthfulness, accuracy, objectivity and impartiality. This chapter discusses in detail the theories and concepts related to ethical journalism as well as qualities of a good journalist.

At the end, I would like to thank all the people associated with this book devoting their precious time and providing their valuable contributions to this book. I would also like to express my gratitude to my fellow colleagues who encouraged me throughout the process.

Kai Hughes

# Introduction to Journalism

The production as well as distribution of information about recent events is known as journalism. Some of the different types of journalism are photo journalism, convergence journalism, citizen journalism and yellow journalism. The chapter closely examines these diverse types of journalism to provide an extensive understanding of the subject.

Journalism means writing for newspapers or magazines. It is the communication of information through writing in periodicals and newspapers. The people have an inborn desire to know what's novel or new. This curiosity is satisfied by the journalists through their writing in the newspapers and journals on current affairs and news.

Journalism is the occupation of reporting, writing, editing, photographing or broadcasting news or of conducting any news organization as a business. The word "Journalism" is derived from the word "Journal" which means a daily register or a diary – a book containing each day's business or transactions. This includes newspapers no matter whether they are published daily or weekly. It also means a magazine to whatever section of the audience it caters to.

When a person writes for a newspaper, magazine or a journal (journalist), such writing is called journalism which means communication of information about daily events condensed into a few words, sounds or pictures. We know that man by his nature is curious to know what is going on in the world around him. Journalism satisfies this vital human need by providing him and other members of the public with the relevant and requisite information. While a historian records what happened in the past, a journalist reports on current events and the latest news.

Journalism draws its inspiration from the present. It depicts the situation as it develops. It is the day to day operation of gathering and transmitting news. It affects everyone. It concerns you; me and the society at large. If a journalist delays reporting of news even by a day, nay, even by a few hours it becomes state. It is not like writing a book at your leisure. Journalism, to be effective, has got to be always kept on the move.

The role of a journalist is not confined to merely reporting the news and events. He is also responsible for interpreting and commenting on the news and events. Thus a journalist's main function is to give out "News and Views". The views to be expressed need not be those of his own. He can elicit and report the views of the knowledgeable cross-sections of people.

The Chambers 20th Century dictionary defines journalism as "the profession of conducting or write for public journals". According to the majority of researchers, journalism means "the collection and editing of material of current interest for presentation, publication or broadcast". In other words, journalism means communication of information to the public by any media, be it a newspaper, radio, or T.V. A person engaged in journalism is called a journalist.

The term journalism embraces all the forms in which and through which the news and the comments on the news reach the public. All that happens in the world, if such happenings hold interest for the public and all the thought, action and ideas which these happenings stimulate become the basic material for the journalist."

According to Leslie Stephens, "Journalism consists of writing for pay on matters of which you are ignorant."

Eric Hodgins of Time Magazine defines it as, "Journalism is the conveying of information from here to there with accuracy, insight and dispatch and in such a manner that the truth is served and the rightness of things is made slowly, even if not immediately, more evident".

According to Websters third International Dictionary Journalism define as "The collection and editing of material of current interest for presentation, publication or broadcast".

The word journalism is derived from Journal which means a daily register or a diary. Today the word journal also connotes a newspaper, published every day or even less often or a magazine. Thus Journalism means.the communication of information regarding the events of a day through written words, sounds or pictures. And a journalist is a person who writes for or conducts a newspaper or a magazine. He is also called a press man.

The oldest journalism is connected with periodical journalism. A periodical, is printed at a regular and fixed interval. A periodical can be called a newspaper if it appears at least weekly in recognized newspaper format and has general public interest.

In the modern age, the press is called the "Fourth Estate". It enjoys a very important place in society and plays a very vital role in a democracy.

Journalism, in its wider sense, includes reporting and commentaries delivered on television and radio. Even news events and film documentaries come within the scope of journalism. The editors, and the reporters working for television, radio or film industry claim that when they deal with news and views, they too are as much covered by the term "the Press" as people belonging to the print media. What qualifies a person to be called a journalist is the nature of the function performed by him and not the media for which he is working.

## Principles of Journalism

### Five Core Principles of Journalism

1. Truth and Accuracy: Journalists cannot always guarantee 'truth', but getting the facts right is the cardinal principle of journalism. We should always strive for accuracy, give all the relevant facts we have and ensure that they have been checked. When we cannot corroborate information we should say so.

2. Independence: Journalists must be independent voices; we should not act, formally or informally, on behalf of special interests whether political, corporate or cultural. We should declare to our editors – or the audience – any of our political affiliations, financial arrangements or other personal information that might constitute a conflict of interest.

3 .Fairness and Impartiality: Most stories have at least two sides. While there is no obligation to present every side in every piece, stories should be balanced and add context. Objectivity is not always possible, and may not always be desirable (in the face for example of brutality or inhumanity), but impartial reporting builds trust and confidence.

4. Humanity: Journalists should do no harm. What we publish or broadcast may be hurtful, but we should be aware of the impact of our words and images on the lives of others.

5. Accountability: A sure sign of professionalism and responsible journalism is the ability to hold ourselves accountable. When we commit errors we must correct them and our expressions of regret must be sincere not cynical. We listen to the concerns of our audience. We may not change what readers write or say but we will always provide remedies when we are unfair.

# Role of a Journalist

In the era of distributed media, the relationship between journalist and audience is asymmetrical. As "audience" transmutes to "community," and the level of communication and information increases exponentially, as news becomes less ecclesiastical and more egalitarian, the role of the professional journalist is changing. Fortunately, there is still a role.

Here are six roles the modern journalist should serve:

- The Ethical Role- Yes, journalists get bashed about because of real and imagined lapses in ethics, but the challenge now is to raise the bar on professional ethics, and then provide ethical guidance to today's participatory audience. We should deal more swiftly and transparently with ethical errors within the profession, but we should also provide teaching tools on information ethics, what ethics means and why it's important, and how to spot compromised ethics.

- The Guide/Filter Role- Editors and reporters should assume some responsibility for providing their audiences with pointers to the best stuff on the web, be it the best-reported of the important news or the most interesting and entertaining articles and videos. In a command-and-control environment, we cared only about directing people to what we ourselves did. Now our role is to help audiences sift through the glut of information assaulting them daily by providing pointers. This is the value-add role, and if done right it can help overcome the digital-age tendency for people to focus too narrowly on their own interests. If done well, it will bring more people to your site or publication.

- The Understanding and Context Role- Why should the best bloggers get to have all the fun? The best journalists should become the best bloggers. I know many really, really smart reporters and editors. These people should have blogs, and they should serve readers better by taking the news of the day and putting it in context, combing articles for the tidbits that need to be weaved together to make a bigger whole, and explaining what it all means.

- The Conversation Leader Role- Already, our news reports start a lot of conversations with our without our consent. The conversation-starter role should become explicit in our job descriptions. Once started, we should guide it. We should thank and encourage the good contributors, and depreciate the bad contributors We should highlight the smartest things people say. We should provide our own insights and supplemental knowledge to any conversation we find. We should be full participants, not just the lurking overlords of top-down media.

- The Aggregator Role- We should aggressively gather data related to the communities we serve. We should make sure that anything that is knowable about a community we serve is findable through resources we provide. While in the Guide/Filter Role we might provide pointers, in the Aggregator Role, we make data available and let people find it for themselves. This is a role that serves the long tail of information, because we never know what other individuals might find useful, important or necessary.

- The Straight News Role- We cannot, even if we wanted to, and should not, cede our professional responsibilities to uncover news. We must know about everything important going on in the communities that we serve, and we should strive to be the first to tell our communities about the important news of the moment. We must still be out in our communities gathering facts and organizing them in a way that is relevant and useful and then reporting the most important facts to our communities.

## Photojournalism

Photojournalists bring us the visual images of a story that back up a writer's words. They are there to cover important events, showcase the faces behind the headlines, and they often force us to feel like we are part of the scene.

Photojournalism started to take shape when photographers could easily transport cameras into war zones. For the first time, ordinary citizens could see the impact of the fighting right there in their newspaper. It was a pivotal moment in photography and it became more and more real between the Civil War and World War II.

Yet photojournalism is not just about war or photographers working the beat for a local newspaper. It's much more than that. Photojournalism tells a story and it often does so in a single photograph. Think of the Depression Era photos of Dorothea Lange or those famous photos of Mickey Mantle hitting home runs. They evoke a feeling, whether its astonishment, empathy, sadness, or joy.

That is the mark of photojournalism; to capture that single moment in time and give viewers the sense that they're part of it.

Put simply, photojournalism is about capturing verbs. This doesn't mean simply taking an action photo. Communicating the verb is much more than that. Stories are captured in slices while photojournalism strives to convey what is happening in one shot.

Although it is great when it happens, photojournalism isn't about the best composition, or the best technical details, or a pretty subject. Photojournalism is about showing the world a story of something that really happened. "Bearing witness" is a phrase that comes to mind in regards to photojournalism.

Photojournalism allows the world to see through the eyes of the photographer for just a moment. When photojournalism is done right, that one moment conveys volumes of time. Conveying the full story is part of environmental portraiture where the setting tells us as much about the subject as the subject themselves.

The emotion is often raw in photojournalism. The photographer is not directing the scene as a portrait or commercial photographer would. Instead, the best of them blend into the background and become a shadow figure (unlike the paparazzi). They are there to observe and capture, not become the story or interrupt it.

It is this attitude, the "You are a mere observer" approach that allows the journalist's subjects to not react to the camera, but to be themselves. The photojournalist has a different attitude than other photographers and it's necessary to capture those memorable photos. Quite often, that single photo can become a call to action for the millions of people who see it.

## Ethics in Photojournalism

Another vitally important part of photojournalism is accuracy. This means that what is in the frame is what happened. The photojournalist is ethically bound not to change the story (though many fall short of this ideal).

Power lines should not be cloned out. More smoke must not be added to a fire scene. What was captured is how it should be. Sadly, the era of digital photography has made it easier than ever to manipulate reality.

The image should be a window into the event. At most, lighten the shadows a touch to see faces or sharpen the image a bit for clarity but do not change the essence of what you capture in the photo. If you do, you change the story.

# Convergence Journalism

Convergence Journalism is bringing together multiple forms of media to tell a more effective story. Rather than just reading an article in a newspaper, news consumers read the article online, scroll through a slideshow, click on a video link, and then listen to the related audio.

The Principles of Convergence Journalism are:

1. The public increasingly wants to access quality news and information at any time through any and all media that are convenient or appealing to them.

2. The audience for news and information is less passive than it used to be. Many people, especially younger people, want to create, respond to, and interact with media. This desire has led to emerging "citizen journalists." Fulltime journalists need to accept this power shift and take advantage of the opportunities it presents.

3. Convergence training should not be "a mile wide and an inch deep." Young journalists will not be equally adept at all storytelling styles and skills, but each student will have the

opportunity to focus in on their desired field. Each student can still be effective in their desired field while understanding and taking advantage of changes in the media landscape.

## Citizen Journalism

Citizen journalism is the journalism that is conducted by people who are not professional journalists but who disseminate information using Web sites, blogs, and social media. Citizen journalism has expanded its worldwide influence despite continuing concerns over whether citizen journalists are as reliable as trained professionals. Citizens in disaster zones have provided instant text and visual reporting from the scene. People in countries affected by political upheaval and often in countries where print and broadcast media are controlled by the government have used a variety of technological tools to share information about hot spots. Swirling in the background of these developments was a debate over whether the term *citizen journalism* was itself accurate.

Both the term and the practice crystallized in South Korea, where the online entrepreneur Oh Ye on-declared in 2000 that "every citizen is a reporter." Oh and three South Korean colleagues started an online daily newspaper in 2000 because, he said, they were dissatisfied with the traditional South Korean press. Unable to afford the costs of hiring professionals and printing a newspaper, they started Oh my News, a Web site that used volunteers to generate its content. In a speech on the site's seventh anniversary, Oh, the firm's president and CEO, noted that the news site began with 727 citizen reporters in one country and by 2007 had grown to 50,000 contributors reporting from 100 countries.

Since then the Internet has spawned thousands of news sites and millions of bloggers. Traditional news media, while battling declining readership and viewership, leapt into the fray with their own Web sites and blogs by their own journalists, and many newspapers invited readers to contribute community news to their Web sites. Some groups started their own "hyperlocal" online news sites to cover happenings in their neighbourhoods or specialized topics of interest that were not reported by larger media organizations.

Among those who studied and nurtured citizen journalism, the phenomenon often went by other names. In a 2007 article, editor J.D. Lasica called it "participatory journalism," though he described it as "a slippery creature. Everyone knows what audience participation means, but when does that translate into journalism?" Dan Gillmor, founder and director of the Center for Citizen Media and author of the book *We the Media: Grassroots Journalism by the People, for the People*, also rejected any single definition for the transformation in news that had begun in the late 1990s. He called this era "a time of incredible exploration" because of the democratization of access to inexpensive and ubiquitous publishing tools.

Citizen journalism has played a major role in 21st-century political events. The Web site Twitter established itself as an emerging outlet for the dissemination of information during the protests following the Iranian presidential election in June 2009. Although the protests did not result in a change in the election results or a new election, the tweets of de facto journalists showed the potential of non-traditional media to circumvent government censorship. In Egypt, activists protesting the government of President Ḥosnī Mubārak during the uprising of 2011 often organized themselves by forming groups on the social networking Web site Facebook.

# Yellow Journalism

Yellow journalism is the use of sensational headlines, rather than factual news, to capture a reader's attention. The hope is that the reader will choose one publication over its competitor. Examples of yellow journalism can be found next to any grocery store's checkout line, with tabloids that boast about "shocking" celebrity news, or the "confirmation" of alien life forms. Modern yellow journalism runs rampant through the internet, daring people to click on scandalous stories, or shocking headlines.

Newspapers were the original source of news, informing people of the goings-on long before radio and television were invented. In order to be successful in business, newspaper publishers began employing new methods to attract readers. This was the start of yellow journalism in the late 1800s, as publishers saw an opportunity to increase their revenue. The question became how they would make their newspapers stand out from the competition.

That's where yellow journalism came in. In the 1890s, newspaper owners William Randolph Hearst (*New York Journal*) and Joseph Pulitzer (*New York World*) came up with the idea to sell their papers using exaggeration, melodrama, and even romance. This style eventually became known as "yellow journalism." Hearst and Pulitzer would exaggerate true events, and fabricate events that had never even happened, just to sell more newspapers. The main goal was to grab the reader's attention, whether or not the details being published were actually true.

In modern times, yellow journalism can be found in grocery store tabloids and news headlines. Typically, if a headline contains an exclamation point, complete with words like "shocking," "unbelievable," or "astounding," then the paper is probably engaging in yellow journalism. One of the most popular tabloids in the United States – *The National Enquirer* – is famous for its use of yellow journalism. Those running the tabloid have been sued several times for their publishing of "facts" pertaining to celebrities that were not, in fact, true, and which were potentially damaging to the celebrity's reputation (slander).

Today, the term "yellow journalism" is used negatively to describe any journalistic style that treats real news either unprofessionally or unethically. or that puts forth information as true, which has no basis in fact. Examples of yellow journalism stories that would be treated in such a way are those that are either scare-mongering or scandal-mongering. The late American historian and journalist Frank Luther Mott said that examples of yellow journalism can essentially be defined by the following traits:

- "Scare" headlines printed in large type, despite the news story itself being minor.

- Generous usage of photos or drawings to accompany the story.

- The writer being overly sympathetic with the "underdog" in the story and overly against "The Man" (the system).

- Using fabricated interviews, deceptive headlines, pseudoscience, and/or false information from so-called "experts" to pad out a story.

Mott also noted that papers would place particular emphasis on the supplements included with the

Sunday edition of each newspaper, including the "funny pages," to sell that particular paper, rather than the substance of its news stories.

## Clickbait

Clickbait is the modern version of yellow journalism. The term "clickbait" is a negative one that describes web content that is only concerned with generating revenue from advertisements. Clickbait overpromises, or misrepresents what it is going to deliver, simply to get people to click on the articles. For instance, it is not uncommon for a click bait article to be paired up with a shocking image that has absolutely nothing to do with that article. The sole purpose of that image is to make people interested enough to click the link. Once readers have followed the link, they will find some non-substantive or even completely false article that is surrounded by, and teeming with, advertisements.

Clickbait articles are famous for using phrases such as "What happens next will shock you!" or "You won't believe what happened when she." Of course, the article does not tell the reader what happened. The headline is meant to spark the reader's curiosity so strongly that he simply must click the link in order to find out what happens next. The sites benefit because the more page views they receive, and the more unique visitors stop by their site, the more advertisers will pay to post ads on their pages. The sites then receive a kick-back from the money that they earn for their advertisers.

The articles themselves are usually not concerned with being wholesome or accurate. Instead, they rely on sensationalist headlines the same way newspapers do. An eye-grabbing thumbnail is usually paired up with the headline to encourage the reader to click on the link, and readers are strongly encouraged to share these articles via their social media networks, such as Facebook or Twitter.

Clickbait headlines are meant to exploit what is known as the "curiosity gap." They are intended to give the reader a quick taste of information to grab their curiosity without providing too much information at once. This is to *bait* the readers, making them want to read more, and to click through to the linked content.

Websites famous for using clickbait in order to get readers to click through to their content include Buzzfeed, ViralNova, and Upworthy. Famous satirical newspaper *The Onion* parodies these kinds of outlets with their own website, *Clickhole*. Ironically, Clickhole has seen significant success due to the fact that the headlines it posts can actually pass for clickbait themselves, encouraging their readers to read more. Facebook announced in 2014 that it was actively taking measures to reduce the number of clickbait articles that show up in users' newsfeeds.

Similarly, websites such as *Huffington Post*, *Salon*, and the late Gawker Media blog have profited from engaging in a practice that current affairs magazine *Slate* describes as an "aggregation of outrage." What this means is that these websites post articles that pair emotional content with blunt headlines to make readers want to read and share them. These pieces are short and simple, offering quick judgments on issues related to politics and culture, rather than in-depth articles that would earn them more respect as journalists.

# Tabloid Journalism

Tabloid journalism is a type of popular, largely sensationalistic journalism that takes its name from the format of a small newspaper, roughly half the size of an ordinary broadsheet. Tabloid journalism is not, however, found only in newspapers, and not every newspaper that is printed in tabloid format is a tabloid in content and style. Notably, many free local publications historically have been printed in tabloid format, and in the early 21st century several traditional British broadsheet newspapers, such as *The Independent*, *The Times*, and *The Scotsman*, changed to the smaller size, preferring, however, to call it "compact" format. On the other hand, one of the most-popular tabloids in Europe, the German *Bild-Zeitung*, was long printed as a broadsheet before shifting, as did many German newspapers, to a format that was smaller than a broadsheet but bigger than the standard tabloid.

The origins of the term tabloid are disputed. According to the most-plausible explanation, the name derives from tablet, the product of compressed pharmaceuticals. Tabloid—a combination of tablet and alkaloid—was a trademark for tablets introduced by Burroughs. Within a couple of years, the connotation of being compressed was transferred to other entities and activities, including a new kind of reporting that condensed stories into a simplified, concentrated style.

## References

- Journalism-meaning-definition-and-scope-of-journalism, journalism-mass-communication: studylecturenotes.com, Retrieved 22 February, 2019

- 5-principles-of-journalism, who-we-are: ethicaljournalismnetwork.org, Retrieved 5 April, 2019

- Six-roles-or-job-duties-modern-journalism: howardowens.com, Retrieved 14 June, 2019

- An-introduction-to-photojournalism-2688644: thesprucecrafts.com, Retrieved 4 August, 2019

- Why-does-convergence-journalism-make-story-more-powerful-16340: pulitzercenter.org, Retrieved 2 January, 2019

- Citizen-journalism: britannica.com, Retrieved 23 May, 2019

- Yellow-journalism: legaldictionary.net, Retrieved 3 July, 2019

- Tabloid-journalism: britannica.com, Retrieved 13 March, 2019

# 2

# Types and Elements of News

The information regarding current events is known as news. The two major types of news are hard news and soft news. This chapter has been carefully written to provide an easy understanding of the varied facets of news such as its elements, its audience and its commercialization.

News is an unpublished account of human activity, which seeks to interest, inform, or educate the readers. The first requirement of news is that a writing should not have been published anywhere before. It should come to the readers to the first time. It is like a hot cake coming straight from the over. Anything, which has come in print before, does not constitute news. It may be anything but not news. The second ingredient is human activity. News must relate in one way or the other to the human activity. Human beings must be involved in an event embodied in news. The Third important factor is that it should be of some interest to the readers. The interest may be physical or emotional. The fourth important pre-requisite is that it should be designed to impart some sort of information to the readers.

The information may be in respect of the reader's interest in specific fields. The best ingredient is that it should be of some education value for readers. The readers ought to be of the progress of the country and making in the specific fields. The countrymen have the right to know as to how strangers their country is. It is for the readers of the country. A news is tomorrows history done up in to-days meal package. News is the flow of tides of human aspirations, the ignominy of mankind and the glory of human race. It is the best record of the incredible meanness and the magnificent coverage of man. The news is current information made available to public about what is going on. It enables the people to make up their minds as what to think and how to act.

News is a truly, concise and accurate report of the event. A news is the report of an event and what an event itself. News means the record of the event that has taken place in a particular era. The significant element of news is that it is an event in which some kind of action takes place. It is a report in which the action is described narrated, highlighted or recorded. News is written in a comprehensive manner. There should be one audience or a class of readership. To whom the description is to be presented in print or on the air or on T.V. or movie screen. News should provoke into recipients or at least some of them to thought or action.

- Oxford Dictionary defines it as "New information, the report of latest incident".

- According to Gerald W. Johnson, "News is the report of such incidents as in writing them, a first rank journalist feels satisfied".

- According to William F. Brook, "News is in fact a synonym of the unexpected."

- According to William Stead, "Everything which is extra-ordinary and unusual is called news".

- According to Carrel Warren, "news is usually a report which is not known to layman before its presentation. This report deals with such activities of man as are a source of interest, entertainment or information to the readers.

- British Journal defines the news as, "any event, idea or opinion that is timely, that interests or affects a large number of people in a community and that is capable of being understood by them".

## Examples

A guide to advanced techniques in journalism brought out by the Editorial Study Centre of the Thompson Foundations has enumerated 20 categories of what makes news. These are "Novelty, Personal impact, Local news, Money, Crime, Sex, Conflict, Religion, Disaster and Tragedy. Humour, Human interest, the Under-dog, Mystery, Health, Science, Entertainment, Famous people, Weather, Food, and Minorities".

A few examples of what makes news are given below:

- "Man bites dog". (Novelty);
- "Pay body recommends raise in pay of Federal Government employees" (Personal Impact);
- "A motorcyclist run over by a Niazi Bus Service near Anarkali, Lahore" (Local News);
- "Prices of T.V., Refrigerator and Cigarettes raised in Federal Budget" (Money);
- "100 persons died in the air crash" (Tragedy).

It is due to the fact that a journalist reports an incident in the same way as he sees it. Although it is possible that a particular journalist gives a dramatic touch to an incident while the others do not. But the original and genuine facts of the happenings are not to be changed at any rate.

## Characteristics of News

The important characteristics of news are-

- Accuracy
- Balance
- Objectivity
- Concise and Clear
- Current and freshness.

## Types of News

Hard news and soft news are considered the two major types of news stories available. Up-to-the-minute news and events that require immediate reporting are considered hard while features and news that is considered background information or human-interest are thought of as soft news.

Subject matter that is usually considered hard news includes: Politics, war, economics, and crime. On the flip side, the arts, entertainment and lifestyle stories are considered to be soft news in nature.

## Hard News

Hard news is a term most often used by journalists and others who work in the media industry, though you may hear others outside the industry use the term. Hard news is the kind of fast-paced news that usually appears on the front page of newspapers. Stories that fall under the umbrella of hard news often deal with topics like business, politics and international news.

What defines hard news isn't always about the subject matter. Some might call a news story hard news because it is heavily reported—even though it is a subject matter considered softer (like entertainment). It is possible to see news features that may be considered both hard and soft, such as a story about the business dealings and private life of a successful media mogul, leaving some to wonder if it is a business or a lifestyle story. Or possibly a story on major style or renovation trends affecting the sale and cost of homes in a booming housing market which again, is a blend of lifestyle and business.

## Soft News

The major difference between hard and soft news is the tone in which the story is presented. Hard news usually takes on a factual approach that explains what happened, who the main people involved were and where and when everything happened and why.

Soft news stories can be presented in a variety of ways, but they usually try to entertain or advise the reader in some way. Lenticels, like "Top 10 Ways to Stretch After a Run to Ease Lactic Acid," are considered soft news, as are more in-depth entertainment features, such as the lives and scandals of famous politicians.

It is important to note that even though some stories may be considered hard news in style, they may use a soft lead-in to capture the reader's interest (and heart).

In general, soft news requires a different approach to lead writing and are often called delayed leads because they start telling a story before getting to the main facts. Soft-news lead-ins tend to be narrative or anecdotal in nature, where they tell a story instead of stating important facts.

Feature stories (soft stories that are a little longer and more reflective) often use soft lead-ins and use more descriptive and colorful language before probing further. Such stories begin with setting the tone and introducing the reader to the atmosphere surrounding the story, before jumping into the who, what, when, where and whys. The story may then be finished up with a conclusion such as those of more traditional structures of storytelling.

## Elements of News

News is a piece of information about an event that would be a matter of interest for a large number of readers. History never actually repeats, but it does seem to repeat tendencies. Similarly, news stories never duplicate each other, but they do have a way of falling into definite categories.

Analyzing them as we read them from day to day or listen to them as they come over through difference source of news like radio, TV or newspaper. We can easily distinguish elements of news interest which recur constantly. Sometimes a news story will contain several of these interest provoking news elements but sometimes one.

There are nine elements of news which enhance the news value:

## Immediacy

Immediacy or timeliness is an important requisite of news. A reporter usually places emphasis on the latest angles of, an event. The words 'today' and 'tomorrow' are related in most of the news stories. Occasionally a story may concern events that happened in the past. In this case, the reporter discusses some present aspect of a past event.

## Proximity

Proximity or nearness refers to geographic nearness. Normally a reader is more interested in an event geographically nearer than the one which has taken place in some remote part of the world.

## Consequences

A reporter should emphasize the angle of a story that will interest most readers, listeners or viewers in terms of consequences.

## Prominence

Prominence means persons, places, things and situations known to the public for their weather, social position, achievement or previous publicity. The reporter should always add as many prominent names and places in news stories, as possible. The more renowned a particular name, place event or situation, the more interest the news will create among its readers.

## Drama

It also promotes the value of a news story. A reporter always tries to find picturesque background and dramatic action for his news.

## Oddity

Oddity or queerness always helps to make facts interesting. The greater the degree of oddity in a story, the greater is its value as news.

## Conflict

It is one of the most important of news elements. It is inherent in nearly all news of sports, war, crime, violence and internal disputes and in all stories involving difference of opinion. Generally, the news of conflict also involves other news values as drama and oddity and therefore, has an emotional impact, a factor that appeals to many people. Many types of stories have conflict as their underlying element the struggle against odd.

Here are some of these types:

1. Man's struggle with nature;

2. Struggle between individual and organized society;

3. Struggle between political and economic groups i.e. wars, campaigns, strikes.

## Sex

It is an integral part of human life. Sex is a vital news element in stories of romance, marriage, divorce and other illicit relationships among members of opposite sexes as readers want their emotions stirred.

## Progress

It involves any significant change for the betterment of humanity. It may also refer to an achievement in the laboratory, industry or a legislative body etc.

A number of factors modify the importance of news elements in actual practice; the policy of a news medium may increase or decrease the importance of a story. The class of readers, listeners and viewers that dominate the audience of a paper, radio or television determines largely what is going to be presented. The amount of space available to a paper or the amount of time available on radio or television determines whether a story is to be told briefly or in detail. Time often alters the value of a story and finally the previous presentation of a story, on any medium, changes its value.

## Commercialization of News

"With TV, the viewer is the screen," said Marshall McLuhan. This symbolizes the power of the television medium which has increased drastically in recent years. With the advent of the age of information, television has become the most potent player in the world of popular culture and has acquired tremendous power in shaping views and influencing every sphere of life. With the drastic increase in the number of television channels and globalization of media, people are being exposed to all king of media programming. Some of these programmes have a strong inherent as well as imposed entertainment dimension, which has not been perceived in conformity with our culture, values and ethos. This trend is reflected in a kind of synchronisation of programming where form is expanding and content is shrinking. The entertainment component of media programming is expanding rapidly to achieve optimum commercial benefit. This trend is becoming dominant obviously at the cost of the public sphere.

Market forces have become an effective instrument in shaping the media content. With the emergence of liberal regimes in the wake of information revolution in the media sector, market requirements and people's taste' as perceived by the producers are playing greater role in determining form and content of media programming. Various channels are opting for more commercially profitable programmes. The market competition to capture prime time slots is getting intense day by day. Satellite television received through cable connection has established a dominant position in urban areas. According to some recent market research, some of the privately owned satellite television channels have left Doordarshan far behind in terms of viewership among additional purchasing power segment of the society which is the key to get advertisements, sponsorship and generate resources to run this high priced medium. The process of globalisation in the field of media and culture is much faster as compared to the political and economic sectors. With the advent of new communication technologies, the global flow of information and media programming has become in stantaneous.

Amidst these processes a new media has emerged which is highly urban-centric and does not at all intend to cater to the information needs of wider sections of society. One of the glaring examples of this phenomenon is the Star Plus programme " Kaun Banega Crorepati" which is said to have stolen the thunder of all other television channels at the super prime time slot of 9.00 p.m. Now the other television channels are bound to offer superior "popular" programmes in competition and are not going to surrender meekly this super prime time slot. Because of fierce market competition, various channels are entering onto the market with highly popular (rather populist) programmes. The first casualty of the inherent tendency of free market to opt for more commercially viable media programming has been healthy entertainment. It has curbed the diversity of human interests and has almost marginalised the public sphere and obviously the public broadcasting. Blatant commercialization has shown little patience with novel voices and fresh visions. The wide range of human interests as reflected in the culture and traditions is not finding adequate expression in the new and emerging media.

The question obviously arises where to put the line separating the public and private. Recently the public sphere of media has come in sharp focus because of its blatant commercialisation. The concept of public sphere is now recognised as an important category for looking at issues of the media, politics and society. It casts light on the structural conditions determining the formation of public opinion through public debate as well as on the relationship between public opinion on the one hand and public policy formation and its execution on the other. Despite differences in views, the public sphere has been defined in relation to the impact and consequences of media in relation to a specific social and cultural setting. The nature of "globalised media" is amply reflected in the form of its negative implications that have already started pouring in. Its "non-globalised" nature is coming in sharp focus in the form of cultural domination of the west which have only facilitated intensification of one way traffic of various kinds of cultural products.

At this juncture of development of communication, the future is blurred. Total clarity on the issue will be too utopian to expect but as of now even a pragmatic vision seems missing. Can the various cultures which exist on our planet with their numerous shades co-exist in any healthy manner? Rather, one way information onslaught has become a problem which should be tackled immediately at least for a large number of developing societies. Prof Nicholas Garnham contended in a recently published article over the issue of line of demarcation between public and private that "the distinction operates normatively as well as descriptively. The conceptualisation of the boundary between the public and the private has shifted historically and it should be examined how the boundary has been mobilised to exclude both topics for debate and action, and social actors from legitimate participation in the public realm. The key argument here is that we can only clarify what the protagonists are actually talking about if we go behind this apparently simple distinction and begin to unpack the range of meanings, both descriptive and normative, that these terms mobilise and the thoughts and associated problems, from which those different meanings are drawn. In particular, in current debates about the media the concepts of public, and private as it's opposite, are mobilised in three ways. First, around the concept of the public sphere within a general institutional debate about the practice of democratic politics in general. Second, in a debate about the content and practice of the mass media, which focuses on issues of privacy. Third, in debates about media regulation which in the face of technological convergence and the growth of the Internet, turn on the distinction between the rights and obligations attaching to public and private communication respectively. In each case two issues are at stake. Where to draw the boundary between the public and private both generally and within specific spheres of social action, which in its turn depends upon how we choose to distinguish the public from the private? And the extent of relative normative valuation to attach to each sphere- that is to say, do we regard, for instance, the private as a sphere to be protected against the encroachment and domination of the public or on the contrary do we regard the public as a sphere of superior shared social values to be fostered at the expense of selfish, corrupting private interests. Because both the boundaries and the relative evaluations are in fact mobilized both for intellectual analysis and political debate in shifting, confused and often matually contradictory ways, it is necessary to unpack the roots of these distinctions and evaluations to clarify their entailments. One of its salient dimensions equally open to the access of all public sphere is citizens.

Another important dimension is for whom and for what purpose standards of public sphere are being defined? The process of formation of public opinion in any society is largely governed by these standards in context of the role of media. Debates over the evaluation of the political implications of talk shows, or other kind of current affairs programmes, has in part turned on the difference between those who stress the populist and emotive nature of discourse as dangerously anti-democratic and anti-social. The primary challenge is how to enlarge the reach of the media to those social segments which are denied legitimate information needs. The media gives rise to cultural incapacities which in turn create barriers to full and effective access to the public sphere and maximally can lead to the elitist defence of rule by experts."

While regulation of the network was considered legitimate, any regulation of the messages passing over the network was and is regarded as in illegitimate infringement of individual freedom, autonomy and privacy. Again, the infringement of the right to free speech cannot be detached from the overall environment in which communication media operate. The thinking on the subject has been influenced by standards set by the Western society without much attention being paid to the specific situations in the developing countries. This kind of standardization is irrational and non-pragmatic. The Internet has created an entirely new communication environment and some of the issues posed by the new situation demand immediate attention. The Internet has created new versions that are going to bring about fundamental changes in communication and media scenario. But in terms of accessibility, it remains highly uneven and does not give developing societies any chance to take a long leap forward and stand on their own in the face of powerful Western media giants. In the new environment, new type of conflicts is bound to occur. For instance, websites on the Internet do have the individual addressability and the nature of communication on the sites does facilitate a series of private individual transactions of the market mould because of its general accessibility. But despite Internet being a tool of public communication, its rights and responsibilities are associated only with those who control and use it. The control and use of new technologies require different set of regulatory mechanisms in differing political, economic, social, and cultural environment. The view that is taken on the issue will make a difference to the normative evaluations of the activity and any resulting regulatory policy that might be enacted. This is an issue which has to be dealt within the national domain. Regulatory mechanism has to be evolved for globalised media within the parameters of national interests. This has been the pattern all over the world and we are no exception to it.

## Alternative Concepts

In the existing media market situation, private interests dominate over the public ones. The situation we are confronted by today cannot be left to the market forces alone. The term public and private and the differential valuations applied to each in different situations register deep unease over the conceptual difficulties that arise from this set of distinctions. These distinctions were developed as a result of complex conceptual, difficulties cultural and political history. They exist within the sphere created by history and are operative within those parameters. The market is set up as a threat to the public sphere the way in which the market and public sphere maps onto the public and private divide. The existing dominant global media systems are colonizing the life world and thus destroying the space of the public sphere. The public sphere is distinguished from the private sphere of the market on the grounds that individuals pursue their private, competitive interests in the market, whereas in the public sphere their actions are oriented to reaching uncovered agreement on the common good or public interest. The public sphere as perceived before the advent of the present information revolution has under gone a radical change in relation to the dimensions of the issues being debated today.

The market, which was considered in the field of media till now, challenge to protect and nurture the public sphere out of the shadow of the market. It is in this background that market is considered as a threat to public sphere but at the same time it would be irrational to segments the media in terms of public and commercial sphere. There is a lot of common but largely undefined areas between the two and elements of being public and commercial are primarily a difference of degrees. In recent past this difference has widened a lot that generated the debate on the erosion of public sphere of the media. With the introduction of new technologies and domination of commercial interests, media's role as means of expression of public thoughts is shrinking and more constraints are developing in the way of free and fair interaction between the media and the public. In most of the developing countries inadequate research and database also often prove a handicap for media, even if it is prepared to experiment and create some space for alternative concepts of programming. This is a reason because of which national media is attempting to be a carbon copy of dominant media concepts of globalised media control by the West. Despite the intense debate on the issue of public broadcasting, the developing countries tend to follow the developed world and are not trying for any kind of leap-frogging. But graphic imagery of public broadcasting has undergone a change in the new situation and some substantial steps are expected in the near future-but nothing can be predicted in relation to the impact and consequences of the scenario which is yet to be unfolded fully.

In highly developed societies public broadcasting has been staging a comeback and its space in media set up has been increasing. The main reason for public broadcasting coming out of hibernation has been the very nature of media programming people in developed societies were subjected to. In the United States (being cited because it is a highly developed information society), there are several studies that look at the long term effects of violence on television.

Television can be a powerful influence in developing value systems and behaviour. Unfortunately, much of today's television programming is violent. Several studies have found that children may become 'immune' to the horror of violence, imitate the violence they observe on television, and identify with certain characters. However, this does not mean that violence on television is the only source for aggressive or violent behaviour, but it is a significant contributor. According to one estimate, by the age of 18 a youngster in the United States will have seen 200,000 acts of violence on television. Some studies indicate that children who watched a lot of TV violence at 8 years of age of 30, including hitting their own children. In America, children watch an average of three to four hours of television daily. The American Academy of Paediatrics suggests children watch no more than two hours of television a day. Even in that recommended time frame, they will have witnessed 8, 000 murders and more than 100,000 other acts of violence by the time they finish elementary school.

Another study undertaken in the United States, titled The National Television Violence Study, discovered that 47 per cent of the violent acts shown resulted in no observable harm to the victim, only 16 per cent of violent shows contained a message about the long term negative repercussions of violence. On television, perpetrators go unpunished in 73 per cent of all violent scenes and only 4 per cent of violent programmes emphasise an ant violent theme. The study found 44 per cent of the shows on network stations contained at least some violence, compared with 59 per cent on basic cable and 85 per cent on premium channels like HBO and Show Time. According to a survey conducted by US News and the University of California Los Angeles with many top-level Hollywood figures, 63 per cent of the Hollywood Elite say the industry glorifies violence. That is because violence is an effective promotional device. There are logical reasons why so many promotions feature scenes of violence. Promos have only a very short time to show something interesting enough to attract the viewer. Most promos contain several scenes thus complicating efforts to explain the plot in 10 or 20 seconds. With so little time, the easiest things to feature are those that requires little time, the easiest things to feature are those that requires little explanation: violence and sex.

## Intensification in the Flow of Images

In our country also a trend is emerging in advertising which glorifies some kind of violence. Recently a number of advertisements have appeared on various television channels showing certain amount of violence, some daring actions and a certain amount of defiance for the rules, especially in the promos of automobiles. A recent study by the National Council of Educational Research and Training has documented growing aggressive behavioural tendencies among children as a result of viewing certain programmes laden with violence, aggression and jealousy. Commenting on the subject Mr Krishna Kumar argues in his article published in the Hindustan Times that," cinema and television have made a substantial contribution to the creation of an unkind, volatile ethos. Bombay films have glamorised certain kinds of violence, certain other kinds of violence they have trivialised. Television has enabled cinema to reach our living spaces, making horror and brutality a homely affair, Watching scenes of cold blooded murder and rape since an early age allows children to develop a kind of derangement which hinders them from coping with the deep anxieties they carry. Why has the Indian State been so easy on the violence depicted in cinema and television? One answer is that it could not cope with the speed at which these media grew. Regulation of the media has proved far too complex for the bureaucracy to handle. The Prasar Bharati initiative was not allowed to work either. Vested interests of both the State and the market wanted it to fail. With

Hollywood cinema determined to appear in Indian languages, we can only expect greater intensity dictum-'if it bleeds, it leads."

But can the steady flow of images watched nightly from television screens across the country be dismissed as simply entertainment? If the sheer volume of absorbed images is considered, how can what is shown on television have no effect on one's own mental images? And if new mental images are created, shouldn't it be logical to say that they can have an effect on behaviour? Each year children read less and less watch more and more television. In fact, people spending more time watching television is increasing and with much faster speed in a country like ours. Watching TV is a passive event. The audience remains completely immobile while viewing the box. Most viewing experiences are both quiet and non-interactive. All attention is given to the images. In order to receive stimulation from the television, the audience must be passive, and accept the predetermined flow rate of the images. The picture on the TV changes every five or six seconds through using various production techniques that are getting more sophisticated day by day. One researcher refers to these events as jolts per minute, noting that as time is cut up, the brain is conditioned to change at the expense of continuity of thought. Adults and children are conditioned to instant gratification and crisis at many levels. Children absorb millions of images from the television just watching it for one session. And what are they watching? With ever-growing number of channels, the choices are expanding. There is much more to watch! Sky is not the limit.

People in developed countries have developed a feeling of frustration over the excessive entertainment loaded with violence and sex. Some 80 per cent of Americans feel that TV violence is harmful to the society and that there is too much of it in their entertainment, according to a study. In several developed countries the situation is heading in a different direction. People are showing more maturity in understanding images bombarded by media as compared to initial phase of the development of new media of information age. In some developed countries public broadcasting stations are presenting provocative public affairs programmes about the vital issues of the day. It is being realized that television can provide high quality public programmes.

An American research project was conducted on the documentary programmes about topics such as nature, history, science, and biography and included focus groups with documentary viewers in Los Angeles, Baltimore, and Portland, Oregon. To stimulate discussion, viewers were shown a series of clips from a variety of documentary programmes. Viewers were able to rate the programmes. The first significant finding from this research is that it is difficult to separate the issue of quality from the programme topic. When asked if the would prefer seeing a programme on a topic of high interest with low quality versus a programme of high quality on a topic of low interest, viewers overwhelmingly chose the high interest topic over quality. Topics that held the highest interest for viewers in order of importance were the following: Nature, Biographies, Medicine, Science, History, Movie Making, Archaeology, and Military. Viewers also expressed an interest in seeing programmes that were timely and new. Viewers generally favoured a strong topic with weak production over a weak topic with strong production. Findings of the survey reveal a clear edge of quality "public" programmes over "pure" entertainment. In a culturally diverse country like ours there is a lot to offer in documentary formats to attract audience and encourage inter-cultural understanding and make television more informative and educational in context of our national perspective without compromising the medium's inherent entertainment dimension. The real challenge is to produce informational and educational programmes of entertainment quality.

Public broadcasting in a developing and diverse society like ours is dominantly targeted at the underprivileged sections of society, which are vital to all our programmes of national development. These sections are information-poor and have to be familiarized with a wide range of issues, such as new government policies and programmes for development, literacy, health education etc. One of the biggest challenges the development programmes have been facing right from the independence has been total lack of information among those people at whom they were targeted. The lack of awareness on the part of the masses has been exploited by the corrupt sections of government machinery to scuttle several development programmes. Media with the help of new technologies can spread awareness about development programmes of the government. The application of new technologies in this direction will make people more demanding towards the implementation machinery and can facilitate development of effective feedback mechanism and better monitoring of implementation of various programmes by the political leadership. An in formed citizenry is the best guarantee to ensure better implementation of all development programmes. All these objectives can be achieved only through public broadcasting. This sector needs more attention specially keeping in view the massive expansion of information and communication sectors. At present these sectors are dominantly governed by the commercial considerations resulting in proliferation of media with little relevant content in relation to information needs for national development.

## Market Pressure

In a developing society like ours an analysis of products of television cannot be carried out exclusively from a study of audience shares among additional purchasing power segments of the society. Rather there is an urgent need to increase the actual reach of media to the people who are not part of the 'market,' and commercially are not a viable proposition. In any given social system and its institutions, it is imperative to understand the process behind the selection of media programmes. The process generates what the market requires. The so called market forces ignore those segments of society which are outside its defined parameters of any kind of media activity. This process is not limited to an in-depth study of each of the phase of television production, but also takes into account the evolution of external contents – political situation, cultural situation, of communications media and the dynamics of the media market. Representation of the public sphere has declined drastically during the recent years – the period of boom in media and information technology. There is an urgent need to understand what is implied by these concepts within the ambit of the communication media. The television programmes can work as spaces where society discusses its objectives and their significance. If this be so, the issue is to see how and in what way it can be achieved within the canvas of production of the audio visual world, finding ways to resolve the contradictions that are implied when making television products conditioned by communication policies close to their respective target groups while at the same time, making productions which are competitive in the audio-visual market. The contradictions of communication systems are being sharply defined on the issue of granting a high degree of autonomy in the editorial field, but with strong financial and structural dependence on the industry. This kind of autonomy by its inherent nature is bound to be hijacked by commercial considerations. Television tends to give higher priority to market pressures and economic factors than to cultural aspects; and more so in the situation the country is facing today. The process of reconciling them is difficult and often incompatible and this leads to a lopsided development of the media that we are witnessing today.

This becomes clear in the tendency of the programmes to take up popular, rather populist, issues that guarantee an audience, choosing participants for their ability to express themselves lucidly or for their extraordinary personal experience. Media industries in our situation cannot be left totally at the mercy of the market forces and certain regulations have to be enacted to ensure a certain semblance of order.

A series of steps have been taken in recent past in this direction, which are reflected in the forms of various regulations enacted and some other under consideration. The fierce competition between networks encourages programmes with a wide audience appeal, and which are far from assuming commitments in context of public sphere of media. This kind of situation, created by market forces is a most difficult challenge to meet for Doordarshan keeping in view its status of the national public broadcaster. This status of Doordarshan does not allow it to enter the market thought it has been making half-hearted attempts now and then. But such attempts have led it to a "neither here nor there situation." The national broadcaster should not panic in the face of ups and downs of a volatile market but win a loyal viewership by the sheer force of informational, educational and healthy entertainment value of its programming.

## Lost Opportunity and New Efforts

The biggest challenge before the national broadcaster is to carve out a significant place for itself in the emerging media market and to strike a balance between the public sphere and the ever-changing concept of entertainment. Privately owned television channels do not face this kind of situation, as there is greater amount of clarity in context of their" market projections". They can allow themselves to be governed solely by market forces and the dominant and saleable concept of entertainment even to the extent of their programmes being addressed to the Lowest common Denominator. Doordarshan is handicapped by the lack of alternative media concepts and this responsibility should be shared by professionals in the field of art, literature, culture, cinema and other creative areas. The national broadcaster can only be expected to be a bit more sensitive on the subject which, tragically it was not when it was required the most during the initial phase of globalisation of media and when international media players were entering the Indian market. At that point of time, Doordarshan was commanding a monopoly in the sky. Though in the initial phase consumers were bound to incline favourably to wards new channels, Doordarshan failed to present its distinct character and kept on trying to follow the new entrants and thus entered into the market war zone of the choice of the commercial outfits. Even today there are moments when people get fed up of the excessive entertainment programmes but alternatives are not there to meet the demand.

Efforts are being made to position the National Public Broadcaster in relation to market situation in a way that it is able to discharge its social responsibilities. An extensive exercise is already underway to chalk out a two pronged strategy for the Public Broadcaster. The premise of this new strategy is to cater to information and entertainment needs of all sections of our society through broadcast of various kinds of programmes through different channels of Doordarshan. This strategy is targeted at striking a right kind of balance vis-à-vis its role as public broadcaster and at the same time not lose out ground to commercial channels in the fast expanding market of entertainment. The Public Broadcaster can do this job even by providing healthy entertainment programmes that are capable of commanding loyalty of viewers and capable of generating revenue. It can very well be achieved even without joining the rat race in the media market which keeps on surfacing now and then with much lesser loyalty factor. The new strategy and vision is amply reflected in the report of the Review Committee on the Working of Prasar Bharati and another bill that is in the drafting stage- the Information, Entertainment and Education Bill and some other bills aimed at evolving a regulatory mechanism. The Review Committee has placed the entire question in the right perspective as it pointed out "as a public broadcaster, advertising revenue should not be the only yardstick for judging the performance of Prasar Bharati. Alternative indices-related to audience size and share, programme content and impact, channel reach and loyalty-are more meaningful and must be used. Once the vision and framework of Prasar Bharati are clearly defined, then, within these, revenue maximisation should be an important goal. Through this recommendation the committee has placed the broad objective of the Prasar Bharati, with its constituents-Doordarshan and the all India Radio-in the national perspective and a certain amount of clarity has emerged regarding how the Public Broadcaster is going to face the challenges of the market while at the same time discharging its social responsibilities. The mission of Prasar Bharati as defined and articulated by the committee further clarifies the following point –"Prasar Bharati will aim to provide, in the most efficient manner possible, media content of the highest quality that will empower and enlighten the citizens of India, and audiences outside the country, through original and relevant programmes which inform, educate and entertain whilst ensuring a sizeable audience and reach."

The hype created by certain kind of television and other media programming has proved to be short-lived on numerous occasions. In the ultimate analysis it is going to be the content and quality of media programming that would decide viewer loyalty despite the fact that a programme loaded with " cheap entertainment" elements may attract a sizable chunk of audience instantly. But there is no denying the fact, that with the media boom its 'consumers' are also becoming 'mature' in choosing programmes to the best of their choice and interest and above all to take care of their information needs.

## Quality Programmes and Loyalty Factor

Some programmes generate a kind of bandwagon effect and there is a tendency to jump for the same kind of media programmes because of often overrated impact on the revenue market. But this should not be allowed to become the governing factor in running the public sphere of the media, specially, Doordarshan and All India Radio. Various studies have pointed out that the media programmes heavily loaded with cheap entertainment elements have an inherent tendency to lose their 'popularity' while informational and educational programmes are capable of sustaining loyalty of their audiences.

To meet the challenges of the unfolding media scenario, a series of measures are being taken and efforts are being made to strike a balance between commercialism of media and to cater to the basic information needs of a diverse developing society like ours. To evolve an integrated approach the government proposes to address the issue through some regulatory mechanism for convergence between information technology, communication and entertainment sectors. The purpose is not to impose any kind of restrictions on the media but to make it compatible with our culture, values and the information needs and not to leave this vital sector solely in the hands of the market forces. Taking this factor into consideration there is an urgent need to protect the public sphere and learn from the Western experience.

The convergence of communication, information technology and broadcasting has become imperative taking into consideration the major advances made in the three areas in the recent past. The proposed IEC Bill- Information, Entertainment and Communication Bill-is expected to take care of this dimension. It will help in creating a new situation, which in turn can introduce new elements in the very concept of entertainment and its impact on the society and hopefully will facilitate emergence of alternative concepts of entertainment. There is wide and intense discussion and debate on the issue. There is a need to evolve a certain kind of regulatory mechanism for the media programming and systems in relation to its role in the areas of information, communication and entertainment. The proposal has been made to set up a Convergence Communication of india (CCI), a regulatory body which will have the powers to grant licenses, assign spectrum, enforce license conditions and act as a content regulator. The Communications authority is expected to play an important role in the vital new areas of telecom, information technology and broadcasting. The authority will function as a regulatory mechanism for telecom, Internet and broadcasting and also voice, data and video with convergence becoming faster. According to media reports, the convergence bill seeks to institute such a body with wide ranging powers in telecom, Internet and broadcasting. The authority will make recommendations to government on laying down conditions for new services in voice, data and video and handle other regulatory issues related to frequency allocation. It will also address the vital issues of terrestrial TV and direct to home TV broadcasting. The report further says the ICE Authority will have the power to regulate Indian web sites as it will be vested with powers to decide on issues such as inter connectivity and spectrum management. The authority will also have the powers to manage the spectrum or allocate radio and telecom frequencies, ensure technical compatibility and effective inter connectivity.

These measures can ensure to a certain extent a significant role for the National Broadcaster and thus can prevent the dangerous drift towards blatant commercialism as reflected in a number of channels having registered their presence in our media market.

The Authority is proposed to have three sections dealing with the transmissions (carriage) and programming (content) and the office of the spectrum manager. There is a need to introduce a broad code to regulate programming and advertisements to protect our national integrity and our unique cultural heritage and bring them as close as possible to be compatible to our values, ethos and traditions. The proposed communications bill envisages the setting up of an apex regulator, the Communications Commission of India, on the lines of the Federal Communications Commission of the US. The challenge for regulators is to develop consistent and relevant regulators, which do not inhibit the growth of the sector, but rather encourage technological innovation. Convergence will make it necessary to ensure adequate spectrum capacity that needs to be regulated. Even in a country like the United States need was felt to enact a communication decency act in 1997 which could not be made operational as it was declared a violation of constitutional provisions of free speech. In the United States, the First Amendment gives sweeping powers to media and again situations are not comparable as the need for such regulatory mechanism in a diverse and developing society like ours entirely different and accordingly our concept of free speech- from constitutional as well as pragmatic point of view.

Any kind of programme or advertisement code cannot be compared with highly developed democratic countries taking into consideration entirely different social and cultural environment and social systems. There are numerous occasions when curbs in different forms were imposed even in these free societies. Now the situation in our country does require some kind of regulatory mechanism to meet the existing and especially the emerging communication situation. Media is allowed to function as much as possible as a self-regulated system but there are times to initiate measures at governmental level. Indian society has always been governed by self-regulating systems in relation to religious, social and cultural structures and traditions.

The sub-continental media market is not only full of entertainment programme of questionable value but also deals with the sensitive news sector. A number of foreign channels have already entered this sphere and some more are to follow. The news packaging of these channels is becoming region-centric and attracting a sizable chunk of audience. The news channels have a direct bearing on the political events in the region. The factor of the news channel acquires. The factor of the news channel acquires added importance keeping in view the volatile political situation that has been created by emergence of fundamental terrorist forces that are well entrenched in our immediate neighbourhood. Robin Day, a television journalist for a decade and a half, says in his article published in the Encounter back in 1970 that, "the fact is that television's dependence on picture (and most vivid pictures) makes it not only a powerful means of communications, but a crude one which tends to strike at the emotions rather than at the intellect. For TV journalism this means a dangerous and increasing concentration on action (usually violent and bloody) rather than on thought, on happenings rather than issues, on shock rather than explanation, in personalities rather than ideas." This tendency of the television medium has grown a lot since 1970 when these comments were made.

Most of the urban areas of the country are hooked to 30-40 channels through cable connection. The number of television channels is increasing day by day. On the one hand international networks are entering with region specific programmes and on the other hand channels in regional languages are also on incline. Television penetration at present is estimated to be 75 sets per one thousand while personal computer and fixed telephones are estimated to be 3 and 22 respectively. By 2008, the figures for television, personal computer and telephones are estimated at 225, 20 and 125 respectively. India has an estimated 69 million TV homes of which 22 million are cable homes. Besides, there are 26 million telephone connections and another 1.8 million cellular subscribers. All these numbers are growing fast. If a single conduit is going to deliver multiple content, then there will be a strong need for legislation to ensure harmony in a field which may experience initial difficulties.

## Redesigning

According to FICCI's Arthur Andersen report, India has a very strong legacy of entertainment industry. It holds the record for producing the maximum number of films, large volume sales of music titles, and it is fast emerging as the global hub for production of TV and radio content. The report further says that the total turnover of this industry, which at present is estimated at $3.5 billion, is expected to go up to $20 billion by 2005 with export revenues of $4 billion. Given the inevitable convergence between entertainment and telecommunication, the potential of this sector is unrivalled. While technology drives this revolution, there is no disputing the fact that "content" is what will fuel the fire of convergence. The report further observes the entertainment industry is unique compared to any other Indian industry, let alone foreign, considering the diverse tastes and cultures the industry caters to. The report suggests that the Indian entertainment industry, currently valued at Rs. 15,400 crore, will grow to nearly Rs. 60,000 crore by 2005. According to the report, Indian film exports, worth Rs. 450 crore in 1999, are estimated to rise to nearly Rs. 12,000 crore by 2005: the Indian music market currently paged at Rs. 1,250 crore, is projected to touch Rs. 2,200 crore by 2005, and TV software revenues are expected to soar from the present Rs. 1,200 crore to Rs. 9,000 crore in 2005.

The public broadcasting in our country is largely left to All India Radio and Doordarshan. They are now covering almost the entire country. Private satellite channels have already established their strong presence in the overall media set-up of the country. Broadcasting uses television, radio, satellites, microwave, videotape and the Internet to distribute its programming. All these technological and other developments suggest that it's time for a fresh look. Any redesign effort begins at the level of concepts- how the organization is now perceived, the services the organization expects to provide and the vision for the future. From these concepts new approaches can be developed. But it is a challenging job taking into consideration the nature of media market and dominance of cheap entertainment and commercial interests. Most importantly, the image must suggest the qualities of the organization. In this age of technology and science more knowledge is available to more people than ever before in history even though its distribution remains highly uneven. Television in particular has an immense power that needs a direction at times through regulations. Television has the potential to be a powerful medium of information and entertainment and if used properly, can be a useful tool for education, especially in this information powered age. But, the way this medium has developed it has been dominantly accepted as a medium of entertainment. Now in the wake of commercialization of the media it is creating new definitions of entertainment some of them quite disturbing. The information explosion as manifested in the television boom has generated fierce competition and resulted into vulgar and highly distorted projection of reality.

The entire media scene is dominated by television at present. It is deeply and widely influencing political, economic, social and cultural life of people. A kind of stage of media saturation has been achieved in a number of highly developed countries and the results have been mixed. It becomes imperative for the developing countries that they take into consideration experience of those countries and opts for leap-fogging instead of following the same path and repeating the misdirected development of media. It is more important for diverse countries like ours that were fully assess the implications of the emerging communication scenario and intervene on time.

In 1977, Jerry Mander, a former advertising executive in San Francisco, published *Four Arguments For The Elimination Of Television*. In the book, Mander reveals how the television networks and advertisers use this pervasive video medium for sales. *Four Arguments* talks about a lot more than just advertising. Mander attacks not only the contents of the television images, but also the effects television has on the human mind and body. His discussions include the induction of alpha waves, a hypnotizing effect on the mind, how viewers often regard what they see on television as real even though the programmes are filled with quick camera switches, rapid image movement, computer generated objects, computer generated morphing and other technical events, the placement of artificial images into our mind's eye, and the effects that large amount of television viewing has on children and the onset of attention deficit disorder.

Mander's work deals with the "abuse" of television and its "harmful effect" and went to the extent of taking a strong anti-television stand and that too back in 1977 when television was in some kind of infant state in our country but the developed countries had started feeling the "heat". Now with the advent of full-fledged information revolution and accelerated pace of process of globalization, Mander's devastating critique deserves some attention. The situation may not be that bad but Mander's observations are worth looking at as they are based on West's experience with television.

"Since television images move more quickly than a viewer can react, one has to chase them with the mind," Mander says in the book. "Every advertiser, for example, knows that before you can convince anyone of anything, you shatter their existing mental set and then restructure awareness along lines, which are useful to you. You do this with a few very simple techniques like fast-moving images, jumping among attention focuses, and switching moods, Television programmes, commercials, news reports and talk show are all designed toward blind acceptance by the viewer. Because, after all if you see it with your own eyes, it must be true, it must be real. Flashing images on the video screen. Reality inside a box, Television offers neither rest nor stimulation. Television inhibits your ability to think, but it does not lead to freedom of mind, relaxation or renewal. It leads to a more exhausted mind. You may have time out from prior obsessive though patterns, but that's as far as television goes. Television technology produces neuron-physiological in the people who watch it. It may create illness; it certainly produces confusion and submission to external imagery. Taken together the effects amount to conditioning for autocratic control."

At the heart of Mander's arguments, lies advertising. His arguments are based on the premise that "television is advertising." It is difficult to accept Mander's argument that television is only advertising and nothing else but the way and direction of programming it has acquired, advertising has definitely become the most important player in the business of television. It is an integral part of the total package of globalization- one creating space for the other. Media and specially television is creating spaces into which other products may fit in. That is a major dimension offered by the present process of globalization. It is a medium whose purpose is to sell, to promote market, In the words of writer Charles Bukowski: "(America is) not a free country-everything is bought and sold and owned." Sales by definition, is the process of convincing someone to purchase what they don't need. Advertising tries to convince someone that the solution to a problem or the fulfillment of a desire can only be achieved through the purchase of a product. "IF we take the word need to mean something basic to human survival- food, shelter, clothing; or basic to human contentment- peace, love, safety, companionship, intimacy, a sense of fulfillment; these will be sought and found by people whether or not there is advertising," Mander writes, "People do need to eat, but the food that is advertised is processed food: processed meat, sodas, sugary cereals, candies. A food in its natural state, unprocessed, does not need to be advertised," He says, "Hungry people will find the food if it is available."

Television commercials and television shows both promote the purchase of commodities. Advertisers and television networks don't want viewers to go out and search for the answers on their own. They want to provide the answers on television. Television is promoting a lifestyle. It is a virtual reality that advertisers and networks seek to promote in order to gain additional revenue. While watching television, the viewer is not seeing the world as it is. He or she is looking at a world created by advertising. Television programmes are put together with the conscious attitude of promoting a consumer society. But what makes television different from other forms of advertising, is that the viewer has absolutely no control over the images. The images flow at the pace of the advertiser; the viewer just watches passively. Bothe the viewer's mind and body do not react, and cannot react. Mander calls television imagery a form of sleep teaching.

Sure you can change the channel, but you're really only watching more of the same. Mander says, "Since there is no way to stop the images, one merely gives over to them. More than this, one has to clear all channels. However, when you watch television, the only way to escape the images is to turn the machine off."

Unfortunately turning off the machine called television is not merely a mechanical action. It is much more than that.

## News Audience

In some ways, the audience for journalistic messages is the most concrete and pre-determined of the three communications professions' work. Journalists write for publications or produce reports for media outlets that have a great deal of information about their subscribers or viewers. With the ability to track digital readership, journalists know what articles people read. At the start of the message analysis process journalists must ask a set of questions about their target audience that will help them identify the treatment of the topic about which they will be writing and make decisions about the kind of reporting they must do.

Understanding the audience that uses the publication or media outlet for which they are producing a news report will help clarify some of the following questions:

- Who: Who reads / views the publication? Who would be interested in this topic? Who needs to know about this topic? Who is the media organization interested in attracting with its offerings?

- What: What would the potential audience member want to know about the topic? What kind of report would be most informative or helpful for the audience? What kind of information will be useful? What does the audience already know about this?

- Where: Where else do people interested in the topic find information? (For freelancers) Where should I pitch my story idea?

- When: When does the audience need to get this information (is this fast-breaking news, or something that will be used as analysis after the event?)

- Why: Why does the audience need to know this? Why does the audience care? Sometimes the audience member just wants to fill empty minutes with a news message (reading news briefs on a mobile device while standing in a line or eating alone at a restaurant). Sometimes the audience member needs to answer a specific question (who won the baseball game this afternoon? when does the movie start?). Each of these "why" questions suggests a different strategy for the communicator?

- How: How can we best communicate to the audience? How much background do they need to understand what we are writing about? How technical can we be? How might the audience react to this report?

# Agenda Setting

Mass communication creates mass culture. Agenda setting is the ability of media to determine salience of issues with news, through a cognitive process called "accessibility", which is the process of retrieving an issue in the memory.

Setting an agenda is also influenced by a person's perception to certain beliefs. For example, a person who is highly sensitive to political issues would regard political news as important.

People have a choice to believe in media or not but people's thinking of obstructiveness and un-obstructiveness of an issue affects it a lot. If the issue affects a large number of people, like increase in price of gas, it will get more coverage as well as a place in the human memory.

So, any issue people would think as important is highly dependent not only on the length of broadcast but also from its position and amount of information. For instance, most people take front page news in newspapers to be more important than other pages. Similarly, if a news article is published frequently and in different media at once, the news gets more value. Media shows its own biased views which is adopted by the audience and deprive the audience from self-thought. Agenda setting comes after gate keeping, which is editing a news by gatekeepers, like editors, before it reaches to the general audience.

Concept of "framing" to the theory was added to this theory in 1998 by McCombs. This concept argues that media can not only direct people on what to think about but also how to think about an issue. It does so by focusing on a particular aspect of the news. For example, agenda setting theory only describes the water scarcity of a place but framing theory talks about how the government is causing water scarcity that defines how people take the issue to be the government's fault. Another theory called Second Level Agenda Setting has been constructed by extending this theory.

## Assumptions of Agenda Setting Theory

- Media distorts reality by filtering and reshaping.

- Media concentrating on specific issues make people perceive that the issues are more important.

## Levels of Agenda Setting

- Deciding what common subjects are important by using objects and issues.

- Deciding parts of subject which are important and how people should think about it.

## Types of Agenda Setting

Types of agenda setting according to Rogers and Dearing in their book Agenda Setting Research are:

- Public agenda setting: Public agenda is the dependent variable.

- Media agenda setting: Media's agenda is the dependent variable.

- Policy agenda setting: Policy makers' agenda is the dependent variable.

## Parts of Agenda Setting Theory

Parts of agenda setting according to Rogers and Dearing in their book Agenda Setting Research are:

- Importance of issues.

- Impact over public thinking or public agenda.

- Effects on policy agenda.

## Examples of Agenda Setting Theory

The Clinton scandal and the Watergate scandal are some of the prime examples. The Clinton scandal, sexual affair of Bill Clinton (U.S. President) and Monica Lewinsky (an intern), created a media frenzy and became sensational news for years. Media gave full pages news as top stories. The media influenced the mind-set of people so much and the news got viral to result in a presidential impeachment. And later, Clinton was acquitted for the crime.

The Watergate scandal was also exposed by media and blown out of proportions. The issue of burglars breaking in at the water-gate office complex was exaggerated by involving President Richard M. Nixon in this scandal. Media created different myths like corruption, the post uncovering the story in the beginning before police, and an increase in enrolment in journalism universities due to the incident.

## Criticisms of Agenda Setting Theory

- Agenda setting of any media or news article is difficult to measure.

- Surveys and studies are very subjective and not very accurate. There are too many variables to consider.

- People have many options to read the same stories from different angles due to new media nowadays. So people have various choices on what to see or hear.

- Nowadays, media uses two way communication unlike when this theory was developed.

- Agenda setting has many benefits as media influences public and public influences policy.

- People might not look at the details and miss some important points resulting in misunderstanding.

- Media effect does not work for people who have fixed mind-set.

- Media is not able to create information but is able to change the priority of the information to the public mind-set.

# Reception Theory

Stuart Hall developed reception theory, popularly known as Audience Theory or reader's reception theory, in 1973. His essay 'Encoding and Decoding Television Discourse' focuses on the encoding and decoding of the content given to the audience no matter the form of media such as magazines/papers, television/radios, games. Today theorists who do the analysis of media through reception theory often derive results from the experience of an audience created by watching a cinema, game or books.

The reception theory concept points out that, a movie, book, or game events though it has none/some inherent meaning, the audience who watch them or experience it make a meaning. The audience comes into an understanding of the happenings of the text or screen.

The audience receives the creative work done and perceives to its content in either similar or different. The meaning of the message can change in the way they see it fit according to their social context.

- Encoding – The encoded messages usually contains shared rules and symbols common with other people. So the (encoder) sender has to think how the receiver will perceive the message.

- Decoding – Decoding would be a successful deliver only if the message sent by the encoder is understood completely to its content as it was intended.

The messages sent with verbal/non-verbal cues and gestures don't bring the same result always as intended by the sender, bringing an altogether different meaning an insight to the concept sent. Thus, the distortion occurs when the audience cannot understand the concept of having a different take on the conclusion itself. Such distortion can be because of the age, gender, religion, race, political views, ethnicity, class, culture and the mood in which the audience receive the message etc.

It is difficult to gather the information necessary to analyze every single audience's experience belongs to a mass. So the media houses and other social handles come in a useful tool to reach the bigger mass as to get to know their experience and understanding.

Press releases, other forms of publicity such as advertisements, the fan letters, celebrity words, fan message boards, reviews, serve as useful materials for the analysts to see how the reception has been.

Here the perceiving of the work can scope in three categories:

- Dominant Reader

- Negotiated Reader

- Oppositional Reader.

## Dominant Reader

They are the audience who take in the work as given by the director which no extra notes attached. Example, Teacher asking the student to submit their assignments or parent implying on the child to clean their room is a direct message. The child understands the messages properly and it is followed by the child. In the Harry Potter Series, Lord Voldemort is a bad guy, and how have the media producers have conveyed it with a bald head, black cloak, sunken eyes, cold and cruel voice, and threatening presence to his surroundings.

## Negotiated Reader

The negotiated reading here is the audiences who thought they know and are aware of the acts made in the film are bad and not right but get on to accept that it is fine because there is a reason behind it. Thus accepting the author's message even though it goes against the audiences' personal convictions. For example, many video games/comics has contents are against our personal views but we still read, enjoy and accept the content given the situation depicted on it for example fictions like zombie hunting, etc.

## Oppositional Reader

The audience has none acceptance for the author's takes on the concept of the film or the subject it handled. It can be morally wrong, emotionally disturbing, unnecessary adult contents of violence and blood gore, religious belief, political outlooks etc., which will make the audience, reject the idea. For example, in 1970-1980 was an era in Indian Films they showed smoking as a sign of prestige, image, wealth, power and flourishing happiness whereas, the reality states otherwise, for it causes cancer. And the pleasant sense of smoking is nothing more than juxtaposed where in reality is an unpleasant smell and is perceived as a very unhealthy habit.

Reception theory is far more complex in understanding as each mind perceives in its own way. A single person can have a mixed reaction of being a dominant, oppositional, and negotiated reader when they are going through the process of receiving the message. The content producer cannot take/judge for every single individual perspective. The conclusion taken by the audience which was/is/will be right for and their perspectives will change as when the time goes by and will feel just right for the conclusion derived at that moment.

## References

- What-is-news-meaning-definition-and-sources-of-news, journalism-mass-communication: studylecturenotes.com, Retrieved 4 April, 2019

- Hard-news-how-does-it-differ-from-other-types-2316022: thebalancecareers.com, Retrieved 18 January, 2019

- Elements-of-news-are-immediacy-prominence-drama-oddity-conflict, journalism-mass-communication: studylecturenotes.com, Retrieved 5 June, 2019

- Commercialization-of-media-and-erosion-of-public-sphere: newswriters.in, Retrieved 11 February, 2019

- 4-12-whos-the-audience-for-news: lib.umn.edu, Retrieved 18 May, 2019

- Agenda-setting-theory, mass-communication: businesstopia.net, Retrieved 9 July, 2019

- Reception-theory: communicationtheory.org, Retrieved 10 March, 2019

# 3

# News Writing

There are a number of different elements which are used to write news reports such as the 5 Ws, the lede and the nut graf. The chapter closely examines the concepts which are used for writing different types of news such as feature writing, opinion piece and editorials in order to provide an extensive understanding of the subject.

News writing follows a basic formula. While styles can diverge more dramatically depending on the kind of story—a feature story may look and sound very different than a hard news story—all news stories are cut from the same mold. The first element of news writing is, of course, to deliver the news.

## The 5 Ws

Many people have heard of the 5 Ws, even if they've never taken a journalism class. The Ws in question refer to the Who, What, When, Where and Why that every story should address. Depending on what the story is, how and when you answer those Ws may change.

If, for example, you're reporting on a drive-by shooting in a city, you'll likely start with where the crime happened (what street or area of town for the local paper) and who was involved.

Figuring out what details to give a reader, and when, is key in constructing a story. The answer, of course, depends on the facts. If you're working on the above story, and the murder happens to be one of a string of similar crimes, that may be the point you open the story with.

If, however, the above story revolved around someone notable being shot, that might be what you start your piece with. However, a story about a notable name being shot is a very different story than one about someone more in the private sector. The latter might speak more to on-going local violence while the former is a story in and of it-self—X person has been killed and here's what X person was known for.

## Crafting a Lede

A lede, which is a journalism slang term for the first sentence or two of a story (i.e. lead), is an incredibly important part of the process. You need to draw readers in with a hook while stating why the story matters.

Like all forms of writing, there's no hard and fast rule about what makes a great lede. A good lede changes depending on the story you're writing. One of the best ways to get familiar with what a good lede is to read.

Read lots of different stories—from breaking news stories to features and reviews. Ledes vary wildly but, you'll start to notice patterns and, more importantly, what kinds of ledes you like and feel are effective.

## Purpose of a Nut Graf

A nut graf, another journalism slang term, is the summarization of what the story's about. A nut graf (or nutgraph, nut 'graph, and nutgraf) can be a sentence or a paragraph and, sometimes, may also be your lede.

A nut graf needs to address why the story is being written, whether the piece is about something like the aforementioned murder, or a profile of a famous celebrity. Like ledes, nut grafs vary wildly from story to story, and they can also be harder to identify than ledes. A good exercise is to read lots of different stories and try to find the nut graf.

## How Style Comes into Play with Different Pieces

The basics outlined above apply directly to all stories but, most obviously, to your classic news story. That said, all stories have ledes and nutgrafs, no matter what they're about or where you find them. These elements are applied differently, and often more subtly, in long-form journalism and feature stories, but they're still there.

One of the best ways to see how the basic elements of news writing can be applied to very different stories is to read, back to back, three very different pieces. For a good exercise, try reading the lead story in any major paper.

The front page of a paper (online and in print) offers the biggest news stories of the day and there you'll find straight, hard news. It might be local or it might be international. Then hit the features section of the paper. Check out the Arts section of the *New York Times* or the *Washington Post*'s Lifestyle section, and read a review, then another trend story.

Then read a piece of long-form journalism in a magazine like *The New Yorker* or *Esquire*. (In *The New Yorker,* nearly every article, save the reviews and pieces from "Talk of the Town," is an example of long-form journalism.) Now think about how different each piece reads.

Find the nut graf in each story and pay attention to how much each lede varies. Notice that some stories have nutgrafs that appear well below the lede, and others begin with the nut graf.

How the nut graf is more obvious in the news stories than in the features or the magazine stories. All these stories rely on the basic elements of news writing but do so in different styles. This exercise is good for giving a sense of the breadth of journalism and how differently the rules of news writing can be applied.

# Inverted Pyramid: Writing for Comprehension

In journalism, the inverted pyramid refers to a story structure where the most important information (or what might even be considered the conclusion) is presented first. The who, what, when, where and why appear at the start of a story, followed by supporting details and background information. This writing style is different than, for example, academic writing, where an abstract may summarize the main findings, but the content typically focuses first on the details, leading to the conclusion which appears at the end of the article.

The name "inverted pyramid" comes from picturing the broad facts at the top of the story, followed by smaller and smaller details, like a triangle balanced on one corner.

This writing style gets to the point quickly and supports all types of readers. Even those who have the time or inclination to read only a single paragraph, or even single sentence will still know what the story is about. The inverted pyramid also helps editors when they need to cut a piece at a certain length to fit a publication: if the paragraphs get less and less important as you advance in the article, the article can easily be trimmed at practically any point.

## Benefits of the Inverted-Pyramid Style for Web Writing

The inverted pyramid is perfectly suited for the web - on any screen size. We know that users don't read carefully online. They have little patience for content that doesn't engage them. Users scroll, but only when they think that the content they want or need will appear on that page. The inverted pyramid style addresses all of these aspects of user behavior.

Using the inverted pyramid style can:

1.  Improve comprehension: Users can quickly form a mental model and a general understanding of the article.

2.  Decrease interaction cost: Users can understand the main point of the page without having to spend a lot of time reading.

3.  Encourage scrolling: This structure can encourage scrolling by engaging the audience with the main point, and drawing them in to the details that follow.

4.  Structure content logically: Starting with broad information sets the stage for what follows. Elements like anchor or jump links can become unnecessary when content is structured to draw the user down the page.

5.  Support readers who skim: Readers can stop reading at any point on the page and still come away with the main point.

## How to Write in the Inverted Pyramid Style

1.  Identify your key points- What piece of information is the key fact you want your readers to know, even if they only read a single paragraph or sentence on the page? What effectively summarizes all the information that will follow?

2.  Rank secondary information- Outline the story details and supporting information, prioritizing the information that is most likely to be of interest to the broadest audience, and moving down the list to the smaller and more nuanced details.

3.  Write well and concisely- The structure only helps readers if the content is strong. Cut unnecessary information. Get to the point quickly. Use straightforward language. Use short paragraphs and bulleted lists.

4.  Frontload all elements of content with important information- The main headline should be descriptive. The story should start with the main point. Each heading or subheading should

be descriptive. The first sentence of every paragraph should be the most important. The first words in each sentence should be information-carrying and indicate what content will follow.

5.  Consider adding a summary or list of highlights- Some sites go a step beyond and add a summary (like this article does) or a bulleted list of key points to further emphasize the main takeaways of the content.

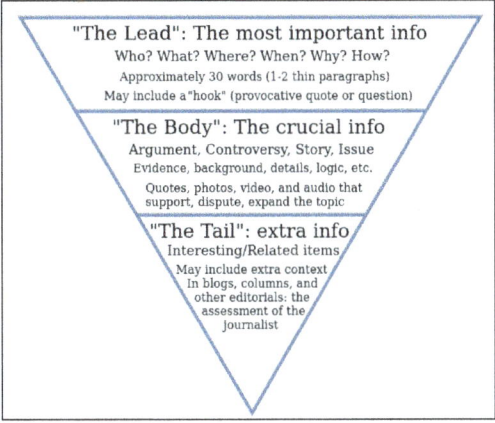

"Inverted pyramid in comprehensive form"

## 5Ws 1H Method

5W1H (who, what, where, when, why, how) is a method of asking questions about a process or a problem taken up for improvement. Four of the W's (who, what, where, when) and the one H is used to comprehend for details, analyze inferences and judgment to get to the fundamental facts and guide statements to get to the abstraction. The last W (why) is often asked five times so that one can drill down to get to the core of a problem.

5W1H is the abbreviation summarising the following six questions: What? Who? Where? When? Why? How? This method consists of asking a systematic set of questions to collect all the data necessary to draw up a report of the existing situation with the aim of identifying the true nature of the problem and describing the context precisely.

Within a critical and constructive analysis process, it is essential to compile exhaustive quality data. Hence the use of open questions requiring supported answers, thereby helping to pinpoint, clarify and delineate the problem.

Better knowledge of all the dimensions of a problem will then make it possible to suggest appropriate measures to take the right corrective actions. Sometimes the method is referred to as the "five Ws" only, with "How" ignored as it does not fit the pattern, but nonetheless used.

Good to know- Another 5W1H variant, especially in business, includes an additional question in the form of "How much?" thus making the 5W2H method. We will mention "How much" later in our list of applications below, but we will keep the 5W1H abbreviation for the rest of the article.

## Applications of 5W1H Method

The 5W1H method has many applications, very different from each other. It is perfectly suited, by virtue of its simplicity and versatility, to a variety of structures, configurations and problems, and so it can be used at all levels of the business:

- At the strategy level to design or improve a market penetration strategy, for instance;

- At the management level to improve organisation and processes during brainstorming sessions;

- At the quality level as a problem-resolution support tool;

- At the innovation level to boost the emergence of solutions and ideas in the cause of progress;

- At the project management level generally.

## The Advantages of the 5W1H Method

The strength of the 5W1H method lies in four key attributes:

- Simple: no need for training or people accredited in the method to successfully ask these questions.

- Systematic: the key to success is to always ask all the questions, each and every time.

- Versatile: it can be used equally well to design a new process as to implement a corrective
- measure.

- Comprehensive: the method can be used to obtain a 360° view of the problem and detect the route to resolution.
- 

## Implementation and Applications of the 5W1H Method

The 5W1H method breaks down into three main stages:

- Describe the initial situation;

- Determine the key factors and prioritise them;

- Propose fitting and, importantly, effective, actions.

The 5W1H questions are used to establish the situation (phase 1). On the basis of the answers and overview obtained, it is possible to find the critical factors (phase 2) and then offer solutions (phase 3).

Keeping it simple, a list of sample questions and explanations follow:

## What?

- Explanation: Description of the task, the activity, the problem, the project purpose.

- Targets: Purpose, actions, procedures, machines, etc.

- Sample questions: What is the problem or risk? What is the situation? What are the product characteristics? How does the service work?

## Who?

- Explanation: Determine the stakeholders involved, the people responsible or affected.

- Targets: Managers, customers, suppliers, victims, those directly involved, etc.

- Sample questions: Who is in charge? Who found the problem? Who will be asked to do the work?

## Where?

- Explanation: Describe the place or location involved.

- Targets: Premises, workshop, workstation, etc.

- Sample questions: Where does the problem apply? Are the premises easy to access? On which machine is the problem located?

## When?

- Explanation: Determine the time when the situation took, takes or will take place.

- Targets: Dates, duration, frequency, etc.

- Sample questions: How long does it take? When is the installation date? How often does the problem arise?

## How?

- Explanation: Determine the way to proceed, the steps and method employed.

- Targets: Procedures, organisational methods, the actions, means and techniques used, etc.

- Sample questions: Under what conditions or circumstances? How is the department organised? What are the methods used? What resources are employed?

## How much?

- Explanation: Determine the resources and equipment needed.

- Targets: Quantities, budget, etc.

- Sample questions: What is the cost? What resources are needed? How many man-days?

## Why?

- Explanation: Describe the motivation, or the objective, or the justification or reason behind a method of working.

- Targets: Goals, purposes, justification, etc.

- Sample questions: What is the targeted objective? Why was this training or this equipment chosen?

The question "Why?" does essential for better understand. Do not hold back from asking it after any answer to the other questions (the other 4Ws and How).

To sum up, the 5W1H method is an outstanding method to better understand and delineate a situation, provided it is controlled properly and used wisely. It is a method that provides effective solutions to problems encountered and helps to create a positive continuous improvement dynamic in the business.

## Feature Writing

Features are not meant to deliver the news first hand. They do contain elements of news, but their main function is to humanize, to add colour, to educate, to entertain, to illuminate. They often recap major news that was reported in a previous news cycle. Features often:

- Profile people who make the news

- Explain events that move or shape the news

- Analyze what is happening in the world, nation or community

- Teach an audience how to do something

- Suggest better ways to live

- Examine trends

- Entertain.

### Hard News and Soft News

A news story can be hard, chronicling as concisely as possible who, what, where, when, why and how of an event. Or it can be soft, standing back to examine the people, places and things that shape the world, nation or community. Hard news events--such as the death of a famous public figure or the plans of city council to raise taxes--affect many people, and the primary job of the media is to report them as they happen. Soft news, such as the widespread popularity of tattooing among athletes or the resurgence of interest in perennial gardening, is also reported by the media. Feature stories are often written on these soft news events.

There is no firm line between a news story and a feature, particularly in contemporary media when many news stories are "featurized." For instance, the results of an Olympic competition may be hard news: "Canadian diver Anne Montmigny claimed her second medal in synchronized diving today." A featurized story might begin: "As a girl jumping off a log into the stream running behind her house, Anne Montmigny never dreamed she would leap into the spotlight of Olympic diving competition." One approach emphasizes the facts of the event, while the feature displaces the facts to accommodate the human interest of the story. Most news broadcasts or publications combine the two to reach a wider audience.

Today's media use many factors to determine what events they will report, including:

1. Timeliness

2. Proximity

3. Consequence

4. The perceived interest of the audience

5. Competition

6. Editorial goals

7. And the influence of advertisers.

All these factors put pressure on the media to give their audiences both news and features. In a version of featurizing, pressure from advertisers or lobbyists often result in writing that appears at first blush to be news when it is, in fact, promotion for a product, idea, or policy.

When a hard news story breaks for example, the sinking of a ferry in the Greek islands it should be reported with a hard news lead. Soft leads and stories are more appropriate when a major news event is not being reported for the first time: a profile of the Canadian couple who had their vacation cut short when the Greek ferry struck a reef and sunk while the crew was watching television. Some editors dispute the emphasis on soft writing and refer to it as Jell-O journalism.

Feature writing can stand alone, or it can be a sidebar to the main story, the main bar. A sidebar runs next to the main story or elsewhere in the same edition, providing an audience with additional information on the same topic.

## Types of Features

1. Personality profiles: A personality profile is written to bring an audience closer to a person in or out of the news. Interviews and observations, as well as creative writing, are used to paint a vivid picture of the person. The CBC's recent profile of Pierre Elliot Trudeau is a classic example of the genre and makes use of archival film footage, interviews, testimonials, and fair degree of editorializing by the voice-over commentary.

2. Human interest stories: A human interest story is written to show a subject's oddity or its practical, emotional, or entertainment value.

3. Trend stories: A trend story examines people, things or organizations that are having an impact on society. Trend stories are popular because people are excited to read or hear about the latest fads.

4. In-depth stories: Through extensive research and interviews, in-depth stories provide a detailed account well beyond a basic news story or feature.

5. Backgrounders: A backgrounder--also called an analysis piec-adds meaning to current issues in the news by explaining them further. These articles bring an audience up-to-date, explaining how this country, this organization, this person happens to be where it is now.

## Writing and Organizing Feature Stories

Feature writers seldom use the inverted-pyramid form. Instead, they may write a chronology that builds to a climax at the end, a narrative, a first-person article about one of their own experiences or a combination of these. Their stories are held together by a thread, and they often end where the lead started, with a single person or event.

Here are the steps typically followed in organizing a feature story:

1. Choose the theme- The theme is similar to the thesis of a scholarly paper and provides unity and coherence to the piece. It should not be too broad or too narrow. Several factors come into play when choosing a theme: Has the story been done before? Is the story of interest to the audience? Does the story have holding power (emotional appeal)? What makes the story worthy of being reported? The theme answers the question, "So what?"

2. Write a lead that invites an audience into the story- A summary may not be the best lead for a feature. A lead block of one or two paragraphs often begins a feature. Rather than put the news elements of the story in the lead, the feature writer uses the first two or three paragraphs to set a mood, to arouse readers, to invite them inside. Then the news peg or the significance of the story is provided in the third or fourth paragraph, the nut graph. Because it explains the reason the story is being written, the nut graph--also called the "so what" graph--is a vital paragraph in every feature. The nut graph should be high in the story. Do not make readers wait until the 10th or 11th paragraph before telling them what the story is about.

3. The body provides vital information while it educates, entertains, and emotionally ties an audience to the subject. The ending will wrap up the story and come back to the lead, often with a quotation or a surprising climax. Important components of the body of a feature story are background information, the thread of the story, transition, dialogue, and voice.

4. Provide vital background information- If appropriate, a paragraph or two of background should be placed high in the story to bring the audience up to date.

5. Write clear, concise sentences. Sprinkle direct quotations, observations and additional background throughout the story. Paragraphs can be written chronologically or in order of importance.

6. Use a thread- Connect the beginning, body and conclusion of the story. Because a feature generally runs longer than a news story, it is effective to weave a thread throughout the story, which connects the lead to the body and to the conclusion. This thread can be a single person, an event or a thing, and it usually highlights the theme.

7. Use transition- Connect paragraphs with transitional words, paraphrases, and direct quotations. Transition is particularly important in a long feature examining several people or events because it is the tool writers use to move subtly from one person or topic to the next. Transition keeps readers from being jarred by the writing.

8. Use dialogue when possible- Feature writers, like fiction writers, often use dialogue to keep a story moving. Of course, feature writers cannot make up dialogue; they listen for it during the reporting process. Good dialogue is like good observation in a story; it gives readers strong mental images and keeps them attached to the writing and to the story's key players.

9. Establish a voice- Another key element that holds a feature together is voice, the "signature" or personal style of each writer. Voice is the personality of the writer and can be used to inject colour, tone, and subtle emotional commentary into the story. Voice should be used subtly (unless you're able to make a fetish of it like Hunter S. Thompson!). The blatant intrusion of a distinctive voice into news writing has been called gonzo journalism-an irresponsible, if entertaining, trend in contemporary writing according to traditionalists.

Conclude with a quotation or another part of the thread- A feature can trail off like a news story or it can be concluded with a climax. Often, a feature ends where the lead started, with a single person or event.

# Opinion Piece

An opinion article, as the name suggests, is an article where you express your opinion on an issue. It is different from an essay in that it deals usually with issues being reported in the news and is written in your own unique tone. Unlike the research paper variant of the essay, it also is briefer and has a clear point of view.

Sure, social media allows us to express opinions like never before, but if you are looking for a larger audience, an opinion article is the solution you are looking for. But this solution also comes with its requirements. Not all opinion articles get noticed or influence other people. If you are looking to write one, it helps to have some tools in hand, especially if you are just beginning to write.

Here then are some easy steps to guide you through writing an opinion article:

1. Be Short and Specific:

If you check the length of an article before deciding to read it, you know what I am talking about. With reducing attention spans, you have to be careful about the space you use and what you do with it.

It makes sense in an opinion article to make those one or two arguments that you can persuasively put forward, and deal with them at length. Making a specific argument isn't limited to finding a specific logic though. It can also include things like a specific location or identity. If you are in an inter-religious relationship, what you have to say about 'love-jihad' is important when the subject is being debated.

## 2. Find new Arguments:

Even in an opinion article, you must try to offer something new. If you are going to tell people that 'violence is bad', there is little incentive for anybody to read on. This is because they have heard this argument earlier, and quite a few times too.

Such new arguments and opinions can range from 'If you look at these numbers, you will get a new perspective on violence', to 'I don't think surgical strikes can end terrorism'. The former makes a new argument through overlooked data, while the latter brings an opinion that is not intuitive.

Similarly, you can look for a specific incident, nuggets from history, and so on. The lesser known or discussed an opinion or argument is, the more likely it is to interest a potential reader.

## 3. Get to the Point Fast:

A reader decides to read the article after reading a title. If you want them to read beyond that, you must make them care about what you have to say. The opening paragraphs or the introduction is one area where you perform this manoeuvre.

For example, do you know of a way in which the issue you are discussing will affect a potential reader? You can draw the attention of the reader to that outcome to make them care about your article. Is there an anecdote relevant to a debate that few people will know? It's good to put it up front.

You also need to tell the reader what new perspective you are bringing to the table early on. It is a good practice to introduce your reader to the specific argument you are going to make in the introduction or immediately after it.

## 4. Structure Your Argument:

Whether it is an emotional argument or a factual one, it becomes convincing only when you explain it. Repeating a statement will only convince those who already believe in it. I structure my arguments usually by first stating what my argument is, then following it up with my reasons. And finally, if possible, I give an example to demonstrate my argument.

## 5. Offer Solutions:

You are not writing a news report showing the existence of a problem. The article is your opinion on the issue. So feel free to offer recommendations or solutions that can solve the problem that you are highlighting.

## 6. Use Active Voice and Avoid Jargon:

Everybody has an opinion once a debate starts. If you have distinguished your opinion by following the above steps, it is important that you also convey your opinion to every reader effectively. So avoid jargon.

It is okay for the Delhi High Court to say: "Any provision of Territorial Army Act barring recruitment of women is ultra vires the Constitution." You are probably better off saying: "Any provision of Territorial Army Act that bars the recruitment of women is unconstitutional."

Using active voice is another way in which you can reduce strain for the reader. Here's an example:

- Passive voice: Students were arrested by the police immediately afterwards.

- Active voice: The police arrested the students immediately afterwards.

7. Give a Winning Conclusion:

If you are offering solutions to a problem at the end of your article, you are already close to summing up what you have argued throughout the article. If you can finish this off with a polished small paragraph that sticks in the mind of the reader, you will have made an impression on them. There are no fixed ways of doing this, but if you can distil everything you have said in the article in as few words as possible, we can say that you have succeeded.

There will always be that opinion article that breaks these rules. But if you are just beginning to write, write routinely, or are writing on a tight deadline, these tools should be useful. Happy writing.

# Editorial

Editorials are not news, but rather reasoned opinion based on facts.

A newspaper publishes its views on current events - both local and national - on its editorial page. This is where letters to the editor, political cartoons, and editorials - unsigned commentary that reflects the collective position of the newspaper's editorial board - appear. Letters are often among the best-read section of any newspaper, for this is where readers express their opinions. Some newspapers limit letters to a certain number of words – maybe 150 or 300 - while others publish letters of virtually any length.

The editorial pages are under the direction of an editor outside the news division. Newspaper people call this "separation of church and state," meaning there is a line between news and opinion that must not be crossed. To do so strips a newspaper of its most valuable asset -- credibility. For that reason, editorial-page editors at some large newspapers report to the publisher, who is the chief executive officer of the company, and not to the executive editor. Other newspapers may have their editorial-page editor reporting to the executive editor. Whatever the organizational model, though, neither department can tell the other what to publish in the newspaper.

# Writing for Television

Writing a TV news script is a lot harder than you might think. Even those skilled in journalism struggle if they have to turn a story meant to be read into a tight script that needs to be heard. However, you can perfect your TV news writing style if you learn the basics.

## Be Sure to Write for the Ear

Always read your script out loud in a conversational tone so you can judge if an audience will be able to understand it. Unlike a newspaper story, your broadcast audience only gets one chance to understand your story.

Also, beware of words that sound alike but mean different things. For instance, words like cite" might be confused with "site" or "sight" and should be avoided. You may have noticed when listening to a newscast that short sentences are easier to digest than long-winded sentences. Just be sure to make your sentences sound lively and interesting—as opposed to flat and monotone.

## Avoid the Passive Voice

Passive voice writing jumbles up the usual sequence of subject, verb, and object in active voice writing. This sounds like a lesson from English class, but it really makes a critical difference in broadcast news writing.

An active voice helps distinguish between verbs and subjects. For example, an active sentence would be, "The burglar fired the gun," as opposed to a passive sentence such as, "The gun was fired by the burglar." You can see in the passive sentence that viewers have to wait until the end of the line to know who did what.

## Use Present Tense wherever Possible

TV news is timely as opposed to print news writing that relates a bigger story, putting facts and information into context. In other words, a 6 p.m. newscast must sound fresh and "of the moment." You need to bring the viewer into the news piece as it's unfolding.

For example, let's look at a mayor's news conference that you covered at 2 p.m. that afternoon to appear on the nightly news. You might want to write, "Mayor Johnson held a news conference earlier today."

However, if you shift the focus of the sentence to the subject of the news conference, you end up putting the sentence in the present tense. This gives it more immediacy and makes it sound less stale. For example, "Mayor Johnson says he intends to slash local taxes by 20 percent. Johnson made the announcement at a news conference."

That example above works because it starts out in the present tense and creates the hook, then shifts to past tense.

## Write Stories for People

It's easy to get mired in what your writing and forget who you're writing for—the people watching your newscast. Viewers need to feel your stories are directed at them, or else they'll turn away. When writing, it's a good idea to pretend that someone is sitting across from you. Direct the story to them.

Let's say your local department of transportation announces plans to overhaul several major thoroughfares in need of repair. Don't just present the institutional information the DOT provided you with. Transform the information into something of consequence for the viewers at home.

For example, you can say, "Your drive to work or school will soon be smoother, thanks to a big project by the DOT to fill in potholes and uneven streets suffering from wear and tear." This way you've telling viewers how an upcoming project will change their lives—for the better.

## Befriend Action Verbs

In news writing, verbs are your best friend. Verbs are the part of speech that adds life and verve to your stories.

For instance- Instead of saying, "Residents are requesting information." Say something like, "Residents want to know." That slight change makes the information more compelling.

If you can, always avoid words like "is, are, was, and were." All of these dilute the impact of the action. "

## Be Careful with Numbers

Numbers are hard to absorb, especially if there are a lot of them. Try to make your point with a number or two then moves on.

"The company's profit was $10,470,000 then fell to $5,695,469 a year later," is just too much information. "The company's profit was about 10 and-a-half million dollars, then fell to about half that the following year." The last example gives the viewer the information without having to listen to every last digit.

## Sell the Story

In most cities, there may be only one or two local newspapers but several stations all vying for an audience. That means a news writer has to be a salesperson and sell the product as something superior to the competition.

"When the school board said there wasn't any money for classroom computers, we decided to dig for answers." A line like that demonstrates that the news team is aggressive, and is taking action to get to the truth. The viewer likes this story because he or she feels someone is championing for them. It personalizes it and brings it home—even if a viewer doesn't have children.

If you can combat the perception that all newscasts are the same by leading the segment with, "We have an NBC exclusive of Kim Kardashian with the woman she got pardoned from prison," viewers will flock to your TV station because you've set yourself apart.

## Move the Story Forward

A good TV news story ends telling the audience what will happen next.

"The school board will take a vote on whether to cut teachers' pay at its next meeting a week from today" doesn't leave the audience hanging and, it forces viewers to tune in next week.

If you wrap-up the segment with, "We will be at that meeting and tell you the outcome of the vote," your viewers know your news team is on top of the story.

## Different Parts of a Script

Let's look at five steps you can take to break down a TV News script. A good example is Pope Benedict's retirement announcement because it was a historic event—no matter what religion you practice. If the story looks at footage of people responding to the Pope's retirement in St. Petersburg Square, you could write the script as follows:

1.  The first line informs the audience about the main point of the story. If you only had one line to tell your story, it would be, "Pilgrims began arriving at St. Peter's Square on Monday, February 11, following an announcement by Pope Benedict that he's resigning at the end of the month."

2.  Provide a line or two of background information that adds context to your first line. For example, "The 85-year-old German-born pontiff said he is no longer strong enough to fulfill the duties of his office, becoming the first pope since the Middle Ages to take such a step."

3.  Next, go back to the pictures being broadcast and what's happening in your story as the news of the Pope's retirement spreads. You could say, "Thousands of people from all over began arriving at St. Peter's Square."

4.  Next, expand on the scene by saying, "People of all religions prayed for the pope and wished him well.

5.  Last, wrap-up the story with concrete information. For example, "The Vatican's spokesman said the pope would step down at 1900 GMT on February 28."

Video may seem like the sexy part of a newscast, but it's the crisp news writing that brings it to life and brings in a bigger audience.

## Writing for Radio

Radio is a fast, easy media that targets everyone, from highly educated people to less knowledgeable ones. The writing must therefore be short, simple, in present tense. easy to listen to and to memorize.

The first rule is to properly understand what you're writing about. If you fail to do so, you will write badly. Understanding is the key to explaining, and the basis to the informal contract between a journalist and his audience.

### Begin with the Freshest News

Your audience is tuning into the broadcast to know what's happening. Each of your scripts must therefore start with the freshest news.

### Hook your Audience

Not only does the first sentence contain the freshest news, it must also catch the attention of the listener. See that your writing is catchy, particularly at the beginning of each piece of news. If the listener is intrigued, he will keep on listening.

## Use the Present Tense

You have to describe events that only just happened or are currently happening. The present tense is the tense to use: it fits with the treatment of the news.

## Write Short Sentences

News is oftentimes complex. Your listeners can't rewind, they must understand straight away. Keep your sentences short and simple: subject/verb/object. A sentence can only carry one idea. Avoid subordinate clauses: end the sentence and start a new one instead.

## Be Precise

Your scripts must be short, every word counts. Choose your words, especially your verbs, wisely. Your scripts must be short: every word counts. Try to avoid "be" and "have", as they are overly vague.

## Stick to the Facts, Avoid Commenting

You are not on air to give out your opinion. Just describe the news and let your listeners make their mind up freely.

## Speak before you Write

A news bulletin is an oral exercise. The anchor reads out the news. Whisper your script as you write it. If you have trouble reading a word, change it : it might just happen to you again, this time on air. If the result does not please you, rewrite the script.

## Speak to your Audience

You're writing your news alone. When talking into the mic, you have no direct contact with the listeners. Still, always try picturing them. Are they going to understand ? Try picturing yourself talking to someone. If you write this way, your audience will feel as though you're talking to them and will keep on listening.

## Describe the News

Radio appeals to the ear. A well-written script creates perfect mental pictures in the mind of the listener. To get this result, use descriptive writing. So as to be sure not to forget anything about a news item, use the 5 Ws. And to describe it, think of the five senses: news get to us through our senses. Let your listeners see, touch, hear, feel and taste the news.

# Writing for Internet

Content is king when it comes to the Web. People will come to your website because of quality content. They will also share your site with others when they feel that the content is worthwhile. This means that your site's content, and the writing of that content, needs to be top notch.

Writing for the Web is an interesting thing. Web writing is similar in many ways to any other kind of writing, but it is also so much different than anything else. Here are some tips you can follow to make your web writing the best that it can be.

## Content

1. Write relevant content: All great content is relevant content. It may be tempting to write about your brother's dog, but if it doesn't relate to your site or page topic, or if you cannot find a way to relate it to your topic, you need leave it out. Web readers want information, and unless the page is information relevant to their specific needs, they really won't care.

2. Put conclusions at the beginning: Think of an inverted pyramid when you write. Get to the point in the first paragraph, then expand upon it in later paragraphs. Remember, if your content does not hook someone early, you are unlikely to get them to read further into the article. Start strong, always.

3. Write only one idea per paragraph: Web pages need to be concise and to-the-point. People don't often read Web pages, they scan them, so having short, meaty paragraphs is better than long rambling ones. On that note, let's move on.

4. Use action words: Tell your readers what to do in the content you write. Avoid the passive voice. Keep the flow of your pages moving and use action words as much as possible.

## Format

1. Use lists instead of paragraphs: Lists are easier to scan than paragraphs, especially if you keep them short. Try to use lists when possible to make scanning easier for reader.

2. Limit list items to 7 words: Studies have shown that people can only reliably remember 7-10 things at a time. By keeping your list items short, it helps your readers remember them.

3. Write short sentences: Sentences should be as concise as you can make them. Use only the words you need to get the essential information across.

4. Include internal sub-headings. Sub-headings make the text more scalable. Your readers will move to the section of the document that is most useful for them, and internal cues make it easier for them to do this. Along with lists, subheadings make longer articles easier to process.

5. Make your links part of the copy.

6. Links are another way Web readers scan pages. They stand out from normal text, and provide more cues as to what the page is about.

## Always

1. Proofread your work: Typos and spelling errors will send people away from your pages. Make sure you proofread everything you post to the Web. Nothing makes you seem amateurish more than content that is riddled with mistakes and spelling errors.

2.  Promote your content. Good content gets found online, but you can always help it along!. Take the time to promote everything you write.

3.  Be Current. Relevance coupled with timeliness is a winning combination. Be mindful of current events and what is happening that is related to your content and write about that. This is a great way to get readers and create content that is fresh and new.

4.  Be Regular. Great content needs to be published regularly. You need to maintain a schedule and you need to keep to that schedule if you want readers to stick with your site and send others to it as well. This can be much easier said than done, but sticking to a schedule is very important when it comes to web writing.

**References**

- News-writing-2316089: thebalancecareers.com, Retrieved 21 August, 2019

- Inverted-pyramid: nngroup.com, Retrieved 27 May, 2019

- Inverted-pyramid-style: pressbooks.pub, Retrieved 7 July, 2019

- Using-five-ws-and-one-h-approach-six-sigma, implementation: isixsigma.com, Retrieved 4 January, 2019

- How-to-write-an-opinion-piece: youthkiawaaz.com, Retrieved 14 April, 2019

- Newspaper: howstuffworks.com, Retrieved 8 February, 2019

- How-to-write-a-news-script-for-tv-news-2315281: thebalancecareers.com, Retrieved 18 June, 2019

- 06-writing-for-the-radio, radio: 24hdansuneredaction.com, Retrieved 29 August, 2019

- Tips-for-good-web-writing-3471335: lifewire.com, Retrieved 30 March, 2019

# 4

# News Editing

The process of selecting and preparing images, writings and sounds in order to efficiently convey information is known as editing. The diverse aspects of news editing such as principles of editing and the importance of editing have been thoroughly discussed in this chapter.

Editing is the process of preparing language, images, or sound for presentation through correction, condensation, organization, and other modifications. A person who edits, especially professionally or as a hobby, is called an Editor.

The five basic rules of Editing are:

1. To process any story the sub-editor ensures the length and style laid down by the News Editor is followed.

2. To mark the news copy with setting instructions so clearly and carefully that there is no possibility of confusion or misunderstanding in the composing room.

3. To ensure that everything that needs to be checked has been checked, that is, names, places, titles, dates and anything else that could possibly be wrong.

4. To write a headline that fits.

5. To make sure, that the copy as edited is intelligible, easy to read and appetizing. Rewriting where it is not necessary is simply a waste of time and in a newspaper organization; time is the most important factor. It is considered in bad taste as it is damaging to the morale of the reporter concerned and danger of committing mistakes is greater.

## Editing Rule 1

Editing involves more than making sure words are spelled correctly, language is used properly, punctuation is in the right places and spelling is accurate. These, however, are important details that separate a polished publication from a sloppy one.

As with reporting and writing, there are big-picture issues that editors must attend to before plunging ahead.

As gatekeepers of a publication, editors must have a clear idea about what the mission is. For instance, the Junior Journal has decided to be a voice for children's issues, a chronicler of Junior Summit action and a vehicle for breaking down barriers of distance and prejudice. Without being too rigid, editors should be sure stories fulfill at least part of the mission.

So part of editing involves being missionaries and a part also involves being ambassadors of ideas.

## Editing Rule 2

What does it mean to be an ambassador of ideas? Bearing in mind that an ambassador is one who exercises diplomacy, let us examine the issue of idea formulation.

It is an experience that the best ideas most often come from the bottom up, not from the top down. So editors should be encouraging writers to pursue their own story ideas. This is done with prompting, nudging, cajoling, pushing--whatever works.

Ask the writer what interests her or him? What issues are writers passionate about? What intrigues them? What are they curious about? What's "hot" where they live (event, trend or issue)?

Editing requires good listening. The writer should be heard first, and then the editor responds. This then is the beginning of a conversation, be it online or by telephone or in person. The conversation process enriches stories, because two heads are better than one. Conversation should be taking place when the idea is first being formulated; it should take place during and after the editing process.

At Reporting phase; it should take place before the story is written and it should take place after the editor has fully processed the story. At each stage the editor should bear in mind that it is the reporter's story on the one hand, but it also is the reader's story. It is not the editor's story.

Thus, the editing should generally take the form of questions readers might ask when they come to the story cold (How was he dressed? When did she say that? Where did it occur?).

What should go into a story, tend to stifle the conversation and the story. On the other hand, editors should speak up if there are gaps in the story; that is, elements that make the story incomplete. And they should speak up when a story is too long, unclear, awkward, meandering, etc. It's a bit like pulling a wagon: the job is easier when two people are pulling, rather than one, especially when the two are pulling together.

## Editing Rule 3

Story ideas are similar to loaves of bread. All of the elements need to be brought together and kneaded. Then the dough is popped into the oven until it rises and is ready to eat.

Editors and reporters should be collaborators in the development of story ideas. Two minds are better than one. It doesn't matter who has the initial idea. What matters is how the idea is molded and framed into a better idea.

Let's say someone wants to do a story on how to make bread. The editor might suggest providing some historical perspective, pointing out that before the 20th Century B.C. There was evidence Egyptians baked bread as did the Swiss Lake Dwellers in the early days of civilized Europe.

That might prompt the writer to recall religious connotations to bread: manna from heaven to feed the Israelites; Jesus calling himself "the bread of life" and the ritual of bread and wine being served in Christian traditions. Soon a simple four-paragraph story can become a story with substance.

The point is that we shouldn't be satisfied with the first idea that comes to mind. That's only the beginning. We should turn it over in our minds, shape it, pull it apart, and push it back together again, just like kneading.

## Editing Rule 4

Lingo means jargon or slang language. The journalism trade is full of lingo. Some of it actually makes sense.

We talk of "heads" for headlines (sometimes spelled "heds"). We refer to the story as "body type". So you can think of a story as having a head and a body.

The head is as important as the body. We need to put more thought into our heads, especially on the web, because readers are browsing fast. So the head has to say, "Hey, wait a minute: you need to look at my body." The tone of the headline should reflect the tone of the story. Don't use funny or flippant headlines on serious stories.

Most heads should contain a verb to connote action. The selection of nouns, verbs, adjectives and adverbs should be done with care. Choosing just the right word can illuminate.

A head in smaller type under the main headline is often called a subhead. Its purpose usually is to expand on the idea in the top headline or to interject a second thought. Generally the main head expresses a single thought or point.

Editor's goal is twofold- To capture the essence of the story and to entice the reader into reading it.

Believe that reporters should submit headlines on their stories. They know what they want to emphasize. However, editors reserve the right to rewrite or polish the wording for the final headline. It's normal for an editor to write a half dozen, dozen or even more versions before being satisfied. You want to put your best head forward.'

## Editing Rule 5

When you're in another country, you would have difficulty getting around without signs. More and more signs are minimizing the use of words and using symbols, because not everyone speaks the native language. So when you are driving and you see a sign with an arrow bending to the right, you know there's a curve ahead. Sometimes one has to look twice to distinguish between the signs for the ladies' room and the men's room, but obviously these symbols are useful guides.

The same is true with punctuation. It has an important function in a story. Its function is to help guide the reader through the sentence or paragraph in a way that will make the wording more understandable.

Commas do not signal a pause; so don't drop them into a sentence without a reason.

The girl went to the store and bought milk (no comma, because "went" and "bought: have the same subject: "girl"); the girl went to the store, and the boy went to school (has a comma, because it is as though two sentences are joined by an "and").

In the beginning the writer did reporting (no comma after "in the beginning", because it is a phrase not a clause; would you put in a comma if it were at the end of the sentence?).

In a series you have a choice as to whether to use two or three commas in the following sentence: She liked vanilla, chocolate, strawberry and chocolate chip. Newspapers generally don't use a comma after "strawberry", because years ago type was handset, so they tried to avoid punctuation marks whenever possible. It saved time and labor.

Most publications have stylebooks to provide consistency when usage and punctuation rules have variables, such as in the last example. Lacking a stylebook, the best thing you can do is use your common sense and think twice before you type a comma or other punctuation mark into a sentence. When in doubt, leave it out. No need to put a bump in the reader's road if you don't have to.

## Basic Editorial Set - up of a Daily

## Newspapers

Editors at newspapers supervise journalists and improve their work. Newspaper editing encompasses a variety of titles and functions. These include:

- Copyeditors;

- Department editors;

- Managing editors and assistant or deputy managing editors (the managing editor is often second in line after the top editor);

- News editors, who oversee the news desks;

- Photo or picture editors;

- Section editors and their assistants, such as for business, features, and sports;

- Editorial Page Editor who oversees the coverage on the editorial page. This includes chairing the Editorial Board and assigning editorial writing responsibilities. The editorial page editor may also oversee the op-ed page or those duties are assigned to a separate op-ed editor;

- Top editors, who may be called editor in chief or executive editor;

- Readers' editors, sometimes known as the ombudsman, who arbitrate complaints;

- Wire editors, who choose and edit articles from various international wire services, and are usually part of the copy desk;

- Administrative editors (who actually don't edit but perform duties such as recruiting and directing training).

A Newsroom is the place where journalists, both reporters, editors, producers and other staffers work to gather news to be published in a newspaper or magazine or broadcast on television, cable or radio. Some journalism organizations refer to the newsroom as the city room.

Copy Editing is the process by which an editor makes formatting changes and other improvements to text. Copy, in this case a noun, refers to material (such as handwritten or typewritten pages) to be set (as in typesetting) for printing. A person who performs the task of copy editing is called a copy editor.

There is no universal form for the term. In magazine and book publishing, it is often written as one word (copyediting). The newspaper industry writes the expression as two words (copy editing) or hyphenates it (copy-editing).

An Editorial is a statement or article by a news organization, newspaper or magazine that expresses the opinion of the editor, editorial board, or publisher. The term op-ed originates from the tradition of newspapers placing such materials on the page opposite the editorial page. The term "op-ed" is a combination of the words "opposite" and "editorial".'

The first modern op-ed page is generally attributed to the New York Times, which initiated its page on September 21, 1970, under editorial page editor John B. Oakes. Oakes had argued for the page's creation for ten years; when it appeared it instantly became one of the paper's most popular features.

## Editorial Boards

The editorial board is a group of people, usually at a print publication, who dictate the tone and direction that the publication's editorials will take. Editorials are typically not written by the regular reporters of the news organization, but are instead collectively authored by a group of individuals and published without by-lines. In fact, most major newspapers have a strict policy of keeping "editorial" and "news" staffs separate.'

In the United Kingdom opinion articles are often referred to as "leading articles" or "leaders."

The editorial board of a newspaper will regularly convene to discuss and assign editorial tasks. If editorials are written by the board, then they generally represent the newspaper's official positions on the issues. Often however, there exist also one or more regular opinion columnists who present their own point of view. Most newspapers also utilize nationally syndicated columnists to supplement the content of their own opinion pages.

## Editorial Guidelines

Editorials are generally printed on their own page of a newspaper, and are always labeled as editorials (to avoid confusion with news coverage). They often address current events or public controversies.

Generally, editorials fall into four broad types: news, policy, social, and special. When covering controversial topics such as election issues, some opinion page editors will run "dueling" editorials, with each staking out a respective side of the issue.

Many magazines also feature editorials, mainly by the editor or publisher of the publication. Additionally, most print publications feature an editorial, or letter from the editor, followed by a Letters to the Editor section.

## Differences

The editorial page contains editorials written by a member of the news organization and the opinion page contains opinion columns and sometimes editorial cartoons:

- Editorials are (usually short) opinion pieces, written by members of the editorial board of the paper. They reflect the stance of the paper and do not have by-lines.

- The opinions expressed on op-ed pages reflect those of the individual authors, not the paper. The articles have by-lines and are written by individual free-lance writers, guest opinion writers, syndicated columnists, or a regular columnist of the paper.

## Managing Editor

A Managing Editor is a senior member of a publication's management team.

In the United States, a managing editor oversees and coordinates the publication's editorial activities. The position is generally the second highest in rank, after the editor-in-chief (also called the executive editor).

In the United Kingdom a managing editor tends to manage budget and staffing issues at a publication, and may have equivalent ranking to a deputy editor in the organization's structure.

Editors review, rewrite, and edit the work of writers. They may also do original writing. An editor's responsibilities vary with the employer and type and level of editorial position held. Editorial duties may include planning the content of books, technical journals, trade magazines, and other general-interest publications. Editors also decide what material will appeal to readers, review and edit drafts of books and articles, offer comments to improve the work, and suggest possible titles. In addition, they may oversee the production of the publications. In the book-publishing industry, an editor's primary responsibility is to review proposals for books and decide whether to buy the publication rights from the author.

Major newspapers and newsmagazines usually employ several types of editors. The executive editor oversees assistant editors, who have responsibility for particular subjects, such as local news, international news, feature stories, or sports. Executive editors generally have the final say about what stories are published and how they are covered. The managing editor usually is responsible for the daily operation of the news department. Assignment editors determine which reporters will cover a given story. Copy editors mostly review and edit a reporter's copy for accuracy, content, grammar, and style.

In smaller organizations, such as small daily or weekly newspapers or the membership or publications departments of non-profit or similar organizations, a single editor may do everything or share responsibility with only a few other people. Executive and managing editors typically hire writers, reporters, and other employees. They also plan budgets and negotiate contracts with freelance writers, sometimes called "stringers" in the news industry. In broadcasting companies, program directors have similar responsibilities.

Editors and program directors often have assistants, many of whom hold entry level jobs. These assistants, such as copy editors and production assistants, review copy for errors in grammar, punctuation, and spelling and check the copy for readability, style, and agreement with editorial policy. They suggest revisions, such as changing words and rearranging sentences, to improve clarity or accuracy. They also carry out research for writers and verify facts, dates, and statistics.

Production assistants arrange page layouts of articles, photographs, and advertising; compose headlines; and prepare copy for printing. Publication assistants who work for publishing houses may read and evaluate manuscripts submitted by freelance writers, proofread, and answer letters about published material. Production assistants on small newspapers or in radio stations compile articles available from wire services or the Internet, answer phones, and make photocopies.

Technical writers put technical information into easily understandable language. They prepare operating and maintenance manuals, catalogs, parts lists, assembly instructions, sales promotion materials, and project proposals. Many technical writers work with engineers on technical subject matters to prepare written interpretations of engineering and design specifications and other information for a general readership. Technical writers also may serve as part of a team conducting usability studies to help improve the design of a product that still is in the prototype stage. They plan and edit technical materials and oversee the preparation of illustrations, photographs, diagrams, and charts.

## Assistant Editor

Assistant Editor may also be called as assistant editor; associate editor. Prepares written material for publication, performing any combination of following duties. Reads copy to detect errors in spelling, punctuation, and syntax. Verifies facts, dates, and statistics, using standard reference sources. Rewrites or modifies copy to conform to publication's style and editorial policy and marks copy for typesetter, using standard symbols to indicate how type should be set. Reads galley and page proofs to detect errors and indicates corrections, using standard proofreading symbols. May confer with authors regarding changes made to manuscript. May select and crop photographs and illustrative materials to conform to space and subject matter requirements. May prepare page layouts to position and space articles and illustrations. May write or rewrite headlines, captions, columns, articles, and stories according to publication requirements. May initiate or reply to correspondence regarding material published or being considered for publication. May read and evaluate submitted manuscripts and be designated Manuscript Reader (print. & pub.). May be designated according to type of publication worked on as Copy Reader (print. & pub.) when working on newspaper; Copy Reader, Book (print. & pub.) when working on books.

## The Editor (ED)

The primary role of the editor is to manage the newspaper:

- Determines whether a submitted manuscript is appropriate for publication.

- Selects expert reviewers (i.e., referees) and an area editor to evaluate the submitted manuscript.

- Renders a final editorial decision on each manuscript based on the AE recommendation, journal priorities, other similar manuscripts in process and related considerations.

- Communicates directly with the author and the review team.

- Schedules accepted manuscripts for publication.

- Balances workloads for the area editors and reviewers.

- Resolves any conflicts.

## Resident Editor (RE)

The primary role of the RE is to make recommendations on submitted manuscripts and, when that recommendation involves revisions, suggesting priorities for the author(s).

- Leads the review team to a recommendation.

- Based on a synthesis of the reviews and a reading of the manuscript, writes a short evaluative and constructive report reflecting the strengths and weaknesses of the manuscript for the authors and the editor.

- Evaluates the relative importance of the issues raised by the reviewers.

- When recommending revisions, provides specific priorities for the author(s).

- Makes suggestions regarding conflicts between reviewer evaluations.

- Makes a recommendation to the Editor regarding the final decision on the manuscript.

## Sub-editor

They are responsible for ensuring that the tone, style and layout of final copy matches the publication's house style and suits the target market. The work involves processing all the copy before it is published to ensure that it is grammatically and factually correct and reads well. Sub-editors also lay out the story on the page, write headings and may be involved with overall page design. Like other journalism roles, sub-editing is demanding and requires constant attention to detail within a fast-paced working environment. They work closely with reporters, editors, designers, production staff and printers.

- Polishes up the language by removing rough edges from the copy and making it readable;

- Fine-tunes the copy to the style of the newspaper;

- Simplifies the language to make it reader-friendly;

- Tailors story length to space requirements;

- Correct factual errors;

- Detects fraud or plant −a plant is falsehood in journalistic garment it promote somebody's interest or discredit somebody;

- Ensure balance and fairness and objectivity in the stories. In case of controversy, both sides get equal space;

- Guard against legal trappings like defamation and copyright violation. The report stories should not defame a person by use of pejorative language;

- Rewrites and restructures stories if necessary. Normally sub editing (subbing) involves looking for errors in spellings and grammar;

- Implement the editorial policy of the newspaper like to maintain good taste, shun sensationalism, etc.

- Thus, a sub editor is responsible for every word that gets printed.

The sub-editor's job is much less glamorous than a reporter's but very important. While a reporter is an out-of-doors man with a 'beat' to cover, a sub-editor is a deskman. Again, while a reporter is well known to newspaper readers as his reports frequently carry a 'by-line', a sub-editor hardly ever sees his name in print. He is an obscure figure working back-stage to give a face-lift to the paper, but even reporters, to whose 'copy' he gives spit and polish, making it readable to the average newspaper reader, rarely acknowledge his worth. Work activities vary and can depend on the extent to which production and layout work falls within a subeditor's remit. To be a good sub, you must be an all-rounder: you need to know the law, government and how to put a story together with speed and style.

## Editorial Set - up of a Magazine

Magazines operate very much like newspaper, with departments, editors, space budgets, and advertising, but magazines differ in a few important ways.

The potential lifespan of a news release is much longer for a magazine. A monthly publication might not use your news for several months. Depending on the printing and preparation schedule, your release could appear as soon as a week or two after you send the release or as late as six-months later. The nice thing is that whenever your news appears, the information remains in front of the reader for a full month instead of just one day.

The editorial focus and format of a magazine are usually more specialized than those of news-papers. "Focus" refers to the subjects a magazine covers; for instance, Linux Journal focuses on Linux in general while Computer World might focus on Linux in the enterprise. "Format" refers to the way in which a magazine's news and information is presented, usually as a particular mix of regular columns, articles, features (main stories), shorter pieces, and editorials (opinion pieces). Magazine stories don't have to be as "newsy" as newspaper stories. To a greater degree, a magazine researches and creates news rather than relying on current events.

General-interest magazines try to appeal to a large segment of the population. (Examples are Ma-cLean's, Readers' Digest, and People.) Special-interest magazines target a limited, well-defined community of readers who share a particular interest along with associated activities and concerns. Special-interest magazines are good targets for the Linux community, especially those focusing on Linux, operating systems, storage, security, computers, and information technology.

Whether special interest or general interest, the closer your news release relates to the audience of a publication and the greater the impact on that audience, the more likely an editor will choose your news to publish. The key factors are editorial relevance and appeal to the publication's target audience.

News Bureau is an accomplished national public relations firm that declines retainers, shares risk, quantifies performance and delivers publicity results before it collects its fees.

News Bureau breaks the rules of traditional PR agency relationships, in which clients assume all financial risk with no assurance of results. By shifting the burden of performance, News Bureau indemnifies qualifying clients from the consequences of rain-or-shine consulting fees and unfulfilled expectations.

## Difference between Editorial Page and other Pages of a Magazine

For magazines to be trusted by consumers and to endure as brands, readers must be assured of their editorial integrity.

- Design: Advertisements should look different enough from editorial pages that readers can tell the difference. To avoid confusion, any ad that looks enough like an editorial story or feature that it could be mistaken for one should be slugged "Advertisement" or "Promotion" at the top of each page in type as prominent as the magazine's normal body type.

- Covers: The front cover and spine are editorial space. Companies and products should appear on covers only in an editorial context and not in a way that suggests advertisement. (This includes use of cover "stickers").

- Adjacencies: Advertisements should not be placed or sold for placement immediately before or after editorial pages that discuss, show or promote the advertised products.'

- Logos: Advertiser logos should not appear on editorial pages except in a journalistic context. A magazine's logo should appear on advertising pages only in connection with advertisements for the magazine and its promotions or when an advertised product is touting editorial awards that it has won.

- Sponsorship: Sponsorship language (i.e., "sponsored by," "presented by," etc.) should not appear in connection with regularly occurring editorial features. Such language may be used in connection with editorial extras (special issues, inserts, onserts and contests) as long as the editorial content does not endorse the sponsor's products and any page announcing the sponsorship is clearly an ad or is labeled "Advertisement" or "Promotion" in a type size as prominent as the magazine's normal body type. Single-advertiser issues that don't include sponsorship language do not have to be labeled, but should include an editor's or publisher's note disclosing the special arrangement to readers. Advertisers may sponsor "out of book" events such as awards shows and conferences, and that sponsorship may be acknowledged without labeling on either advertising or editorial pages.

- Advertising sections: Editorial-looking sections or pages that are not produced by a magazine's editors are not editorial content. They should be labeled "Advertisement," "Special Advertising Section" or "Promotion" at the top of every page in type as prominent as the magazine's normal body type.

- Product Placement: Advertisers should not pay to place their products in editorial pages nor should they demand placement in return for advertising. Editorial pages may display and credit products and tell readers where to buy them, as long as those pages are solely under editorial control.

- Editorial Staffing & Titles: A magazine's editorial staff members should not be involved in producing advertising in that magazine. Advertising and marketing staff should not use titles that imply editorial involvement (e.g., merchandising editor).

- Editorial Review: In order for a publication's chief editor to be able to monitor compliance with these guidelines, every effort must be made to show all advertising pages, sections and their placement to the editor far enough in advance to allow for necessary changes.

- Advertising Review: While editors or publishers at their discretion may share the general topic matter of upcoming editorial content with advertisers, specific stories, layouts or tables of contents should not be submitted for advertiser review.

## Editing in Magazines

It may be a trade, technical, political, or popular magazines in any event it is well planned and every feature carefully edited by the editor himself if it is a one-man production, or by one of his assistant if it is bigger enterprise.

The magazine aims at informing and entertaining its readers. Since it contains matter, which is likely to remain fresh and interesting for some time, it is able to reach every nook and corner of the country. It has a wider and more extensive range of readers, and accordingly the scope of writings contained in it is larger than that of the newspaper, which circulates among a small group and deals in an easily perishable commodity-news. The magazine has to compete with newspapers conducting magazine sections, radio, and other media of information and entertainment. As such it has to be physically more attractive and from the point of view of contents more varied and perfect then the Sunday newspaper.

Magazines are read and appreciated at leisure. They are written and produced at leisure. The magazine sub prepares the dummy of his next issue several weeks in advance. He has no dread of the deadline. He knows what his readers want, and he gives it to them.

The front page is gay and colourful. The reader cannot resist it. The inside is equally enchanting. The table of contents promises a sumptuous feast- an intellectual treat. Every item is laid out with care and precision. Headings are attractive. They arouse curiosity. An artist to suit the atmosphere has carved them out. They have been appropriately displayed at the top, with the sub heads inside.

The magazine is richly illustrated with graphs, charts, comics, and photographs, and some of them are beautifully placed with the reading matter all around them. Magazine stories begin and end in continuation. There is no jumping for the reader to get the tail ends of stories somewhere on the back pages. Stories are measured and cut to fit the space assigned. The magazine sub is able to present a model of attractiveness and contents since he has time and also the resources. Since magazine articles are written in advance, quite often the lead paragraphs of special articles and features on current problems have to be rewritten by the magazine or sub editor. Only a few Indian magazines care for looks and contents. Those few are popular and successful.

## Into the Newsroom

## Role of a News Editor

"The job of an Editor is, among other things, to prod, shape, wheedle, cajole, mediate, challenge, anticipate, nit-pick, rebuke, inspire, support, confront, defend, criticize, and, as required, suggest different words, phrases, or grammar."

The eventual success of your organization's public and media relations efforts depends mainly on how often your news releases are issued and, more importantly, how often the news they contain is selected to run. The latter decision is in the hands of a person whose title is usually editor. Understanding an editor's job will help you do your job better.

Can you name the editor of your local computer magazine or local newspaper? The editor is a very important ally in public relations. The editor (whose title might also be managing editor or editor in chief) has overall responsibility for the publication's content. Below him or her, depending on the periodical's size, are subject editors who are assigned to specific beats (often called "departments"). These editors oversee the content for their departments. Sometimes each editor has additional staff, such as reporters, freelancer writers, photographers, copy writers, copy editors, etc.

The information contained in news releases is the primary source of information for most editors. Newsworthy releases are selected and edited or worked into an article. The selected releases are the lucky ones; most never see the light of day. When you consider that the editor at a daily publication receives upwards of 500 news releases on any given day, gauging the statistical possibility of an individual release being picked up for coverage is easy.

Newspaper Editors have overall responsibility for the quality, accuracy and tone of their publication, or a section within it. Their main responsibilities may include:

- Deciding on which stories to run

- Interviewing and writing

- Editing other writers' work

- Designing layout

- Recruiting and training

- Meeting distribution and advertising targets.

Most of the work is done at a computer. A newspaper editor works closely with the editorial team, reporters, advertising staff, printers and publishers to meet deadlines. It can be a highly pressured job.

Newspaper editors generally work around 40 hours a week. They often work into the evening and may work some weekends. If a big story breaks, they could be expected to cover it, even on a day off. The work is office based.

A newspaper editor needs to:

- Have excellent oral and written communication skills

- Be creative with a good command of English

- Have good organizational and time-management skills

- Be able to remain calm under pressure

- Be able to work to deadlines

- Be flexible and adaptable

- Have an interest in current affairs.

A successful editing career may begin with the post of copy sub-editor, leading to an editorial assistant or sub-editor position. Editors may move into related work with PR organizations or press offices.

Newspapers don't mean just the regular daily newspapers targeted at the general public. There are special-interest newspapers for business, computers, information technology, telecommunications, and other fields. The specialty papers may run weekly instead of daily, but, like their daily counterparts, they are primarily news-driven rather than feature-driven (which is more the case with magazines).

Newspaper editors reject many more releases than they use. The larger the paper's circulation or the more active the area being covered, the more releases the editor has to sort through.

Most newspapers have a space budget. The space budget consists of the total number of pages printed, divided between advertising and news articles. Advertisements are the lifeblood of a newspaper; ads consistently provide the largest portion of income. The ads must be accommodated first, after which the issue's remaining space is allocated to specific stories and departments by the key editors.

The selection of news releases to cover is based on the editor's personal and professional judgment. The main factor in that judgment can be summed up in a single word: "newsworthiness". Unfortunately, newsworthiness is defined by individual editor's opinions. Newsworthy stories are generally those that offer the most information with the most urgency to the most people.

If a news release issued on particular day is not covered in the following day's paper, this does not mean the news will not appear at all. Releases not considered newsworthy enough to appear in a weekday edition may be suitable for the weekend paper, where there is more room and less emphasis on breaking news. Even if a news item is selected for use, the article may still get pulled at the last minute. Perhaps an advertiser cancelled a large insert just prior to deadline, necessitating a layout change, or a big story emerged late in the day. When this happens, more expendable news is sacrificed.

What happens to releases that aren't selected for immediate coverage? Some are kept for future use, but more likely they are sent into the editor's trashcan.

## Editing Desk v/s Reporting

### Reporter

A Reporter is a type of journalist who researches and presents information in certain types of mass media.

Reporters gather their information in a variety of ways, including tips, press releases, and witnessing events. They perform research through interviews, public records, and other sources. The information-gathering part of the job is sometimes called "reporting" as distinct from the production part of the job, such as writing articles. Reporters generally split their time between working in a newsroom and going out to witness events or interview people.

Most reporters working for major news media outlets are assigned an area to focus on called a beat or patch. They are encouraged to cultivate sources to improve their information gathering.

A correspondent or on-the-scene reporter is a journalist or commentator who contributes reports to a newspaper, or radio or television news, from a remote, often distant, location. A foreign correspondent is in a foreign country. The term correspondent refers to the original practice of filing news reports via postal letter.

### Reporter v/s Correspondent

A Correspondent generally interjects some of his/her own opinions into the reported news. A reporter on the other hand in general considered to be impartial, i.e. only reports and nothing more. The term and spirit of the reporter is found more in British news, such as the BBC. While the correspondent is more of an American term, used in media outlets such as NBC or Fox News.

In Britain the term 'correspondent' usually refers to someone with a specific specialist area, such as health correspondent. A 'reporter' is usually someone without such expertise who is allocated stories by the news desk on any story in the news.

### On-the-scene TV news

In TV news, a "live on-the-scene" reporter reports from the field during a "live shot". This became an extremely popular format with the advent of Eyewitness News.

A recent cost-saving measure is for local TV news to dispense with out-of-town reporters and replace them with syndicated correspondents, usually supplied by a centralized news reporting agency. The producers of the show schedule time with the correspondent, who then appears "live" to file a report and chat with the hosts. The reporter will go do a number of similar reports for other stations. Many viewers may be unaware that the reporter does not work directly for the news show.

### Stringer

In journalism, a stringer is a freelance journalist, who is paid for each piece of published or broadcast work, rather than receiving a regular salary. They are heavily relied upon by most television news organizations. They mostly specialize in breaking news. In American newspapers the word carries a connotation of no-nonsense professionalism as compared to "freelancer," a term more likely to be used by newcomers to the business. The etymology of the word is uncertain. Newspapers once paid stringers per inch of printed text they generated, and one theory says the length of this text was measured against a string. More likely is the theory given in the Oxford English Dictionary: that a stringer is a person who strings words together.

## Freelancer

A Freelancer or Freelance worker is a person who pursues a profession without a long-term commitment to any one employer. The term was first coined by Sir Walter Scott in his well-known historical romance Ivanhoe to describe a "medieval mercenary warrior." The phrase later transitioned to a figurative noun around the 1860s and was then officially recognized as a verb in 1903 by various authorities in etymology such as the Oxford English Dictionary. Only in modern times has the term morphed from a noun (a freelance or a freelancer) into various verb forms (a journalist who freelance), and an adverb (she worked freelance).

Freelance practice varies greatly. Some require clients to sign written contracts, while others may perform work based on verbal agreements, perhaps enforceable through the very nature of the work. Some freelancers may provide written estimates of work and request deposits from clients.

Payment for freelance work also varies greatly. Freelancers may charge by the day or hour, or on a per-project basis. Instead of a flat rate or fee, some consultants have adopted a value-based pricing method based on the perceived value of the results to the client. By custom, payment arrangements may be upfront, percentage upfront, or upon completion. For more complex projects, a contract may set a payment schedule based on milestones or outcomes.

## Benefits and Drawbacks

Freelancers generally enjoy a greater variety of assignments than in regular employment, and almost always have more freedom to choose their work schedule. The experience also allows the opportunity to build up a portfolio of work and cultivate a network of clients in hopes of obtaining a permanent position.

Sometimes a freelancer will work with one or more other freelancers and/or vendors to form a "virtual agency" to serve a particular client's needs for short-term and permanent project work. This versatile agency model can help a freelancer land jobs which require targeted, specific experience and skills outside the scope of one individual. As the clients change, so too may the players chosen for a virtual agency's talent base.

A major drawback is the uncertainty of work — and thus income — and lack of company benefits such as health insurance or retirement pay. However, many freelancers, journalists specifically, have found security in a new option. Many periodicals and newspapers have recently offered the option of ghost signing. Ghost signing occurs when a freelance writer signs with an editor, but their name is not listed on the by-line of their article(s). This allows the writer to receive benefits, while still being classified as a freelancer, and independent of any set organization.

Another drawback is that freelancers often must handle contracts, legal issues, accounting, marketing, and other business functions by themselves. If they do choose to pay for professional services, they can sometimes turn into significant out-of-pocket expenses. Working hours can extend beyond the standard working day and working week.

## Principles of Editing

The main consideration in editing is to tell the story in the fewest words possible. Condensation is essential because there is more material than can be used. The second consideration is clarity, which is obtained by avoiding intricate sentence structure and by using familiar words. The third consideration is forceful expression. The sub-editor must constantly seek the most effective way to express the ideas of the story. The forth consideration is respect for accuracy. It means looking out for small factual errors, which disfigure an otherwise good story.

Editing involves more than making sure words are spelled correctly, language is used properly, punctuation is in the right places and spelling is accurate. These, however, are important details that separate a polished publication from a sloppy one. As gatekeepers of a publication, editors must have a clear idea about what the mission is. So part of editing involves being missionaries and Part also involves being ambassadors of ideas.

It is with experience that the best ideas most often come from the bottom up, not from the top down. So editors should be encouraging writers to pursue their own story ideas. This is done with prompting, nudging, cajoling, pushing-whatever works.

Editing requires good listening. The writer should be heard first then the editor responds. The conversation process enriches stories, because two heads are better than one. Conversation should be taking place when the idea is first being formulated; it should take place during and after the reporting phase; it should take place before the story is written and it should take place after the editor has fully processed the story. At each stage the editor should bear in mind that it is the reporter's story on the one hand, but it also is the reader's story. It is not the editor's story.

Story ideas are similar to loaves of bread. All of the elements need to be brought together and kneaded. Then the dough is popped into the oven until it rises and is ready to eat. The punctuation has an important function in a story. Its function is to help guide the reader through the sentence or paragraph in a way that will make the wording more understandable.

### Revision

Editorial changes, normally made in ink for the printer, are better made clearly in pencil on the typescript if the writer is going to see the changes. A reasonably legible photocopy can then be sent to the author for checking and revision process. The editor can draw attention to doubtful points with a marginal note.

### Structural Reorganization

Reorganizing a whole write up, argument or section ought to be the writer's responsibility, but the editor must have good reasons for asking for major reorganization, and they should suggest how it should be done.

## Expansion

If a step in the argument is missing, or if further experimental evidence is needed, only the writer can supply the missing material.

## Shortening

Shortening an article to a given length may be done by the author but is often better done in the editorial office. If the writer is asked to do the work the editor must indicate how it might be done, which sections, paragraphs, tables or illustrations could be deleted, which part could be condensed, and which marginally relevant theme might be cut out.

## The Title

A title that conveys the main subject or the message in a few words as possible is easy retrieval. Since editors know more about the use of titles in information retrieval than most writers, editors should have a major say in re-titling stories where necessary.

## Spellings

The difference between American and British spelling produce problems in these days of international journals largely in English. If the editor, publisher or printer cannot accept inconsistency between articles, the editor or copy-editor should change the spelling, where necessary, to whichever version is more common in the country of publication.

Guidelines for rewriting, revising and some basic principles of editing:

1. Give the main points of the news in the first paragraph.

2. Tell the story in headline and use a verb to give it vigor.

3. Check names, titles, facts, figures, dates, and address where ever slightest doubt exists. The sub-editor know the reference book which will clear the doubt.

4. Both sides of the story in a dispute must be given.

5. Use short sentences and short paragraphs.

6. Repeat names in court cases rather than refer to them as accused, witness, etc.

7. Indicate correctness of doubtful spelling by saying 'correct' within brackets.

8. Beware of foreign names.

9. Define long, unfamiliar words, especially scientific and medical terms.

10. Do not begin sentences with words like 'despite' or 'because'.

11. Do not use vague phrases like a ' serous charge' or a 'certain offence'.

12. Reporters to give a rather artificial flow to the story 'meanwhile' often use the word. Cut it out.

13. Use concrete words, words that make the reader see, hear, smell or taste. Test the story for concrete images and visual word pictures.

14. Be careful about pronouns. The misuse of the relative pronoun and punctuation are the most common grammatical errors in the news stories.

15. Editorializing any trace of personal opinion or a value judgment should be eliminated from the copy unless it is a feature or news analysis.

## Importance of Editing

The importance of editing are followings:

1. Ensures your written message matches what you were trying to say.

2. Helps to condense and improve the efficiency of your writing.

3. Questions your flow of thoughts, ensuring there's good logic.

4. Tells you if your content is too technical or if it doesn't make sense, at least to the general public; it is very easy to "get into the weeds" about a topic you are very knowledgeable about.

5. Asks questions or presents an alternative perspective that you might not have considered; in the case of a blog, this feedback might be an excellent follow-up for a new post.

## Editing for TV

We do post production editing to combine diverse elements, to trim existing elements, to correct mistakes and to build up shows from smaller segments.

The simplest editing is when you combine program portions by simply cutting the various video-taped pieces together into the proper sequence. The more care that was taken during the pre-production, the less work you have to do in the post production stage.

Many editing assignments involve trimming the available material to make the final videotape fit a given time slot or to cut all extraneous material. This occurs in ENG editing, where you may have 10 minutes' worth of exciting fire footage, but only 20 seconds to tell the story.

Editing is often done to correct mistakes, by cutting out the bad parts, and replacing them with good ones. This can be quite simple and may only involve cutting out a few seconds during which the talent made a mistake. It also can become quite challenging, especially if the retakes do not quite fit the rest of the recording, as to colour temperature, background sounds, continuity, or field of view.

The most difficult, but most satisfying editing assignments are those in which you must build a show from a great many takes. In this case, the edit is the major production phase. This is especially true in EFP post production, when all takes are shot with a single camera to be combined later.

## On-line and Off-line

Off-line editing produces a work print, a preliminary and usually lower-quality tape dubbed from the higher quality master. On-line editing produces that master copy that is used on the air or for dubbing off copies. The terms off-line and on-line don't refer so much to the tape format used, but rather the intent of the edited product.

The major advantage of off-line editing is that you can take time for reviewing the unedited material and deciding where to cut, without tying up expensive equipment. With burn-in dubs (those with a window featuring time code numbers "burned into" the bottom of the frame), you can identify the exact spot where you'll cut, and note these decisions on an editing shot list. Later, you can proceed with the actual editing.

Too many times, however, people start editing without having properly thought about the editing sequence. This can sometimes help to save time, but more often than not you will get lost in a maze of detail. In all but the most routine editing jobs, you will need to do an editing outline, a list of the desired event sequences and the necessary transitions.

## Analog Video Editing

### Assemble and Insert Modes on Analog VTRs

One's first thought is that, if you wanted to assemble a series of shots back to back, you'd use the assemble edit mode, and when you wanted to insert a shot somewhere to replace existing video, you'd use the insert mode. This is not exactly true.

When in the assemble mode, you dub onto the record tape so you always add new, fresh control track. The recording VTR is supposed to make perfectly continuous control track in this mode. Unfortunately, even the best machines sometimes fail in this regard. As a result, some assemble edits experience sync roll or momentary tearing.

When editing in insert mode, on the other hand, you do not transfer fresh control track to the record videotape. Instead, you use it as a guide and position reference for laying down the inserted video on the tape. Therefore, to do insert edits, you must first lay down a control track by recording black on the record tape, before using it for editing. This takes time, but you gain roll-free edits.

### Time Code

Time code is a way of representing time and position information about a tape in either an audio or visual form. To identify and mark where all segments occur, various address code systems have been developed. The two most common are the control track or pulse-count system, and SMPTE time code.

## Control Track Counter

The control track counter takes advantage of the control track pulses on the tape. These are counted, one by one, as elapsed time - one pulse per frame. The advantage of this system is that no special code needs to be recorded onto any videotape - either during the original shoot, or on the master edited reel. The disadvantage of control track counting systems is that they are not always frame accurate. You may lose one or two frames over the course of stopping, starting, and shuttling the machine.

## SMPTE Time Code

SMPTE time code, on the other hand, is an electronic signal that provides an address for each frame of video. This address is recorded on the time code track of the videotape.

If you look at the audio time code signal as an audio wave, it appears as a sort of square wave at a frequency of somewhere between 2400 Hz and 4800 Hz. This signal, upon closer inspection, is actually at least 80 transitions (cycles) about every 1/30 second. The code itself is made up of 80 binary digits (bits) of information:

| Time Code Bits | |
|---|---|
| Bit | What It Does |
| 0-3: | Frames units |
| 4-7: | [Assignable bits] |
| 8-9: | Frames tens |
| 10: | Drop Frame bit |
| 11: | [Unassigned bit] |
| 12-15: | [Assignable bits] |
| 16-19: | Seconds units |
| 20-23: | [Assignable bits] |
| 24-26: | Seconds tens |
| 27: | [Unassigned bit] |
| 28-31: | [Assignable bits] |
| 32-35: | Minutes units |
| 36-39: | [Assignable bits] |
| 40-42: | Minutes tens |
| 43: | [Unassigned bit] |
| 44-47: | [Assignable bits] |
| 48-51: | Hours units |
| 52-55: | [Assignable bits] |
| 56-57: | Hours tens |
| 58-59: | [Unassigned bits] |
| 60-63: | [Assignable bits] |
| 64-79: | Synchronizing word |

As you can see there are several groups of "assignable" bits for reel and show IDs and the like, as well as some future expansion room in the form of "unassigned" bits. These single digits can be any hex (base 16) value (0-9 and A-F). These can be used as a date, a "scene and take" number, or even as a source identifier.

The remainder make up the "hours:minutes:seconds:frames" we're familiar with, and a synchronizing word that always contains the same information to provide time code readers with a clue to when each time code word begins and ends and in which direction the tape is moving. The sync word of the time code frame must correspond exactly with the vertical interval of the matching TV frame.

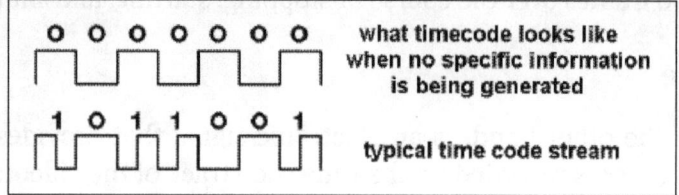

The figure on the left shows the basic signal when no specific information is being generated - actually, it's sending constant zeros. Keep in mind that the time code signal always changes polarity at the end of each bit interval, regardless of whether changing information is being sent. Sending these continuous signals - on, off, on, off - with no other aberrations sends a series of zeros to the time code reader. Changing the polarity within one of these half-cycles sends a one.

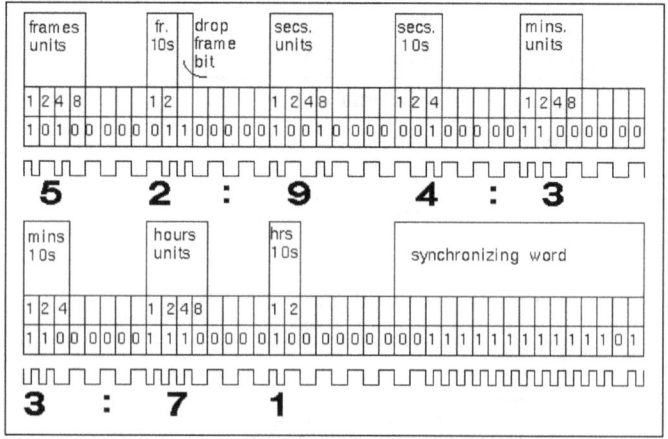

It's important to realize that while time code can be heard as an audio signal (a sort of rasping noise), it is in fact an audio representation of a digital signal that is read, decoded and turned into the familiar numbers. There's another way that time code can be encoded on the tape: vertical interval time code.

Vertical interval time code is another analog representation of time code. VITC (its abbreviation) is located in the vertical interval of a signal where it can be read back by equipment capable of doing so. It's essentially a series of white and black patches on one line of video. These segments are interpreted as "1s" and "0s" in the time code reader.

The time code reader, in its simplest form, is a box that takes the audio or VITC representation of time code, and converts it into a displayed set of numbers. It can display on an LED or LCD readout or on a "burn-in" within a video signal.

Frequently, there is a time code generator built into the same box as the reader. It can generate fresh code from numbers manually dialled in, or can frequently be "jammed" with time code from another source. This means that it reads in the time code, and locks its generator to that incoming source, creating fresh code.

Why generate fresh code? Time code is a square wave. It's read back most reliably when that square shape is preserved. Electronic devices will decay that shape, rounding off the sharp corners of the wave, making reading unreliable. Jam sync code helps prevent the problem by making new sharp square waves, identical to the incoming set. Also, if the incoming time code is interrupted, the jam synced generator will continue to create fresh code.

## Drop Frame Time Code

Regular time code counts 30 frames per second. Colour television has, in fact, 29.97 frames per second.

In drop frame time code, frames 00 and 01 are dropped from the counter every minute, except multiples of 10 minutes (10, 20, 30, 40, 50, 00).

Therefore, 108 frame numbers are dropped every hour (3.6 seconds), or one frame about every 33.3 seconds. Notice that it's digits from the numbering system that are dropped, not actual frames of video. You still have all of your video information with drop frame time code.

## Rule of Thumb when Spinning Shows

"Spinning a show" is the act of quickly fast-forwarding the program, to get the final running time, instead of watching the tape in real time.

To calculate the real duration of a show that has been spun using non-drop-frame control track pulse counters, multiply the result on the non-drop frame counter by .999. If you've spun a show using a non-drop frame control track pulse counter by accident, subtract 3.6 seconds per hour, or 1 second for every 16.67 minutes. This is a ball park estimate; your mileage may vary.

- If your show runs shorter than it was supposed to, you possibly did your timings using non-drop-frame on the control track pulse counter.

- If your show runs longer than it was supposed to, you possibly have your show material time-coded with non-drop-frame time code.

A 24-hour broadcast day can be out by about a minute and a half in one direction or the other, if all control track pulse counters or time code generators are in the non-drop-frame mode by accident.

## Analog Editing Systems

When videotape was first introduced, tape was actually cut with a razor blade and spliced together like audio tape. It was important to cut between the individual tracks of video, otherwise jumping or rolling of the video picture would occur. You can see a video editing suite in the picture, circa early 1960s.

Videotape editing "suite", early 1960s.

The microscope thing is what was called a Smith splicer, and allowed precision physical edits to be made. To make an edit in these days, you as the editor would push the stop button where you wanted the edit to occur. You'd mark the tape with a grease pencil, carefully unthread the tape from the quad machine then put it in the Smith splicer.

Developing the video tracks.

You can't see video tracks, so you would then wipe a "developer fluid" (essentially very fine iron filings suspended in alcohol) over the videotape which would magically reveal the tracks. You'd find the nearest control track pulse, and gingerly make your edit with the hinged blade. The second piece of tape (the continuation of your show) would be stopped, marked, developed and hacked in a similar fashion, and then the two pieces would be put together with adhesive splicing tape.

If you were good, the picture wouldn't roll or break up (or the join fall apart) as each splice went through the high speed rotating heads with a distinctive "zinging" noise.

With today's helical scan VTRs, this procedure is impractical if not impossible.

Making the splice.

Developed sync pulses, along with video tracks.

Despite the array of available equipment, videotape editing comes down to two basic systems: single-source editing and multiple-source editing.

## Single-source Editing

Single-source editing simply involves a playback VTR and a recording VTR. The *in* point of the record VTR's edit switches the record VTR from playback to record mode; the *out* point cues the machine to go back to play mode. This is a "straight cuts only" system, since there is not a second source to which you may perform transitions.

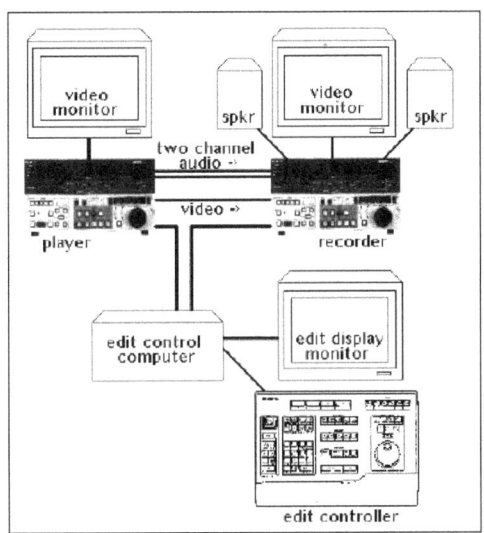

The two machines are operated via an editing control unit that allows: selection of precise edit points; control of VTR rolls; control of play and record modes (assemble, insert) and editing of audio and video tracks separately or together. Most units also allow you to: see and hear the tape at other than normal speeds; run a trial edit so you can rehearse it before actually performing it; trim the editing point frame by frame; perform split edits (edit video and audio separately without their affecting each other); and review the edit once it's been performed.

## Multiple-source Editing

The multiple-source editing system consists of two or more sources (VTRs, character generator, still store, etc.) generally labelled with letters (A, B, C, and so forth), and a record VTR. Most of the time, multiple-source systems are also interfaced with a switcher, audio console, audio tape machine, special effects and signal processing equipment. Most multiple-source editing systems use SMPTE time code.

The key element of these systems is the computerized editing control unit, capable of storing and performing many different editing functions automatically. In addition to the functions performed by a single-source editing unit, it can: locate any frame on either the source or record VTRs; pre-roll and run all VTRs in sync, simultaneously or staggered; preview and perform a variety of switcher-type transitions; do audio crossfades and other transitions; store many editing decisions (in an "edit decision list," or EDL); shift any one edit point, with all the others moving accordingly; print a hard copy of the EDL; interface with a wide variety of VTRs and other production equipment; use the "user bits" in SMPTE time code for scene numbers or videotape reels. Because of this increased complexity, when working with multiple source editing units, you have to learn a few more controls and procedures than when using single source units.

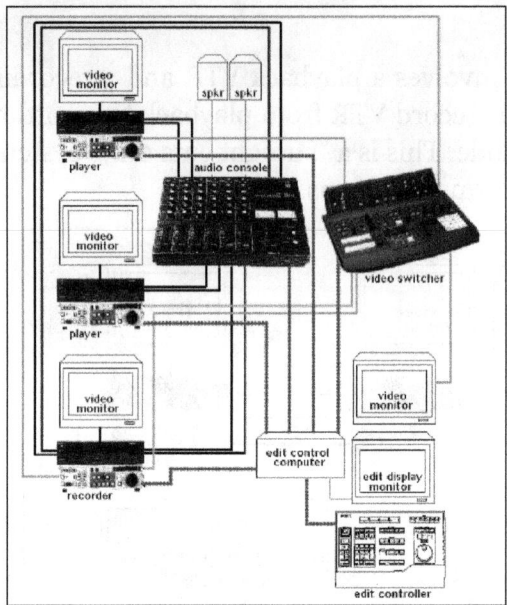

Typical A/B roll suite.

## Non-linear Editing

Now that you've studied a whole chapter on analog videotape machines, the future of video recording and editing may not be based on tape at all.

In the beginning, to get moving pictures recorded, there was motion picture film. Editing film meant finding the right shot on the reels (via a Movieola or flat bed editing machine); cutting on the individual frame lines; and splicing using tape, film cement, or a hot splicer. To keep track of all of these shots, the ribbons of cut film would be hung on a rail with a box below it (to catch the tail ends) - this was called a film bin. The process was slow and tedious, but very direct, and the editor felt in control. There's nothing quite like touching the actual frames of the shot. You could actually see how long a shot was, by looking at the film strip. The process was not perfect, however. Film would get shredded or sometimes lost somewhere in the bottom of the bin (or on the floor, whereupon the cat would eat it).

For television people, when videotape came along, it was a whole new ball game. There was no negative or work print developing - the shots were simply reproduced on a second VTR. However, once you had laid down 50 shots or so, it was very difficult to insert another piece between, say, shots 27 and 28. Your choice was to insert the extra shot, and overwrite the rest of your hard-earned editing session, or make a dub of the end of the edit, insert the shot, and dub back the remaining program again (losing two generations in the process.) Somehow, something had been lost in the editing process, which can be so much a matter of cutting and re-cutting, inserting new material, and experimentation.

Now, the phrase nonlinear editing is the buzz word in the electronic editing field. Nonlinear editing systems digitize and store analog footage onto computer hard disk drives, providing random access from that digital storage. The editing process takes place on a computer, running appropriate software to perform various functions. The video and audio information is stored on large computer hard drives, where it can be viewed, modified, and eventually played back in real time from the system. The concept of having quick access to video information is a very powerful one. This allows the editor to arrange and re-arrange material to his or her heart's content, when the work can then be output directly to air or to more traditional videotape.

Despite the initial high cost of using this type of technology, specialized off-line applications have been using it for years. Today, these systems have on-line quality output and user-friendly interfaces. Recently, prices have decreased, making nonlinear video editing cost effective for an even wider range of applications and for consumer use as well.

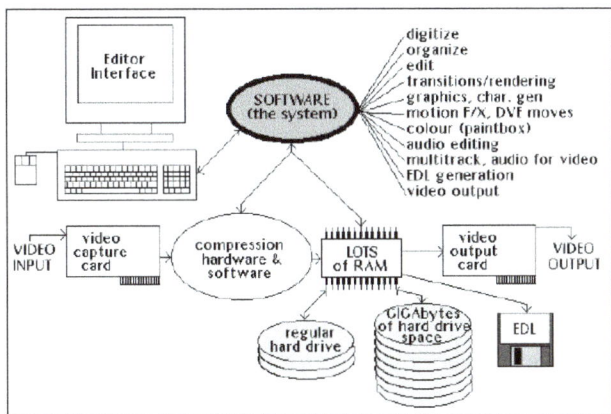

In many systems, shots are displayed on the computer screen as being stored in a list, contained within a bin - the old film term comes back. This list can be displayed and sorted according to name, length, or any of several other categories. To view any shot, you just click on it with a mouse or trackball interface, and drag it onto the source screen where it's available for viewing. With nonlinear, there is no waiting for tapes to spool to preview a segment.

One of the best things about nonlinear editing, is that the edit is instant - no splicing and waiting for the glue to set as in film, and no having to actually play back the entire shot for its full duration, as in videotape. One mouse click and it's done - on to the next edit. And the shot can, of course, be placed absolutely anywhere, even in between two frames of a previously laid down shot.

Another advantage of nonlinear editing can be its reduced VTR cost. Obviously, to have instant access to all of your shots, you have to shoot on a non-digital camera and VTR, and dump the raw footage into the nonlinear editing system, but this requires only one VTR (you can use the same videotape machine to record the finished product afterwards, too.) The down side of this, however, is the cost of hard drive storage - many editors only dub over the final takes of their shoot, not all of their raw footage.

Well, you may not believe it, but there are still a lot of linear editing suites in use in major broadcasting enterprises all over the world. They may be as simple as a straight cut Betacam set-up, or they may be a multi-VTR, multi-format, multi-million dollar conform suite that can play back everything from analog, to digital, to formats even considered obsolete. There is still (and will probably always be) a large demand for a linear system that can handle many formats, get the job done as efficiently as possible and at reasonable cost.

As well, television stations over the last few decades have poured millions of dollars into analog VTRs and linear editing systems. Economically speaking, they're going to want to get their full money's worth out of this equipment, and won't simply discard it because it's not the latest and greatest gear - especially if it is getting the job done already, quickly and effectively.

Consider another editing situation. Suppose you have a multi-hour live television special that was recorded on videotape and now has to be cut down into a one-hour special, involving a handful of edits. Would it be economical (in terms of time and image degradation) to digitize all that footage into a computer, make your few edits, and then play out the finished product back onto another piece of tape? It would be far quicker to simply assemble the finished show from the original record tapes straight onto the master tape – you'd be done in a little over an hour. In a nonlinear environment, it would take you that long just to digitize the original footage! So, in some cases, linear editing is far better than nonlinear.

## References

- Editing-Concept-Process: nraismc.com, Retrieved 3 April, 2019

- Reporting-Editing: nraismc.com, Retrieved 13 January, 2019

- The-importance-of-editing: gordonbenzie.com, Retrieved 17 July, 2019

- Editing-for-television: danalee.ca, Retrieved 7 May, 2019

# 5

# News Reporting

The process of discovering and selecting the relevant facts as well as weaving them into a comprehensible story is known as news reporting. Some of the different kinds of news reporting are sports reporting, political reporting, crime reporting, investigative reporting and education reporting. The topics elaborated in this chapter will help in gaining a better perspective about the types of news reporting.

News reporting involves discovering all relevant facts, selecting and presenting the important facts and weaving a comprehensive story. Reporting involves hard work, which in turn involves stamina and patience. The main function of journalistic profession is news reporting.

A reporter needs not only energy to spend long hours chasing a story, collecting facts from various sources in an effort to dig up the truth, he needs must have the will to pursue the course of his investigation to the very end in order to produce a really comprehensive story without any missing links or unanswered questions.

In the modern age news journalism the responsibilities of the press have grown manifold. These days, the people are governed by multiplicity of authorities, viz. Municipality, District Administration, State Government and the Central Government. Even non-governmental authorities are involved in the lives of the people in one-way or the other. Man cannot live alone. He is a social animal. The way his neighbours behave or act affects him. Man is thus anxious to know more about the world he lives in. Satisfaction of this curiosity is the major task of a good journalist.

The variety and the depth of news has, of late, increased manifold. In fact, newspapers, magazines and periodicals have become the main source of information for the people. This fact underscores the need for accuracy in news reporting. Giving inaccurate news or putting out news in a casual manner is fraught with grave dangers. A journalist, who is careless in news reporting or indulges in lies, is a disgrace to the profession. It is better to ease him out from this profession. If a journalist reports that 50 persons belonging to a particular community ,died as a result of communal riot when in fact only 5 persons had lost their lives, his misreporting can trigger off a major communal flare up and pose grave threat to law and order.

A News Reporter should follow the following steps-

1. A reporter must appreciate the importance of having a good reputation for absolute reliability. For this purpose he must be systematic in his habits and punctual in keeping his appointments. By observing these principles, every reporter can make his path smooth and trouble free.

2. A reporter should have the ability of news reporting and writing skills in the language of his paper. He should possess the quality to compose in a condensed manner as per allowable space.

3. The reporter of any local newspaper occupies a unique position and he becomes quite popular with the people of his town. He reports the local events, functions, fairs, socials etc. and comes closer to the social life of the town. A reporter should follow some professional ethics in his work. Sometimes, while engaged in his profession, he may come to some persons and develop confidential relations with them.

4. Sometimes, a reporter may be asked to write short length paragraphs regarding the local intelligence or about the city news. For this he should keep his eyes and ears open and develop a nose for local news. He should develop a system to ensure that none of the interesting news is missed by him. He should try to know the secretaries of social, religious, political, musical dramatic, legal, official and other organizations and should call upon them regularly to get some interesting stories. He should make inquiries from the police regarding news of accidents and crimes. He should also contact the fire-station for the particulars of local fires.

5. Every reporter should keep an engagement diary. In this way he can systematize his working and attend to all his appointments properly and punctually. By keeping an engagement diary he can know about the important engagements and other events in the future and cover them without fail.

6. The reporter should not forget to give a head line to his typed copy. Every copy which goes to the printer to be set is given a catch line. The catch line is a key word, because during the production it identifies all the sheets of the copy. Tile catch line is given on each sheet so that the printer can collate the whole story. The catch line should be chosen very carefully. It is better to choose an uncommon word, which may not resemble with another news catch line.

## Sports Reporting

Sports reporting are a type of reporting that reports on sports topics and events. While the sports department within some newspapers has been mockingly called the toy department, because sports journalists do not concern themselves with the 'serious' topics covered by the news desk, sports coverage has grown in importance as sport has grown in wealth, power and influence.

Sports journalism is an essential element of any news media organization. Sports journalism includes organizations devoted entirely to sports reporting—newspapers such as L'Equipe in France, La Gazette dell Sport in Italy, and the now defunct Sporting Life in Britain, American magazines such as Sports Illustrated and the Sporting News, all-sports talk radio stations, and television networks like ESPN.

Sports journalists, like any other reporters, must do their own reporting to find the story rather than simply relying on information given to them by the sports team, institution or coaching staff. Sports journalists must verify facts given to them by the teams and organizations they are covering. Often, coaches, players or sports organization management rescind sports journalists' access credentials in retaliation for printing accurate yet disparaging information about a team, player, coach or coaches, or organization.

Access for sports journalists is usually easier for professional and intercollegiate sports such as American football, ice hockey, basketball, baseball, and football.

## Famous Pioneers

### Grantland Rice

Grantland Rice was a early innovator for sports journalism and is best known for his work covering college football teams starting in 1925. Rice is also the writer known for naming the Notre Dame backfield of 1924 after the "Four Housemen of the Apocalypse." He covered exceptional athletes like Babe Ruth, Knute Rockne, and Bobby Jones, among others, helping make them into American icons. Rice has a scholarship given in his name by Vanderbilt University for a freshman intending to become a professional sports writer.

### Henry Chadwick

Henry Chadwick was known as the father of baseball for his work editing The Beadle Baseball Player, the first guide for sale on baseball. He was one of the first promoters of sports journalism and helped start the National Baseball Club.

### Leonard Koppett

Kopett was an established and influential sports writer who wrote for The Sporting News, New York Times, and New York Post among others. His best work was in baseball, writing stories on the game, and the inspirations that come from it. He received the Curt Gowdy media award by the Basketball Hall of Fame in 1994 and the J.G Taylor Spink Award by the Baseball Hall of Fame in 1992.

## Socio-political Significance

Major League Baseball once gave print journalists a special role in its games; they were named official scorers and kept statistics that were considered part of the official record of the league. Active sportswriters were removed from this role in 1980. Although their statistical judgment calls could not affect the outcome of a game, there was still the perception of a conflict of interest.

Sports stories often transcend the games themselves and take on socio-political significance; Jackie Robinson breaking the color barrier in baseball is a good example. Modern controversies regarding the compensation of top athletes, the use of anabolic steroids and other, banned performance-enhancing drugs, and the cost to local and national governments to build sports venues and related infrastructure, especially for the Olympic Games, show that sports still can intrude onto the news pages.

Sportswriters face much more deadline pressure than most other reporters, because sporting events tend to occur late in the day and closer to the deadlines many organizations must observe. Yet, they are expected to use the same tools as news journalists, and to uphold the same professional and ethical standards. They must take care not to show bias for any team. Sports journalists usually must also gather and use voluminous performance statistics for teams and individual athletes in most sports.

Many of the most talented and respected print journalists have been sportswriters.

## Sports Journalism

The tradition of sports reporting attracting some of the finest writers in journalism can be traced to the coverage of sport in Victorian England, where several modern sports—such as association football, cricket, athletics and rugby—were first organized and codified into something resembling what we would recognize today.

Cricket, somewhat like baseball in the United States, has regularly attracted the most elegant of writers due to its esteemed place in society. The Manchester Guardian, in the first half of the twentieth century, employed Neville Cardus as its cricket correspondent as well as its music critic. Cardus was later knighted for his services to journalism. One of his successors, John Arlott, who became a worldwide favorite because of his radio commentaries on the BBC, and was also known for his poetry.

The first London Olympic Games in 1908 attracted such widespread public interest that many newspapers assigned their very best-known writers to the event. The Daily Mail even had Sir Arthur Conan Doyle at the White City Stadium to cover the finish of the first ever 26-mile, 385-yard Marathon.

Such was the drama of that race, in which Dorando Pietri collapsed within sight of the finishing line when leading, that Conan Doyle led a public subscription campaign to see the gallant Italian, having been denied the gold medal through his disqualification, awarded a special silver cup, which was presented by Queen Alexandra. And the public imagination was so well caught by the event that annual races in Boston, Massachusetts, and London, and at future Olympics, were henceforward staged over exactly the same, 26-mile, 385-yard distance, the official length of the event worldwide to this day.

The London race, called the Polytechnic Marathon and originally staged over the 1908 Olympic route from outside the royal residence at Windsor Castle to White City, was first sponsored by the Sporting Life, which in those Edwardian times was a daily newspaper which sought to cover all sporting events, rather than just a betting paper for [horse racing]] and greyhounds that it became in the years after the Second World War.

In France, L'Auto, the predecessor of L'Equipe, had already played an equally influential part in the sporting fabric of society when it announced in 1903 that it would stage an annual bicycle race around the country. The Tour de France was born, and sports journalism's role in its foundation is still reflected today in the leading rider wearing a yellow jersey—the color of the paper on which L'Auto was published (in Italy, the Giro d'Italia established a similar tradition, with the leading rider wearing a jersey the same pink color as the sponsoring newspaper, La Gazetta).

## Specialist Sports Agencies

The 1950s and 1960s saw a rapid growth in sports coverage, both in print and on broadcast media. It also saw the development of specialist sports news and photographic agencies. For example, photographer Tony Duffy founded the picture agency AllSport in south London shortly after the 1964 Tokyo Olympics, and, through some outstanding photography (such as Duffy's iconic image of the American long jumper Bob Beamon flying through the air towards his world record at the 1968 Mexico City Olympics) and the astute marketing of its images, saw the business grow into a multi-million pound, worldwide concern that ultimately would be bought and re-named Getty Images.

McIlvanney and Wooldridge, who died in March 2007 aged 75, both enjoyed careers that saw them frequently work in television. During his career, Wooldridge became so famous that, like the sports stars he reported upon, he hired the services of IMG, the agency founded by the American businessman, Mark McCormack, to manage his affairs. And Glanville wrote several books, including novels, as well as scripting the memorable official film to the 1966 World Cup staged in England.

## Investigative Journalism and Sport

Since the 1990s, the growing importance of sport, its impact as a global business and the huge amounts of money involved from sponsorship and in the staging of the Olympic Games and football World Cups, has also attracted the attention of well-known investigative journalists. The sensitive nature of the relationships between sports journalists and the subjects of their reporting, as well as declining budgets experienced by most Fleet Street newspapers, has meant that such long-term projects have often emanated from television documentary makers.

Tom Bower, with his 2003 sports book of the year Broken Dreams, which analyzed British football (soccer), followed in the tradition established a decade earlier by Andrew Jennings and Vyv Simson with their controversial investigation of corruption within the International Olympic Committee. Jennings and Simson's The Lords of the Rings in many ways predicted the scandals that were to emerge around the staging of the 2002 Winter Olympics in Salt Lake City; Jennings would follow-up with two further books on the Olympics and one on FIFA, the world football body. Likewise, award-winning writers Duncan Mackay, of The Guardian, and Steven Downes unraveled many scandals involving doping, fixed races and bribery in international athletics in their 1996 book, Running Scared, which offered an account of the threats by a senior track official that led to the suicide of their sports journalist colleague, Cliff Temple.

But the writing of such exposes—referred to as "spitting in the soup" by Paul Kimmage, the former Tour de France professional cyclist, who now writes for the Sunday Times—often requires the view of an outsider who is not compromised by the need of day-to-day dealings with sportsmen and officials, as required by "beat" correspondents.

The stakes can be high when upsetting sport's powers: when in 2007, the English FA opted to switch its multi-million pound contract for UK coverage rights of the FA Cup and England international matches from the BBC to rival broadcasters ITV, one of the reasons cited was that the BBC had been too critical of the performances of the England football team.

## Some Leaders in Sports Journalism

### ESPN

ESPN or the Entertainment and Sports Programming Network launched in 1979 as a sports channel that covered low-awareness sports. Its signature show, Sports center, originated to show a larger package of sports highlights than local news programming. Since its inception, ESPN has grown into one of the largest players in the sports media industry. They currently offer sports television channels of ESPN, ESPN2, ESPNews, ESPNClassic, ESPNU, ESPN Deportes, ESPN

International, ESPN Brazil. ESPN also covers sports with their magazine, ESPN sports radio, and their streaming website.

ESPN fills their sports television stations with coverage and live broadcasting of sporting events from the NBA, NFL, MLB, college football, college basketball, PGA, PTA, PBA, Nascar, WNBA, and others.

## Sports

Sports is a well-known weekly sports magazine that has been covering sports since its inception on August 16, 1954. What started out as a magazine that covered yachting and polo has grown into a news source for all kinds of sports.

The early times of Sports Illustrated were anchored by the outstanding sports journalist of Dan Jenkins, Tex Maule, and Robert Creamer. More recently the great work of writers such as Rick Reilly has helped keep Sports Illustrated as a popular source for sports news.

## Fox Sports

Fox broadcasting company entered the world of sports journalism in 1993 when in bid 1.58 billion dollars to be the NFC conference television carrier in 1993 for the NFL. Since then, Fox Sports has become a large part of the sports journalism world with its regional television networks for many parts of the United States, and with its Fox Sports World channel. Fox Sports carries the rights to the Bowl Championship Series for college football, and also broadcasts NBA, NFL, Nascar, and other major sports leagues.

## Health Reporting

Medical journalism is news reporting of medical news and features. Medical journalism is diverse, and reflects its audience. The main division is into (1) medical journalism for the general public, which includes medical coverage in general news publications and in specialty medical publications, and (2) medical journalism for doctors and other professionals, which often appears in peer-reviewed journals. The accuracy of medical journalism varies widely. Reviews of mass media publications have graded most stories unsatisfactory, although there were examples of excellence. Other reviews have found that most errors in mass media publications were the result of repeating errors in the original journal articles or their press releases. Some web sites, such as Columbia Journalism Review and Hippocrates Med Review, publish and review medical journalism.

Medical journalism can come from a variety of sources including:

- Television news programs
- Newspapers
- Internet websites
- Scientific journals (those that report health- and medical-related news).

## Accuracy

Most inaccuracies and speculations in news coverage can be attributed to several barriers between the scientific community and the general public that include lack of knowledge by reporters, lack of time to prepare a proper report, and lack of space in the publication. Most news articles fail to discuss important issues such as evidence quality, costs, and risks versus benefits. However, medical journalism is not only what is being commercialized and covered by news and mass media. There is also another extensive, more academic branch of medical journalism which is based on evidence. Evidence-based research is more accurate and thus it is a much more reliable source than medical news disseminated by tabloids. Medical journalism in this regard is a professional field and is often disregarded. There are also some medical journalism institutions that provide assistance to medical researchers to enable them to perform more reliable studies. A 2009 study found small improvements in some areas of medical reporting in Australia, but the overall quality remained poor, particularly in commercial human-interest television programs.

More recently, the use of medical writers has become more popular as a way to produce medical literature that is clear, concise, and easier to read by the lay person.

The ICMJE, International Committee of Medical Journal Editors, is a committee that specifically deals with this kind of issue. This organization is committed to keeping medical reporting as true as possible by setting a standard known as URM, or the Uniform Requirements for Manuscripts. These requirements do not only specify technical points such as bibliographical references and copyrights but also regarding ethical issues that may arise. For example, a submitter must disclose any personal or professional relationships that might even slightly have a bearing on the submitted work.

To this end, it is not uncommon for researchers to hold a press conference or interviews before publishing significant research to prevent any misconstruing of any data or methods.

Although medical news articles often deliver public health messages effectively, they often convey wrong or misleading information about health care, partly when reporters do not know or cannot convey the results of clinical studies, and partly when they fail to supply reasonable context. This can result in unrealistic expectations due to coverage of radical medical procedures and experimental technology. Mass media news outlets can also create a "communications storm" to shift attention to a single health issue. The lack of health knowledge in the general public creates a situation where a person can be easily swayed to a certain point of view that is cast in the manner in which information is reported. Consequently, this can create a potentially unhealthy focus on an illness that in actuality is relatively rare.

Medical journalism can also influence an individual's quality of health care. Due to the relative ease at which information can be obtained on the internet, many people will now question doctors on new medications and treatments for their conditions. In more extreme cases, people will compare their symptoms, real or imagined, to various illnesses in attempts to diagnose themselves. There have been a few recent studies that have tried to explore the availability of health information as complement to health care or as a substitute yet no direct relationships have been found. This is most likely caused by a lack of knowledge or a lack of the ability in the individual to apply the health information once found resulting in seeking health care.

# Political Reporting

Politics is a big area which provides a very large part of the media's diet of news. Politics is about relationships within and between societies, about the use of power and authority, and about the government of countries or communities. For journalists, politics can range from stories about individuals competing for power in minor organisations to nation competing against nation in international affairs.

It is difficult to define where politics ends and government begins - or even if there is a dividing line. In this and the following chapter, we will look at the ways of reporting power struggles as news, at the coverage of elections, and at government - the practical application of politics.

## Principles of Political Reporting

The most important thing to remember about politics is that it involves people. It involves the politicians who make decisions, the public servants who carry out their orders and - most important - the people affected by their actions. Your job as a journalist is to serve the people affected, to explain how the decisions will affect their lives. You should also give them knowledge they need to take part in debates and vote for the people who will serve them best. You should not be writing for the politicians or public servants concerned in particular issues; they should know already what is going on. Whenever you report on any political story, always ask yourself: "How will it affect my readers' or listeners' lives?"

There is a further reason for reporting politics. If you tell the people what is happening, they can give their reactions to it. They can write letters to the editor give their opinions in pops or express their feelings directly to the politicians and public servants themselves. In this way, those in power know what the people they are governing think. This is important in any democracy.

## Explain Events and Issues

One of your main tasks as a journalist is to explain events and issues in a way your readers or listeners can understand. If you only report what happens or what is said, you will give your readers or listeners a fragmented picture of the world. They also need to know how and why things happen. Your stories must always put events and issues in context, showing how they affect people.

Explanations do not have to be long descriptions. It can often be done in one or two sentences. In the following example, we explain why it is significant that Parliament has extended its sitting to debate a finance bill.

Parliament is to sit for an extra day, to complete debate on a bill to introduce deep sea fishing licences. The Government wants the Fishery Control Bill passed this session, in order to raise revenue. Fisheries Minister Alva Maifu hopes that the licensing system will raise more than $1 million. If the bill is not passed by Parliament tomorrow, it will have to wait for the next session in three months' time.

Such explanations are particularly important in politics, where there is often a lot of debate and dealing in the background before decisions are reached which affect the lives of your readers or listeners. The change of one key person in a political structure may alter the whole nature of that structure and, as a result, change the lives of your readers or listeners.

## Explanation not Advice

There is an important difference between explaining events and giving advice on how to alter situations. Explanation is clearly one role of the journalist. Leave the political activist or the expert in that field to give advice. Your job as a journalist is to report different opinions, not to judge them. Be objective.

For example, while you should report that your country has signed a new trade treaty with Japan, and explain what it will mean for imports, exports, prices and jobs, you should not give your personal opinion on whether you think the treaty is a good or a bad thing. Your job is to tell the news, put it in context, report some expert opinion - and leave your audience to make up their own minds.

## Know your Audience

As with any area of news, it is important that you know your readers or listeners. You can then adapt your news-telling style to their general level of interest and understanding, remembering always that you should aim to inform the less-educated members of your audience as well as the educated ones.

It is worth adding here that some societies or communities are more "political" than others. By this we mean that they see politics at work in issues more often than the members of some other communities.

An awareness of the general level of political consciousness in your community will help you to determine which issues you need to cover - and how.

Do not confuse your community's general level of political consciousness with your own interest in political affairs, which might be greater because you work in the media. If readers or listeners are not interested in politics, you should not force them. However, even a lack of interest in politics should not cut them off from receiving news of a political nature about things which affect their lives.

For example, your readers or listeners may have little interest in debates in parliament over transport policy. However, if the debate ends in a decision to increase bus fares by 20 percent, you must tell them this.

## Be Suspicious

It may seem obvious, but remember that you cannot believe everything you are told in politics. Always be suspicious about what people say, especially when they make promises or boast about their achievements.

When a politician or political activist speaks just to appear good (or to keep in the public eye for the next election), you should treat what they say as personal advertising.

When they speak on a current issue, you should ask whether their comments add to the people's understanding of the issue. If they do, that is news. If they do not, that is just personal advertising.

## Cultivate Sources and Contacts

Even though you may be suspicious of the motives of politicians, you should still try to make a wide range of contacts among them. You may need to put aside your personal dislike for a politician or his philosophy. You should judge politicians you dislike in the same way as you judge those you admire. Whenever they speak on an issue, you must ask:

- Do they have the power to do anything practical about what they are saying? Can they change words into deeds?

- Are they influential in shaping opinion?

- Does their specific comment increase your audience's understanding of the issue?

If the answer is "yes" to any of the above, they may be worth reporting.

On a practical level, even politicians you personally dislike will give you stories if they believe that you will treat them fairly.

Politicians in opposition often provide useful information about abuses by those in power. Both you and they are there to monitor the performance of the rulers, whether national or local.

You may, of course, be working in a country where confrontation is not encouraged in politics. In some countries, politicians not in power are meant to support the leaders, not oppose them. Everyone is urged to work together to achieve certain national goals. Even in situations such as these, criticism is usually allowed as long as its aim is to suggest improvements to the system, not simply to oppose it on ideological grounds.

In most political systems, the leaders and the people try to work together to improve their society. They can do this by exchanging views. Try to keep a balance between reporting the achievements of the powerful and reporting the concerns of the powerless.

## Protect Confidentiality

Because political reporters have to deal with both sides in an argument, you have a duty to respect the confidentiality of sources - you must keep any promises you give to keep certain information to yourself. For example, you should not tell an interviewee what you have just learned in confidence from their opponent unless you know that the opponent will not mind. If people feel that they can talk in confidence to you, they will often give you plenty of material, both on and off the record. On the record comments can be reported. Off the record comments are usually given on agreement that they will not be reported.

## Know your Subject

Knowing your subject and being properly prepared is vital in all fields of journalism. Before you do any interview, you need to know something about the issue, its latest developments and history; the interviewee's background and politics; and the political system applicable to the issue. It could, for example, be pointless interviewing a local council leader about defence policy when defence is a central government responsibility. Equally, it could be embarrassing to ask a person why he opposes a measure when, in fact, he supports it in principle.

Always try to prepare some searching questions. Some stories will demand a very critical approach, others may only need a clear explanation and some questions to make some points clearer.

You must always pursue a line of questioning until you get an answer that will satisfy your readers or listeners. They cannot ask the party leader, association chairman or minister directly, so your readers or listeners rely on you to know what kind of questions they want answering. You may think you already know the answers, but the purpose of journalism is not to educate you. You exist as a journalist to inform your readers or listeners, so keep asking questions until you are sure that they will be satisfied with the answers.

It is important that you keep up-to-date records of any changes in government structures or political office. Whenever you write a story about any political or government changes, also make the necessary changes in the newsroom reference file. For example, if there is a cabinet reshuffle, get a full list of the new ministers and put it in the news desk file. Regularly update your files and check contact numbers.

# Crime Reporting

Crime reporting teaches some of the essential techniques of journalism. You learn how to dig for a story, how to follow leads, how to interview people to extract information and how to write crisp, clear, interesting stories under pressure of a deadline.

In small newspapers, radio and television stations, general reporters cover crime stories, while in bigger organisations there may be a specialist crime reporter or team of reporters who cover nothing else but crime.

These specialist reporters are occasionally called police reporters, although this title gives a misleading idea of their task. It suggests that all they do is report on what the police are doing when, in fact, crime reporting should cover all aspects of law-breaking - the police, the criminals and the victims.

Crime reporting has long been a central part of news coverage in free press societies, because crime stories are usually newsworthy.

There are several reasons why you should report crime and why people want to read about or listen to stories of crime:

- Readers or listeners often want an explanation of why crimes happen. They ask: "Could it happen to me?" They may want to know so that they can prevent a similar thing happening to themselves.

- Your readers and listeners need to know how laws are broken, and how people who break laws are caught and punished. This helps them understand what laws are and what the penalties for breaking them are.

- Most people obey the law, so crime stories are about unusual events - one of the criteria for news.

- Some people are interested in the way criminals get something without much effort. For example, although a gang of crooks may spend weeks or months planning a robbery to net them $100,000, it might take ordinary workers many years of effort to earn that much legally. Some crimes may fascinate people who obey the laws but who wonder what it might be like to break them.

- Criminals take risks and face punishment if they are caught. This may make them fascinating to read about.

You have a role to play, in providing information to counteract rumour. People will hear about crimes through casual conversations or rumour, or they may hear a siren as a police car dashes along the road; they will be only half-informed. It is your job as a journalist to tell them the truth about the rumoured crime or explain why the police car went past. If you can establish a reputation for reliability in this field, people will buy your paper or tune into your station as a way of making sure they know what is happening.

## Types of Crime

There are many types of crimes, criminals and victims. There are serious crimes and small offences. There are professional criminals and ordinary people who occasionally break the law. There are crimes which have obvious victims and there is the so-called victim-less crimes (although, as we shall see in a moment, all crimes have a victim somewhere).

It is not always the major crimes which make the most interesting news. Of course, your readers or listeners will be interested to know about an armed hold-up which netted a million dollars. But they may also be interested in the story of a sneak thief who broke into a poor widow's home and killed her much-loved cat. As with all news, crime stories should be new, unusual, interesting, significant and about people.

- New - Crime reporting has to be as up-to-date as possible. This is partly because some crimes depend for their news value on being current. For example, a story about a violent killer on the loose will lose much of its impact (and its value in alerting your audience to danger) once he is captured. Also, because in some societies crimes are a regular feature of life, todays break-and-enter quickly replaces yesterday break-and-enter in the public's attention. Crime stories get stale quickly.

- Unusual - Murders or armed robbery are not everyday events in most communities, and so have news value. However, less serious crime can also have unusual elements. Someone who sneaks on to a bus without paying or throws rubbish on the street may be breaking the law, but it is not very newsworthy. However, if a person stows away on an international airliner, that free flight becomes newsworthy. If the rubbish someone dumps fills three garbage trucks, that too is newsworthy.

- Interesting or significant - As we have said, most law-abiding citizens are interested in people who break the law in big or unusual ways. Crimes which by themselves are ordinary can become significant when placed in context. For example, the car theft can be one of hundreds in a city, but it may become significant if it is the hundredth car to be stolen this year.

- About people - Crimes involve people, as criminals and victims. The so-called victim-less crime does not really exist. The motorist parked in a No Parking zone at the very least may inconvenience other people and at worst may cause an accident. People who make false declarations to claim government benefits are taking money which could have gone to other people.

Always try to tell a crime story in human terms. Do not concentrate all the time on the police or the criminals. Look at what has happened to the victim. Your readers or listeners are more likely to be victims of crime than they are to be either police officers or criminals.

Remember too that the person the police refer to as "the victim" or "the deceased" is (or was) a real, living, breathing person. Try to visualise what their life was like before and after the crime. How did the crime affect them, their family or community?

## News Value

Most stories about crimes will have some news value. Exactly how much depends on several factors, which you will have to consider.

## Seriousness

We usually assume that more serious crimes are more newsworthy. A murder is more important than an armed assault, which is more serious than a break-and-enter, which is more serious than a parking offence. In terms of money, the bigger the amount stolen the more important the crime. Remember, however, that money has a different value to different people. The theft of $100 will be more newsworthy when it is money taken from a poor widow that when it is stolen from a rich businessman.

## Unusual Nature of the Crime

The more unusual crimes are generally more newsworthy. A break-and-enter at a school may be more newsworthy than a break-in at a home, but a burglary at a crocodile farm may be more newsworthy still.

## Size of the Community

Crimes are usually viewed as more important by smaller communities. If you are a journalist on a big city newspaper, an ordinary car theft may not be newsworthy at all. If you are a journalist in a small community, a car theft may be the biggest news of the week. Everybody may know the owner - they may all know the car. It is a sad fact that quite horrible crimes do not make the news in a big city because they are so common and because the chances are small of readers or listeners knowing the victims or caring about them.

## Identity of the Victim or Criminal

Crimes become more newsworthy if they involve people who are themselves newsworthy. An ordinary person attacked on the street may not be big news, but if that person is a local chief, that will be very newsworthy. A fraud case becomes more important when it involves a leading politician. A robbery becomes bigger news when police reveal that the robber was an escaped prisoner with convictions for murder and rape. It is generally true that a crime becomes more newsworthy if there is a strong chance of it happening again - usually because the criminal is known and likely to strike again.

## Investigative Reporting

Investigative journalism is finding, reporting and presenting news which other people try to hide. It is very similar to standard news reporting, except that the people at the centre of the story will usually not help you and may even try to stop you doing your job.

The job of journalists is to let people know what is going on in the community, the society and the world around them. Journalists do this by finding facts and telling them to their readers or listeners.

In much of their work, the facts are easy to find in such places as the courts and parliaments, disasters, public meetings, churches and sporting events. People are usually happy to provide journalists with news. Indeed, in many countries, thousands of people work full time in public relations, giving statements, comments, press releases and other forms of information to journalists.

Throughout the world, though, there are still a lot of things happening which people want to keep secret. In most cases these are private things which have no impact on other people - such as relations within a family or a bad report from school. These personal things can remain secret.

In many other cases, governments, companies, organisations and individuals try to hide decisions or events which affect other people. When a journalist tries to report on matters which somebody wants to keep secret, this is investigative journalism.

The great British newspaper publisher Lord Northcliffe once said: "News is what somebody somewhere wants to suppress; all the rest is advertising."

There are several reasons why societies need investigative journalism. They include:

- People have a right to know about the society in which they live. They have a right to know about decisions which may affect them, even if people in power want to keep them secret.

- People in power - whether in government, the world of commerce, or any other group in society - can abuse that power. They can be corrupt, steal money, break laws and do all sorts of things which harm other people. They might just be incompetent and unable to do their job properly. They will usually try to keep this knowledge secret. Journalists try to expose such abuse.

- Journalists also have a duty to watch how well people in power perform their jobs, especially those who have been elected to public office. Journalists should constantly ask whether such people are keeping their election promises. Politicians and others who are not keeping their promises may try to hide the fact; journalists should try to expose it.

Of course, journalists are not the only people in society who should expose incompetence, corruption, lies and broken promises. We also have parliaments, councils, courts, commissions, the police and other authorities. The police often take people to court for breaking laws. But sometimes they do not have the time, staff or skills to catch and correct every case of abuse. Also, they cannot do anything against people who behave badly without actually breaking any laws.

So journalists have a role as well. The difference is that when journalists expose wrongdoing, they cannot punish people. Journalists can only bring wrongdoing into the light of public attention and hope that society will do the rest, to punish wrongdoers or to change a system which is at fault.

## Who should we investigate?

Journalists should be able to expose abuse, corruption and criminal activities in all fields of public life, but the main areas include the following:

### Governments

These range from local councils to national parliaments and foreign governments. Sometimes politicians and public servants are actually corrupt and should be exposed and removed from office. But often they hide a decision because they know the public may not like it. They might keep a deal they have made with a foreign timber company secret because it will harm the environment or destroy people's homes. Often politicians and public servants spend so long in office that they forget that the public has the right to know what is happening. If the public elects people to office and gives those taxes and other forms of wealth to administer, the public has the right to know what they are doing. The electors should also know so that they can decide how to vote at the next election.

### Companies

Some companies break the law and should be exposed. But companies usually like to keep activities secret for other reasons. Perhaps they have made a mistake or lost money. Perhaps they do not want competitors to steal their secrets or they do not want people to oppose a development they are planning. However, even private companies have some responsibility towards the public. Companies are part of each society. They usually make some use of natural resources, take money from customers and shareholders, provide jobs for people and use services provided by all taxpayers. Where their activities affect the rest of the community, the community has a right to know what they are doing.

### Criminals

Although governments and companies can be corrupt, criminals make their living at it. They act like leeches on the community, so your readers and listeners have the right to know about them. Fighting crime is, of course, mainly the job of the police and legal system. But sometimes they do not have enough resources to do their jobs properly. Sometimes the law itself limits their powers. Also, the police and judiciary can sometimes be corrupt themselves. So journalists - like every law-abiding citizen - have the duty to expose wrongdoing.

There are, of course, all sorts of other individuals and organisations who like to hide things which affect the public. A charity may try to hide the fact that it is not doing a good job with money it has been given. A football club might be secretly negotiating to move its ground against the wishes of its fans. A man might be selling coloured water as a cure for every illness. All these things need to be exposed so that the public can make up its mind whether to support them or not.

## Some Basic Principles

Let us discuss some basic rules about investigative reporting before we move on to the practical techniques.

## News Value

Most newspapers, radio and television stations get a lot of requests from people to "investigate" some alleged wrongdoing. In many cases these are silly matters, lies or hoaxes. But you should spend some time on each tip-off, to decide whether or not it will make a story.

You should judge all topics for investigative reporting on the criteria for what makes news. Is it new, unusual, interesting, significant and about people? Sometimes, the story might only affect one person and be so trivial that it is not worth following up. Remember you have limited time and resources, so you cannot follow every story idea. Use your news judgment.

## Keep your Eyes and Ears Open

Always be on the lookout for possible stories. Sometimes people will come to you with tip-offs, but often you must discover the stories yourself. Story ideas can come from what you read or overhear or even a sudden thought while you are brushing your teeth. Good investigative reporters do not let any possible story clues escape. They write them down because they might come in useful later.

Listen to casual conversations and rumour, on the bus, in the street or in a club. Careless words give the first clues to something wrong, but *never* write a story based only on talk you have overheard or on rumour.

## Get the facts

Because investigative reporting means digging up hidden facts, your job will not be as easy as reporting court or a public meeting. People will try to hide things from you. You must gather as many relevant facts as you can, from as many people as possible. Your facts must be accurate, so always check them.

And do not expect dramatic results. Real life journalism is seldom like the stories you see in films. Most investigations need many hours of work gathering lots and lots of small details. You and your editor must realise this. If you are not given enough time, you may not be able to do any successful investigative reporting.

## Fit the Facts Together

As you gather the facts, fit them together to make sure that they make sense. Investigative reporting is often like doing a jigsaw. At the beginning you have a jumble of pieces. Only slowly will they emerge as a picture. Unlike a jigsaw puzzle, you will not have all the pieces at the beginning. You have to recognise which pieces are missing then go and find them.

## Check the facts

Remember you are trying to find information which some people want to keep secret. They will not help you in your investigation, so you cannot check your facts with them. They will probably oppose you and look for mistakes in everything you write or broadcast. If you make a mistake, they will probably take you to court. You must always check your facts. Take a tip from the most famous example of investigative reporting, the so-called Watergate Affair. *The Washington Post* reporters Bob Woodward and Carl Bernstein investigated a crime which eventually led to the downfall of US President Richard Nixon. They knew their enemies would be waiting for them to make a mistake, so they made it a rule that they would never use any fact unless it was confirmed by two sources. This is a good rule to try to follow.

However, remember that many people you might interview about corruption could be corrupt themselves. Criminals lie, so be suspicious of what you are told - and check their words with someone else, preferably someone you trust.

## Evidence

In addition to gathering facts, you should also gather evidence to support those facts. This is especially important in case you are taken to court for defamation as a result of your investigation. Courts will only accept facts which can be proved. If someone tells you something on the record, you can show the court your notes, but it would also be useful to get a signed statutory declaration from them. This is a kind of legal statement given under oath. Original documents will usually be accepted as evidence, but photocopies may not, unless they are supported by evidence from the owner of the original, who may not choose to help you.

## Confidential Sources

When investigating corruption or abuse, you will meet people who will only give you information if you promise never to reveal their identity. This is very common in criminal matters, where people are scared of pay-back.

You can agree to these conditions but remember sometime in the future a judge examining the same matter in court may order you to reveal the name of such a confidential source of information. You will be breaking the law if you refuse to name your source, and could go to jail for contempt.

If you promise to protect a confidential source, you must do so until the source himself or herself releases you from that promise. So if you are not prepared to go to jail to protect a source, do not promise in the first place.

## Threats

People may threaten you to try to stop your work. This could be a threat of physical harm or a threat by a company to stop advertising with your newspaper or station. It could even by a vague threat to "do something" to you. Most threats are never carried out. The people making them realise that harming you will only make their situation worse.

But all threats should be reported immediately to your editor or your organisation's lawyer. This will share the burden of worry with someone objective. It will also act as extra protection if the person making the threat knows that it is public knowledge. If you have a witness to the threat, you might be able to include it in your eventual story, after getting legal advice.

Investigative journalism *always* leads to some unpleasant conflict. If you cannot cope with conflict, stay out of investigative journalism.

## Work within the Law

Journalists have no special rights in law, even when investigating corruption. Unlike the police, journalists cannot listen in to other people's telephone calls or open their letters. Journalists cannot enter premises against a person's wish.

You must work within the law, but more than that, you should not use any unethical methods of getting information. For example, you should not pretend to be someone to whom people feel obliged to give information, such as a police officer or a government official.

However, there are situations where you do not have to tell people that you are a journalist when gathering information. If you have any doubts about legal matters, consult your editor or your organisation's lawyer.

# Education Reporting

The education beat is a wide umbrella, covering everything from preschool through higher education, and from school funding to learning outcomes. The beat has become even broader and more complex in recent years in part because of the expansion of charter schools, the increasing popularity of home schooling, and federal achievement standards. These days, education stories are often political stories as well, and reporters on the beat frequently have to navigate overlapping layers of authority to get the information they need to understand what's really happening in the schools.

If you're on the education beat, you'll probably spend time attending school board and PTA meetings, not so much to report on them as to look for sources and story ideas. Celeste Ford, formerly of WABC-TV in New York, once found a story by scanning the agenda for an upcoming meeting and noticing a proposed city resolution that would ask the state to tighten beeper requirements on school buses. At the time, the state required back-up beepers only on buses built after 1990, but thousands of city school buses were older than that. Ford located statistics through the Board of Education and the Department of Motor Vehicles. She did the math, determined how much it would cost to install beepers on the buses that lacked them, and then took that number to a city official for comment. Her story included the voices of schoolchildren, parents, a deputy chancellor of city schools, a school bus company executive and a representative of a school where a student was killed when a bus without a beeper backed over her.

Reporters covering education need to understand the structure, staffing and economics of the school systems they cover, which may vary widely. They should be prepared to decipher statistics and to compare budgets over time to see where the money goes and what happens as a result. Covering education also means tracking statistical data such as dropout and graduation rates, teacher retention and vacancy rates, principal turnover and the results of high-stakes testing. Following the numbers helped WFAA-TV in Dallas expose fraud by for-profit schools in a series of stories, Bitter Lessons, that won both a DuPont-Columbia and a Peabody Award.

Some news organizations use education data to create their own measurements, like the Washington Post's "challenge index" that ranks high schools based on the percentage of students who take Advanced Placement, International Baccalaureate or other college-level tests.

When education reporters cover policy issues like the certification process for teachers or efforts to end social promotion, they need to know how these issues have been handled in the past or in similar school districts, and what research has shown about the effectiveness of these policies. When they cover test results, they need to examine the details behind the data. Ranking schools' performance without considering demographics like race, income or parents' education, for example, will produce a misleading story.

One of the toughest challenges many education reporters face is a lack of access to schools and students; superintendents often cite privacy concerns to keep reporters out. It's difficult to put a human face on education stories if you can't shoot pictures in classrooms or talk to students and teachers on school grounds. Reporters who invest time in developing relationships with individual students, parents, teachers and administrators can eventually earn their trust and gain the access they need to tell compelling stories on the education beat.

As an education reporter, you should read school newspapers and websites, subscribe to parent newsletters and e-mail discussion lists, and check local university alumni reviews to see which issues are bubbling up.

## Online Reporting

Online Reporting, also known as digital reporting is a contemporary form of journalism where editorial content is distributed via the Internet, as opposed to publishing via print or broadcast. What constitutes digital journalism is debated by scholars; however, the primary product of journalism, which is news and features on current affairs, is presented solely or in combination as text, audio, video, or some interactive forms like newsgames, and disseminated through digital media technology.

Fewer barriers to entry, lowered distribution costs, and diverse computer networking technologies have led to the widespread practice of digital journalism. It has democratized the flow of information that was previously controlled by traditional media including newspapers, magazines, radio, and television.

Some have asserted that a greater degree of creativity can be exercised with digital journalism when compared to traditional journalism and traditional media. The digital aspect may be central to the journalistic message and remains, to some extent, within the creative control of the writer, editor, and/or publisher.

It has been acknowledged that reports of its growth have tended to be exaggerated. In fact, a 2019 Pew survey showed of 16% decline of time spent on online news sites since 2016.

There is no absolute agreement as to what constitutes digital journalism. Mu Lin argues that, "Web and mobile platforms demand us to adopt a platform-free mindset for an all-inclusive production approach – create the [digital] contents first, then distribute via appropriate platforms." The repurposing of print content for an online audience is sufficient for some, while others require content created with the digital medium's unique features like hypertextuality. Fondevila Gascón adds multimedia and interactivity to complete the digital journalism essence. For Deuze, online journalism can be functionally differentiated from other kinds of journalism by its technological component which journalists have to consider when creating or displaying content. Digital journalistic work may range from purely editorial content like CNN (produced by professional journalists) online to public-connectivity websites like Slashdot (communication lacking formal barriers of entry). The difference of digital journalism from traditional journalism may be in its reconceptualised role of the reporter in relation to audiences and news organizations. The expectations of society for instant information was important for the evolution of digital journalism. However, it is likely that the exact nature and roles of digital journalism will not be fully known for some time.

Digital journalism allows for connection and discussion at levels that print does not offer on its own. People can comment on articles and start discussion boards to discuss articles. Before the Internet, spontaneous discussion between readers who had never met was impossible. The process of discussing a news item is a big portion of what makes for digital journalism. People add to the story and connect with other people who want to discuss the topic.

Digital journalism creates an opportunity for niche audiences, allowing people to have more options as to what to view and read.

Digital journalism opens up new ways of storytelling; through the technical components of the new medium, digital journalists can provide a variety of media, such as audio, video, and digital photography.

Digital journalism represents a revolution of how news is consumed by society. Online sources are able to provide quick, efficient, and accurate reporting of breaking news in a matter of seconds, providing society with a synopsis of events as they occur. Throughout the development of the event, journalists are able to feed online sources the information keeping readers up-to-date in mere seconds. The speed in which a story can be posted can affect the accuracy of the reporting in a way that doesn't usually happen in print journalism. Before the emergence of digital journalism the printing process took much more time, allowing for the discovery and correction of errors.

News consumers must become Web literate and use critical thinking to evaluate the credibility of sources. Because it is possible for anyone to write articles and post them on the Internet, the definition of journalism is changing. Because it is becoming increasingly simple for the average person to have an impact in the news world through tools like blogs and even comments on news stories on reputable news websites, it becomes increasingly difficult to sift through the massive amount of information coming in from the digital area of journalism.

There are great advantages with digital journalism and the new blogging evolution that people are becoming accustomed to, but there are disadvantages. For instance, people are used to what they already know and can't always catch up quickly with the new technologies in the 21st century. The goals of print and digital journalism are the same, although different tools are needed to function.

The interaction between the writer and consumer is new, and this can be credited to digital journalism. There are many ways to get personal thoughts on the Web. There are some disadvantages to this, however, the main one being factual information. There is a pressing need for accuracy in digital journalism, and until they find a way to press accuracy, they will still face some criticism.

One major dispute regards the credibility of these online news websites. A digital journalism credibility study performed by the Online News Association compares the online public credibility ratings to actual media respondent credibility ratings.

The effects of digital journalism are evident worldwide. This form of journalism has pushed journalists to reform and evolve. Older journalists who are not tech savvy have felt the blunt force of this. In recent months, a number of older journalists have been pushed out and younger journalists brought in because of their lower cost and ability to work in advanced technology settings.

## Impact on Publishers

Many newspapers, such as *The New York Times*, have created online sites to remain competitive and have taken advantage of audio, video, and text linking to remain at the top of news consumers' lists as most of the news enthusiasm now reach their base through hand held devices such as smart phones, tables etc. Hence audio or video backing is definite advantage.

Newspapers rarely break news stories any more, with most websites reporting on breaking news before the cable news channels. Digital journalism allows for reports to start out vague and generalized, and progress to a better story. Newspapers and TV cable are at a disadvantage because they generally can only put together stories when an ample amount of detail and information are available. Often, newspapers have to wait for the next day, or even two days later if it is a late-breaking story, before being able to publish it. Newspapers lose a lot of ground to their online counterparts, with ad revenue shifting to the Internet, and subscription to the printed paper decreasing. People are now able to find the news they want, when they want, without having to leave their homes or pay to receive the news, even though there are still people who are willing to pay for online journalistic content.

Because of this, many people have viewed digital journalism as the death of journalism. According to communication scholar Nicole Cohen, "four practices stand out as putting pressure on traditional journalism production: outsourcing, unpaid labour, metrics and measurement, and automation". Free advertising on websites such as Craigslist has transformed how people publicize; the Internet has created a faster, cheaper way for people to get news out, thus creating the shift in ad sales from standard newspapers to the Internet. There has been a substantial effect of digital journalism and media on the newspaper industry, with the creation of new business models. It is now possible to contemplate a time in the near future when major towns will no longer have a newspaper and when magazines and network news operations will employ no more than a handful of reporters. Many newspapers and individual print journalists have been forced out of business because of the popularity of digital journalism. The newspapers that have not been willing to be forced out of business have attempted to survive by saving money, laying off staff, shrinking the size of the publications, eliminating editions, as well as partnering with other businesses to share coverage and content. In 2009, one study concluded that most journalists are ready to compete in a digital world and that these journalists believe the transition from print to digital journalism in their newsroom is moving too slowly. Some highly specialized positions in the publishing industry have become obsolete. The growth in digital journalism and the near collapse of the economy has also led to downsizing for those in the industry.

Students wishing to become journalists now need to be familiar with digital journalism in order to be able to contribute and develop journalism skills. Not only must a journalist analyze their audience and focus on effective communication with them, they have to be quick; news websites are able to update their stories within minutes of the news event. Other skills may include creating a website and uploading information using basic programming skills.

Critics believe digital journalism has made it easier for individuals who are not qualified journalists to misinform the general public. Many believe that this form of journalism has created a number of sites that do not have credible information. Sites such as PerezHilton.com have been criticized for blurring the lines between journalism and opinionated writing.

Some critics believe that newspapers should not switch to a solely Internet-based format, but instead keep a component of print as well as digital.

Digital journalism allows citizens and readers the opportunity to join in on threaded discussions relating to a news article that has been read by the public. This offers an excellent source for writers and reporters to decide what is important and what should be omitted in the future. These threads can provide useful information to writers of digital journalism so that future articles can be pruned and improved to possibly create a better article the next time around.

## Implications on Traditional Journalism

Digitization is currently causing many changes to traditional journalistic practice. The labour of journalists in general is becoming increasingly dependant on digital journalism. Scholars outline that this is actually a change to the execution of journalism and not the conception part of the labour process. They also contend that this is simply the de-skilling of some skills and the up-skilling of others. This theory is in contention to the notion that technological determinism is negatively effecting journalism, as it should be understood that it is just changing the traditional skill set. Communication scholar Nicole Cohen believes there are several trends putting pressure on this traditional skill set. Some of which being outsourcing, algorithms, and automation. Although she believes that technology could be used to improve Journalism, she feels the current trends in digital journalism are so far affecting the practice in a negative way.

There is also the impact that digital journalism is facing due to citizen journalism. Because digital journalism takes place online and is contributed mostly by citizens on user generated content sites, there is competition growing between the two. Citizen journalism allows anyone to post anything, and because of that, journalists are being forced by their employers to publish more news content than before, which often means rushing news stories and failing to confirm information.

## Work outside Traditional Press

The Internet has also given rise to more participation by people who are not normally journalists, such as with Indy Media (Max Perez). Bloggers write on web logs or blogs. Traditional journalists often do not consider bloggers to automatically be journalists. This has more to do with standards and professional practices than the medium. For instance, crowdsourcing and crowd funding journalism attracts amateur journalists, as well as ambitious professionals that are restrained by the boundaries set by traditional press. However, the implication of these types of journalism is that it disregards the professional norms of journalistic practices that ensures accuracy and impartiality of the content. But, as of 2005, blogging has generally gained at least more attention and has led to some effects on mainstream journalism, such as exposing problems related to a television piece about President George W. Bush's National Guard Service.

Recent legal judgements have determined that bloggers are entitled to the same protections as other journalists subject to the same responsibilities. In the United States, the Electronic Frontier Foundation has been instrumental in advocating for the rights of journalist bloggers.

In Canada, the Supreme Court of Canada ruled that:" A second preliminary question is what the new defence should be called. In arguments before us, the defence was referred to as the responsible journalism test. This has the value of capturing the essence of the defence in succinct style. However, the traditional media are rapidly being complemented by new ways of communicating on matters of public interest, many of them online, which do not involve journalists. These new disseminators of news and information should, absent good reasons for exclusion, be subject to the same laws as established media outlets.

Other significant tools of on-line journalism are Internet forums, discussion boards and chats, especially those representing the Internet version of official media. The widespread use of the Internet all over the world created a unique opportunity to create a meeting place for both sides in many conflicts, such as the Israeli–Palestinian conflict and the First and Second Chechen Wars. Often this gives a unique chance to find new, alternative solutions to the conflict, but often the Internet is turned into the battlefield by contradicting parties creating endless "online battles."

Internet radio and podcasts are other growing independent media based on the Internet.

## Blogs

With the rise of digital media, there is a move from the traditional journalist to the blogger or amateur journalist. Blogs can be seen as a new genre of journalism because of their "narrative style of news characterized by personalization" that moves away from traditional journalism's approach, changing journalism into a more conversational and decentralized type of news. Blogging has become a large part of the transmitting of news and ideas across cites, states, and countries, and bloggers argue that blogs themselves are now breaking stories. Even online news publications have blogs that are written by their affiliated journalists or other respected writers. Blogging allows readers and journalists to be opinionated about the news and talk about it in an open environment. Blogs allow comments where some news outlets do not, due to the need to constantly monitor what is posted. By allowing comments, the reader can interact with a story instead of just absorbing the words on the screen. According to one 2007 study, 15% of those who read blogs read them for news.

However, many blogs are highly opinionated and have a bias. Some are not verified to be true. The Federal Trade Commission (FTC) established guidelines mandating that bloggers disclose any free goods or services they receive from third parties in 2009 in response to a question of the integrity of product and service reviews in the online community.

## Citizen Journalism

Digital journalism's lack of a traditional "editor" has given rise to citizen journalism. The early advances that the digital age offered journalism were faster research, easier editing, conveniences, and a faster delivery time for articles. The Internet has broadened the effect that the digital age has on journalism. Because of the popularity of the Internet, most people have access, and can add their forms of journalism to the information network. This allows anyone who wants to share something they deem important that has happened in their community. Individuals who are not professional journalists who present news through their blogs or websites are often referred to as citizen journalists. One does not need a degree to be a citizen journalist. Citizen journalists are able to publish information that may not be reported otherwise, and the public has a greater opportunity to be informed. Some companies use the information that a citizen journalist relays when they themselves can not access certain situations, for example, in countries where freedom of the press is limited. Anyone can record events happening and send it anywhere they wish, or put it on their website. Non-profit and grass roots digital journalism sites may have far fewer resources than their corporate counterparts, yet due to digital media are able to have websites that are technically comparable. Other media outlets can then pick up their story and run with it as they please, thus allowing information to reach wider audiences.

For citizen journalism to be effective and successful there needs to be citizen editors, their role being to solicit other people to provide accurate information and to mediate interactivity among users. An example can be found in the start up of the South Korean online daily newspaper, OhMyNews, where the founder recruited several hundred volunteer "citizen reporters" to write news articles which were edited and processed by four professional journalists.

## Legal Issues

One emerging problem with online journalism in the United States is that, in many states, individuals who publish only on the Web do not enjoy the same First Amendment rights as reporters who work for traditional print or broadcast media. As a result, unlike a newspaper, they are much more liable for such things as libel. In California, however, protection of anonymous blog sources was ruled to be the same for both kinds of journalism.

## Extra-jurisdictional Enforcement

In Canada there are more ambiguities, as Canadian libel law permits suits to succeed even if no false statements of fact are involved, and even if matters of public controversy are being discussed. In British Columbia, as part of "a spate of lawsuits" against online news sites, according to legal columnist Michael Geist, several cases have put key issues in online journalism up for rulings. Geist mentioned that Green Party of Canada financier Wayne Crookes filed a suit in which he alleged damages for an online news service that republished resignation letters from that party and let users summarize claims they contained. He had demanded access to all the anonymous sources confirming the insider information, which Geist believed would be extremely prejudicial to online journalism. The lawsuit, "Crookes versus open politics", attracted attention from the BBC and major newspapers, perhaps because of its humorous name. Crookes had also objected to satire published on the site, including use of the name "gang of Crookes" for his allies. Subsequently, Crookes sued Geist, expanding the circle of liability. Crookes also sued Google, Wikipedia, Yahoo, PBwiki, domain registrars and Green bloggers who he felt were associated with his political opponents. Crookes' attempt to enforce BC's plaintiff-friendly libel laws on California, Ontario and other jurisdictions led to an immediate backlash in bad publicity but the legal issues remain somewhat unresolved as of November 2009. Crookes lost four times on the grounds that he had not shown anyone in BC had actually read the materials on the minor websites, but this left the major question unresolved: How to deal with commentary deemed fair in one jurisdiction but actionable in another, and how to ensure that universal rights to free speech and reputation are balanced in a way that does not lead to radically different outcomes for two people who might for instance participate in a conversation on the Internet.

## International Issues

Non-democratic regimes that do not respect international human rights law present special challenges for online journalism:

- Persons reporting from those regimes or with relatives under those regimes may be intimidated, harassed, tortured or killed and the risk of their exposure generally rises if they become involved in a private dispute and are subjected to civil discovery, or if a plaintiff or police officer or government official pressures an international service provider to disclose their identity.

- If print and broadcast journalists are excluded, unverifiable reports from persons on the spot (as during the Iran election crisis of 2009) may be the only way to relay news at all— each individual incident may be unverifiable though statistically a much more representative sample of events might be gathered this way if enough citizens are participating in gathering the news.

- Court processes that do not explicitly respect the rights of fair comment on public issues, political expression in general, religious freedoms, the right to dissent government decisions or oppose power figures, could be imposed on persons who merely comment on a blog. If judgments can be enforced at a distance, this may require expensive legal responses or chill on comment while cases move through a remote court, with the proceedings possibly even being heard in a foreign language under rules the commentator never heard of before. If people from relatively free countries engage in conversations with those from oppressive countries, for instance on homosexuality, they may actually contribute to exposing and loss of human rights by their correspondents.

## Science Reporting

Science journalism is an increasingly imperilled occupation that, perversely, is needed now more than ever. In a world where both citizens and advertisers increasingly control their own delivery of information via online channels, the kind of legacy mass media that have long served as the principal employers of science journalists – newspapers and magazines – are faltering in many countries. Journalists cut loose from these media organisations are scrambling to find their footing elsewhere. It will be years before successful models for delivery of substantive science journalism emerge from the bevy of experiments now under way.

And yet, science journalism has never been more important. Citizens of the globe are buffeted by one issue after another – the potential impacts of GM crops; the mysterious die-off of bees; individualised medical treatment via genomics; climate disruption; the prospect of bringing extinct species back to life – and have few places to turn for independent, evidence-based information. Historically, most people have depended on mediated channels, those ubiquitous packagers of information intended for large numbers of readers/listeners/viewers, where they typically encounter science information almost inadvertently as they watch TV news, read their morning newspaper or page through a magazine from the corner news stand. While that is still the case in many countries, today's citizens rely increasingly on volitional searching of the Internet for their information. The science journalists are there, blogging and placing stories in a variety of web-only outlets. But finding that good information requires effort on the part of the individual searcher, effort that the typical individual rarely expends.

Science stories have appeared in the mass media for as long as these channels have existed. Who wrote those stories, on the other hand, has varied over time and across cultures. Scholars in a number of countries have sought to track the evolution of *popular science* in their respective cultures. What they find is a process initially characterised by scientists' efforts to share knowledge as widely as possible, followed by a retrenchment that moved scientists away from direct contact with publics and, in Broks's words, transformed the public 'from participants to consumers'. In this characterisation of the process in Britain, scientists in the late eighteenth century sought to diffuse scientific understanding throughout the culture, assuming substantial benefits would accrue in the course of the integration of science with the workaday world of ordinary folks. By the nineteenth century, however, the relentless advance of specialised knowledge began to create a chasm between scientists and society. Broks describes this as evolution from 'the Enlightenment ideal of "experience"' to 'the early nineteenth-century construction of "expertise"' with scientists morphing even further by the end of the nineteenth century into an even less accessible category of beings called the 'professional expert'. As scientists withdrew from the world of popularisation, the construction of popular science narratives was turned over increasingly to journalists.

Captures the same trend in the United States. By the late nineteenth century, several popular science magazines were already established – pre-eminent among them *Scientific American* and *Popular Science Monthly* – and newspaper editors were happy to reprint texts of science lectures and to publish scientists' reflections on natural phenomena such as meteor showers. The scientists themselves were equally willing to invest time and energy in public communication endeavours. Scientists in the latter part of the nineteenth century tended to view popularisation as part of their job.

In the early twentieth century, however, increasing specialisation and professionalization pushed scientists to see themselves as apart from everyday people. As scientists developed their own languages, their own training regimens and their own reward systems, communication with others outside the occupation became less of a priority. To make matters worse, major scientific societies began to punish scientists for daring to popularise by ostracising offending individuals and even denying them access to rewards, such as membership in honorific societies. Goodell's classic book *The Visible Scientists* is replete with examples of how even senior, accomplished scientists were subjected to sustained repercussions as a result of their popularising efforts. Although, as popularisation has again become *au courant* for many scientists, residual hostility within the scientific culture makes it a risky behaviour even today. But, back in the early twentieth century, too much of an investment in popularisation could ruin a scientist's career, so many scientists left the world of popularisation to journalists and the mass media.

The mass media's interest in science has remained steady throughout the centuries. The technology of warfare, discoveries of planets and entire galaxies (not to mention Martian canals!) and advances in medical care were easy for journalists to *sell* to their editors. These editors did not care that a topic was scientific, only that it was novel and likely to grab the attention of their readers. Canvas the issues of any newspaper of the eighteenth, nineteenth and early twentieth centuries and you are likely to find stories that we would today classify as 'science' in the broadest sense.

Still, few journalists by the mid-twentieth century would have defined themselves as science writers. Specialist reporters are expensive and, consequently, rare in most media organisations. Editors believed strongly in the ability of a good generalist to cover anything and worried more about the by-products of cozy relationships between journalists and their sources than about the need to apply specialised knowledge to complex topics. Through much of the twentieth century, in fact, a common practice in American news media was to rotate reporters across beats every few years to prevent the pitfalls of reporter/source intimacy.

A few specialised science reporters did gain a foothold in newspapers and wire services early in the twentieth century in Britain and the United States. But it took the technological innovations catalysed by World War II, post-war decisions by governments in several countries to invest in scientific research, the space race of the 1960s and the growing environmental concerns of the 1970s and 1980s to galvanise media organisations into finding science and environmental reporters to cover what loomed as some of the major stories of the century. ) characterise this post-war period as the time when science journalism became an organised, visible and increasingly powerful presence in journalism.

The numbers of science reporters burgeoned in many countries over the course of the twentieth century. In addition to the establishment of country-specific organisations of science writers, global associations such as the World Federation of Science Journalists arose, and formal science journalism training was provided at universities around the world. With increased numbers of journalists, coverage also increased as a number of longitudinal studies demonstrated for the latter part of the twentieth century.

Despite the flowering of science journalism during this time, it is important to remember that science reporters – like most classes of specialist reporters – have always constituted a small subset of all journalists in media organisations around the world. Thus, science stories remained relatively minor components of media coverage. An analysis of science coverage by four Greek newspapers, for example, found that the proportion of the news hole given over to science ranged from 1.5 to 2.5 per cent; similar to what found in the United States and to what ) found in Australia. In Greek newspapers, political coverage accounted for some 25 per cent while sports made up 15 per cent of stories.

By the end of the twentieth century, a sea change was under way. New communication channels were cropping up that permitted readers/viewers to implement their own information-seeking practices. While the legacy media – newspapers, television, radio – continue to play important roles in the science information diet of many consumers around the world, today's lay person re-lies increasingly on the Internet. A Welcome Trust survey of British adults and young people found the Internet to be the channel of choice for information about medical research for 23 per cent of adults and 35 per cent of young people; adults were more likely to indicate a preference for tele-vision (29 per cent) while young people were less likely to prefer these channels (27 per cent and 13 per cent respectively). [2] American data from 2010 showed that, while television has long been the preferred channel for science information, for the first time the Internet was running neck and neck with television.

The increasing popularity of the Internet as a channel for information meant something had to give. And that *something*, in many countries, has been citizens' reliance on newspapers. The de-cline in newspaper advertising and the slower but steady decline in buyers over the years have led newspapers to shed staff and, in many places in the United States, even to reduce frequency of publication. Figures from the US Department of Labor's Bureau of Labor Statistics indicate that the newspaper industry as a whole in the United States declined by 40 per cent over the course of a decade. There has been a correspondingly large drop in dedicated science sections. In 1989, weekly science sections in US newspapers numbered 95; by early 2013, only 19 survived. Since the prima-ry employer of science journalists in the United States has long been newspapers, this change has forced many journalists to redefine what it means to be a journalist.

So where does all this leave the science journalist? In some countries, these journalists feel embattled. But in other cultures, they continue to thrive and the occupation, by all accounts, continues to grow. Systematic data are hard to find, but anecdotal accounts suggest that sci-ence journalists in the United States increasingly find themselves on their own, in the ranks of freelancers as their former media organisations downsize. Conditions in Canada and Britain, while not yet critical, show similar patterns. Faced with the need to become entrepreneurs, science journalists in these countries have embraced new media as a cheap and sometimes effective way of reaching publics.

Elsewhere in the world, science journalists seem to be holding their own, according to an analy-sis of data from hundreds of science reporters from around the world. Taking advantage of data from four surveys of science journalists archived at SciDev.Net, Bauer and colleagues sought to construct a picture of 'global science journalism' in the twenty-first century. The researchers used data from a survey of 179 participants in the 2009 World Conference of Science Journalists, held in London; a survey of 320 journalists from Latin America conducted in 2010 and 2011; a subset of data from a larger survey project from six regions, primarily developing countries; and original survey data from 93 additional journalists primarily from Africa and Asia, gathered in 2012. While the researchers caution that the complex nature of this aggregated analysis makes it hard to argue for the generalisability of the sample, global comparative data are so rare that this study deserves some attention.

Found that, while men continued to hold the majority of science journalism positions in Europe, Africa and Asia, women accounted for fully 45 per cent of the sample and actually trumped men in Latin America (55 per cent women versus 45 per cent men). University degrees were common attributes, as was journalism training; 26 per cent indicated receiving science writing training spe-cifically while 19 per cent had general journalism training. One in ten held a doctorate. More than half had worked as science journalists for ten or fewer years, and half reported being in full-time positions. While these journalists reported they were writing more stories for the Web, they also noted that their work for more traditional print sites had increased. Among these working journalists, job satisfaction remained high. That is, respondents were reasonably satisfied with their autonomy, with access to scientists and with their ability to serve their audiences responsibly. What that last factor meant, according to these journalists, was the opportunity to inform and explain.

So science journalism sounds like great work if you can get it. But like all occupations, it is beset by its own sets of issues, some of them grounded in journalism generally and others driven by the idiosyncrasies of science. Below, I discuss a few of them before returning to further consideration of the shift to the Internet and its implications for the roles of science journalists.

## Science News is Overwhelmingly about Medicine and Health

For media outlets in many countries, the bulk of what passes for science writing is all about medicine and health. Bauer tracked what he called 'The medicalisation of science news' (1998) in the British press in the latter half of the twentieth century, and found that a set of elite US newspapers focused on medicine and health in more than 70 per cent of their stories during the same period. Encountered a similar dominance of health topics in an analysis of science stories in seven Canadian newspapers. Television is a more eclectic medium in most countries, with an often strong focus on natural history and environmental issues. But here, too, medicine and health often dominate.

In a study of science coverage in a leading Italian newspaper over the course of 50 years, also found that biology and medicine accounted for more than half of the stories. But they noted that the medicalisation of science was particularly pronounced in stories written for the newspaper's special supplements and sections, while science news featured on the front page was dominated by physics and engineering stories. This suggests that science journalists may be making a conceptual distinction between news and *news you can use*, with the latter focusing more heavily on health and medicine topics.

## Science News on Television Remains Scarce

Analyses of science news on television in Europe find not much of it. Television news typically attends only sporadically to science topics, and broadcast stories emphasise the entertainment aspects of scientific discoveries and processes at the cost of in-depth, explanatory and critical treatment. A recent analysis of science in BBC news programming offered a slightly more positive picture of the situation in the UK. Analysis of news coverage over the course of three months in both 2009 and 2010 found that one in four news programmes included at least one science news item, as well as that fully half of the main television news bulletins contained science news reporting.

What about television programmes dedicated to science? In an analysis of television science programmes in 11 European countries, found great variation in the number and nature of such programmes and concluded that market structure was a major predictor of that diversity. For example, with the exception of Britain, most science programming occurred on public service channels. The more such channels available in a country, the study found, the more science programming. However, few science programmes in any of these countries were dedicated to science *news*. The most common types of programming were either longer-form, magazine-style coverage of science issues (such as Britain's *Horizon*, Germany's *Terra X* or Austria's *Newton*) or what the team called 'advice' programmes, often health-related with question and answer structures.

An early analysis of a set of British documentary science programmes noted the heavy overlay of certainty that accompanied the programmes: 'Television presents science as producing unambiguous and intractable knowledge'. Recent studies also found that TV coverage of science – like much of science journalism – neglects uncertainty. A content analysis of BBC science coverage, for example, noted that only one in five sources in broadcast news stories urged caution in evaluating scientific claims.

Drama plays a major role in much of science television programming and, according to scholars, can often trump public understanding of science goals. Studied the making of a science documentary for the BBC *Horizon* series and tracked the gradual takeover of the storyline by producers. Scientists eventually lost control of the narrative, he concluded, via a production process that privileged the kind of dramatic tension that only skilled film-makers could provide. In a similar vein, Hornig concluded of *Nova* documentaries that the programmes maintained the 'sacredness' (1990: 17) of science by portraying scientists as special and distinct from others.

## Coverage of Science follows Journalistic Norms

Media coverage of science looks a lot like coverage of other arenas, principally because the primary drivers of coverage patterns are not the content areas on which stories are focused but, instead, the production infrastructure through which that content must pass.

For example, science stories – like all journalistic accounts – tend to be *episodic* in nature. That is, journalists are more likely to produce shorter stories about concrete happenings than longer, thematic stories about issues. Underlying this pattern is the rapid pace of most media production processes. Daily or, in the case of Internet news sites, hourly production cycles cannot wait for months-long scientific processes to spool out. Journalists produce stories about pieces of processes and hope that faithful readers will be able to knit together a larger picture from these bits of narrative fabric.

Episodic coverage does not lend itself well to discussions of process. So, not surprisingly, analyses of science stories find few descriptions of the research methods employed. found that nearly 75 per cent of the science stories they analyzed from four Greek newspapers contained no reflection on the methodological *how* of the scientific process, and discussion of that dimension in the remaining stories was brief and superficial. too, noted that most of the Canadian stories her team analyzed virtually ignored process details. And a study of the coverage of scientific research in Dutch newspapers found, similarly, that most stories eschewed complex process information.

Science journalism, again in ways typical of other types of journalism, seeks to hang stories on *traditional news pegs*, characteristics of real-world processes that are proven audience attention-getters. Those pegs include timeliness, conflict and novelty. Thus, for example, rather than dip into a scientific research process at some haphazard stage, the science journalist waits until the completed work is on the cusp of publication in a scientific journal. That moment of publication offers a prized timely angle, an opportunity to grab the attention of a reader/viewer with the words: 'In today's issue of *Nature*'.

These moments also tend to coincide with points in a process recognised – or designated – as salient by the scientific culture. Journalists typically *buy* into the legitimising structures of sources, uncritically accepting sources' designation of what is important and worthy of notice. Scientists, thus, can easily sell the argument that journalists must respect scientific process and, for example, wait for peer review to take place before embarking on a wider dissemination of research results. Scientists often complain that journalists pay undue attention to mavericks and outliers, but studies of media coverage of contested science suggest that those stories overwhelmingly reflect the views of the scientific mainstream.

This reliance on news pegs also means that coverage of a long-running issue waxes and wanes with the presence/absence of pegs. Scientists and policymakers will struggle for decades, for example, to understand the mechanisms of cloning and to explore means for society to adapt to the technique's many tantalising and alarming possibilities. But coverage of the issue will erupt only when *something happens* in a journalistic sense – when a prime minister formally announces a new initiative, when a team of scientists unveils the first cloned cat, when a religious group lodges a complaint. While the disjunction between coverage and process can be disconcerting to some scientists, others have learned to take advantage of reporter dependence on news pegs and have become facile at guiding coverage. For example, if an important paper is about to be published in a journal, scientists may hire consultants to help them *market* their discovery to the press by appealing to the demand for news pegs. The resulting press conferences and reporter *exclusives* may be more influential in generating coverage than the original papers themselves.

The most important *audiences* for journalists have long been their editors and their sources. While their *real* audiences – members of the public – have historically had only sporadic access to the newsroom, a science writer is in daily touch with her sources and her bosses. Thus, coverage is more likely to be responsive to the priorities of these individuals. This may seem unpersuasive to scientists, who feel that journalists often run roughshod over them and treat their information in cavalier manner. But studies of media coverage of science have demonstrated repeatedly that the scientific culture is a powerful driver of what becomes news about science. Dorothy Nelkin, in her seminal book *Selling Science*, reflected that media science stories overwhelmingly represent scientists as successful problem-solvers. Such coverage is not accidental, she notes; the scientific culture actively cultivates its image as society's major tool for reducing uncertainty. The invisibility of audiences is changing with the increased access that the Internet affords readers/viewers to journalistic work.

Two long-standing journalistic norms – objectivity and balance – have come under intense scrutiny in the twenty-first century. Both arose as surrogates for validity, that is, as ways of compensating for journalists' inability to determine whether their sources' assertions are true or not. They are particularly salient in science journalism as much of science is contested terrain. What is a journalist to do when credible scientists make contradictory claims about a particular issue? The occupation responds: default to objectivity and balance.

In a world where the science journalist cannot declare what is most likely to be true, *objectivity* demands that the reporter go into *neutral transmitter* mode and focus not on validity but on accuracy. That is, rather than judging the veracity of a truth claim, the journalist concentrates instead on representing the claim accurately in her story. The issue is no longer whether the claim is supported by evidence but, rather, the goodness of fit between what a source says and what a journalist presents.

Similarly, when a science reporter cannot determine who is telling the truth, the norm of *balance* suggests that he represent as many truth claims as possible in the story. When validity is impossible, in other words, a good fall-back position is comprehensiveness. The journalist is, in effect, telling the reader: 'The truth is in here somewhere'.

But, for example, argue that balance too often means giving truth claims equal space even when they are not, in fact, equally valid. They use the example of global warming coverage in US newspapers to demonstrate that, even in the face of burgeoning consensus among scientists that humans are making a substantive contribution to warming, many media accounts still give significant play to global warming outliers who dispute the trend. Find similar patterns in coverage of the debate in the United States over teaching evolution in the biology classroom; attempts to *balance* the arguments of biologists and creationists, they claim, confers legitimacy on both sides in the minds of readers.

At least one American study indicates that journalists are keenly aware of the problems created by objective, balanced accounts but feel that journalistic norms prevent them from abandoning these behaviours. Found the expected balancing of extreme points of view in coverage of several scientific issues where healthy majority viewpoints were being contested by outliers. In interviews, the journalists readily acknowledged the likely bogus nature of the mavericks' positions but then indicated that both editors and audiences expected their stories to treat those positions with respect.

## Training Remains Contentious and Under-studied

Should science writers be formally trained in science, or should they more properly come up through the ranks of journalism? If one looks across countries, the former seems to trump the latter. In some countries, doctoral degrees are highly sought by newsrooms; in others, science writing training programmes increasingly privilege those applicants who have science credentials. The argument embedded in these preferences is not that journalistic training is irrelevant but that a marriage of scientific and journalistic skills will yield better results than will journalistic skills alone.

The value of formal science training seems obvious and, not surprisingly, is strongly endorsed by the scientific culture, which feels that such grounding will produce more accurate and responsible stories. Many science graduate students in search of alternative careers find that science writing has intuitive appeal. Given the robustness of these training beliefs, it is interesting to note that there is little empirical evidence to support them. Only a few studies have been conducted in the United States to explore differences in journalistic quality that can be pinned to differences in training, and none of those studies have found formal science training to be strongly predictive of that quality. For example gave American environmental journalists a global warming knowledge test and then compared the answers of those journalists with formal science training to the answers of those without such training. While formal science education made a modest difference in reporter knowledge, it was trumped by another variable: number of years on the job. Years on the job has proved the best quality predictor in a variety of studies of journalistic work in the United States. As is the case for most skilled occupations, experiential learning is probably the most critical predictor of job performance.

## Great and General shift to the Internet

The availability of the Internet as an information channel has profoundly affected audiences' patterns of information-seeking. In many countries, traditional, mediated channels are either in holding patterns (television) or are in decline (newspapers) as the public adjusts to the enormous amount of information available to it electronically.

A dominant Internet environment does not, however, necessarily mean an *anything goes* pattern of information-seeking. The worldwide popularity of sites such as Yahoo! News, CNN, MSNBC, Google News and the New York Times suggests an enduring need for a credible, initial filter on information. We are hungry to keep up with current events, but we continue to depend on journalism to make reasoned choices and to craft readable narratives.

Science journalists have also embraced the Internet as, among other uses, a primary site for story searches. Respondents in one recent study reported spending more than three hours a day, on average, on the Internet. This survey of science writers in 14 European countries found that the journalists relied on a relatively small group of sites – among them Eurek Alert, Nature, BBC News, and New Scientist – for story ideas, and they overwhelmingly agreed that 'the Internet has made my job easier. Many of them also admitted, however, that such reliance increases their focus on breaking news, a trend that may exacerbate the dominance of episodic narratives over more thematic ones.

Scientists' use of the Internet, on the other hand, remains more muted. Although many scientists have embraced Internet communication and its promise to link them directly to audiences, others continue to rely on more mediated paths. A recent survey of neuroscientists in Germany and the United States, for example, found that although the respondents believed that *new media* such as blogs and online social networks do influence public opinion and policy decisions, they reported that they themselves use more traditional outlets – newspapers, television, magazines (both legacy and online) – to keep up with scientific developments.

Finally, the Internet has opened direct communication lines between audience members and both scientists and journalists. Several scholars have begun to study the online interactions between journalists and audiences, particularly through the lens of comments by audience members in response to online science journalism stories. Both and characterise this process as the evolution of *unfinished stories*. The initial science story, rather than deemed a final product, serves instead as a catalyst for an on-going narrative construction process in which both journalists and readers participate., among others, documents the dynamic nature of such narratives in a couple of case studies in which stories whose narratives become contested disappear from the online sites of major media organisations.

## Scientists Losing and Gaining Control

For much of the twentieth century, scientists avoided public contact and, as a result, knew much less about public communication processes than did the journalists who contacted them. That gave journalists an edge in their relationships with their sources, but that has begun to lessen as scientists have come to realise the value of public visibility and take active steps to structure their own public images. Twenty-first-century scientists increasingly come equipped with media training, and have begun to communicate directly with publics on their own through popular science books, blogs and websites.

Such visibility can be harmful, as many *burned* scientists still ruefully report, but the social and scientific legitimacy that can attend such visibility is luring many scientists into acquiring greater communicative expertise. Several studies demonstrate that media coverage makes a scientist's work look more important not only to members of the public (including funders) but also to other scientists; for example, media visibility of peer-reviewed, published work increases the number of citations of that research in the scientific literature. As a result, scientists in all disciplines are acquiring communication skills and are learning to take advantage of communication professionals employed by their organisations. These scientists report not only regular interactions with journalists but also beliefs that those interactions are good for their careers.

On the other hand, the onslaught of new information channels and the increasing ubiquity of user control means that all information creators are increasingly finding themselves buffeted by audience reactions. Scientists have always chafed at their perceived lack of control over public representations of their work. In 2002, scientists in the UK established the Science Media Centre, initially through the Royal Institution of Great Britain. The centre defines its mission as one of helping scientists to become better communicators, but it also seeks to intervene early in the course of media coverage of science issues by staging briefings and otherwise providing expert reactions to breaking news, compiling fact sheets about specific science topics that are becoming newsworthy and even by engaging in independent analyses of scientific papers for journalists. These efforts have been welcomed by many but have led some journalists to suggest that the centre functions as a large-scale science PR agency that tries to control the science agenda, as seen in a series of articles in *Columbia Journalism Review*'s online version. Despite this controversy, similar centres now exist in other countries and are proposed for yet more.

## Whither the Science Journalist?

Have we entered an era in which science journalists gradually lose their media platforms and find themselves increasingly eclipsed by savvy scientists keen to promote their research *brands*? Not yet. But as legacy media platforms struggle to maintain audience share, science journalists are being forced to become more entrepreneurial and to look for new ways to explain to their audiences the profound scientific developments under way. These journalists have embraced social media channels – Facebook, Twitter – not only to maintain contact with sources and peers but also to build their own personal brands. Today's successful science writer may work from home, where she maintains a highly visible blog (ideally hosted by a legacy media website), tweets regularly about topics that fit within her declared area of expertise (specialisation is the name of the game), freelances articles (again focused on her niche) to magazines and online sites and hopes that the synergistic effect of these activities will give her visibility, credibility and a book contract.

In some countries, journalists are banding together in non-profit organisations in order to maintain traditions of investigative and explanatory journalism. The groups rely on a wide variety of funding mechanisms, principally foundation and private donations, and often give their work free of charge to media organisations willing to publish the stories. One of those non-profits, Inside Climate News – which specialises in covering energy issues and environmental science – was awarded a Pulitzer Prize in 2013 for its reporting on an oil spill in the Midwestern United States that journalists broadened into an analysis of national pipeline safety issues.

In a special issue of the journal *Journalism*, devoted to 'Science Journalism in a Digital Age', contributors pondered the impact of the channel revolution on science journalism. Issue editor

Stuart notes that the those impacts may be both salutary and daunting. The Internet *wild west* offers science journalists the opportunity to engage directly and transparently with a variety of audiences, from everyday people to scientists; the interactive nature of social channels makes it possible for users to understand science in more profound ways; science journalists who build storytelling skills across platforms have the potential to communicate science in ways far more powerful than before. The *New York Times'* multi-platform story, 'Snowfall: The Avalanche at Tunnel Creek', chronicling the death of a group of world-class skiers caught in an avalanche in the mountains of the north-west United States, offers an example of that potential.

But Allan also asks us to be aware of the possible downsides of this brave new world. The Web, like a black hole, demands constant feeding. Journalism becomes a 24/7 occupation in which stories becomes rapid-fire processes with no obvious end points. Building science news stories for Internet consumption presents many challenges, among them the need for constant updating, managing the speed with which information must be turned into narrative and maximising the brevity of those narratives, so critical to audiences with only seconds to spare.

Suggest that journalistic roles will expand to accommodate these twenty-first-century changes. While some journalists will continue to embrace such longstanding roles as the need to analyse and then explain, the need to illuminate wrongdoing, the need to monitor the landscape in order to alert audiences to important changes, new communication modes will draw science journalists into new roles. Among them, note Fahy and Nisbet, are the role of curator, who aggregates and makes sense of existing news and commentary; the role of civic educator, who uses the news of science as a means of informing audiences 'about the methods, aims, limits and risks of scientific work' and a role that they label the 'public intellectual', journalists who not only synthesise but also interpret via a point of view.

We are too early in the process of change to determine what occupational modifications will strengthen and which ones will fade. Scholars are just beginning to explore the impacts of these changes, making it difficult to assess the societal risks and benefits that accompany them.

Other difficulties also will attend future efforts to study the behaviours and products of science journalists. Prominent among them is the question of just who constitutes a science journalist. Studies in the past have relied on organisational affiliation as an important component of that definition. But in a world filled with freelancers, many of whom work for a magazine on one day and for a government research laboratory on another, separating the science journalist from the non-journalist will prove daunting.

Similarly, what is a science news story? Does a tweet count? A blog post? And even when a story looks like the traditional stereotype of a news narrative, when is it a *finished* narrative? In an electronic publishing environment where reporters and editors can make corrections, fiddle at will with content and even remove a story altogether, how do scholars determine the point at which story evaluation should take place?

What has not changed, however, is the commitment and passion of science journalists. In my home town of Madison, Wisconsin, the local newspaper's long-time science writer Ron Seely retired, in part, because he was disheartened by the decline of journalism in these smaller urban areas. While the newspaper, regretably, has no plans to replace him, Seely quickly found a new home with the non-profit Wisconsin Center for Investigative Journalism, where he will continue a 30-plus-year career of covering complicated science and environmental issues. His excitement about this next stage of his career is infectious and serves as a reminder that science journalism done well can have tremendous societal value. Societies now need to figure out how to maintain this capacity.

## Environment Reporting

Environmental reporting is the communication of environmental performance information by an organisation to its stakeholders.

Information on environmental performance includes among others:

- Impacts on the environment,

- Performance in managing those impacts, and

- Contribution to ecological and sustainable development.

Nowadays, such information is becoming increasingly important to satisfy the expectations of stakeholders groups like: employees, shareholders, the public, regulators, contractors/suppliers, customers and other interested parties, who have varying objectives and expectations.

Sustainable consumption and production activities, for example, must/can be reported, such as buying environmentally preferred goods and services like recycled paper, energy efficient devices etc.

### Report

The main reasons for reporting are:

- Transparency: In line with Sustainable Development objectives, many stakeholders want to integrate environmental and social information in their decision making processes. Information flow increases the visibility of the organisation's activities. As a result, several organisations are voluntarily choosing to be more transparent.

- Accountability: Organisations are becoming increasingly accountable for their actions. For instance, adverse criticism on environmental and social performance can put at risk the significant economic value of good corporate reputation and well-regarded brand.

- Multi-way Stakeholder Dialogue: More and more non-traditional stakeholders (NGOs, media, suppliers/partners, employees, consumers and shareholders) are demanding information in environmental and social performance. Organisations are finding satisfaction and detainment of both traditional and non-traditional stakeholders on their willingness to openly communicate.

### Benefits of Reporting

Some common benefits include:

- Creation of market opportunities: Environmental reporting is closely linked to business performance and raises the profile of an organisation and gains recognition of potential customers. Investors are increasingly choosing to invest in 'clean and green organisations' and may appreciate the availability of public environmental performance information.

- Indirect improvement in internal environmental performance: An environmental report that details resource use, waste discharges and impacts of the organisation's operations can highlight inefficiencies in production processes. Commitment to public environmental reporting will result in increasing internal awareness and focus on improving environmental performance.

- Increased confidence of investors and other financial institutions: Environmental liabilities and risks are increasingly becoming the focus of lending institutions, investors and insurers. It is good business to ensure that these stakeholder groups are kept well informed of the organisation's environmental performance.

- Improvement of relationships with local communities, regulators & NGOs: Local communities will be more tolerant and even supportive of organisations that openly communicate with their stakeholders.

- Greater control of environmental disclosure: Reporting allows organisations to present information on their environmental performance thereby avoiding involuntary disclosure by other parties including media, non-government organisations, etc. This control can enable organisations to ensure that the public is also aware of the measures being taken to improve performance.

- Increased staff commitment: Environmental reporting can raise the environmental awareness and commitment of an organisation's employees and management. Environmental performance may be related to the personal health of employees, the surrounding environment where they reside or simply raise their level of confidence in the organisation by creating a sense of pride.

## Financial Reporting

This is an increasingly important field of journalism, and covers such areas as industry and agriculture, commerce, finance and economics - the ways wealth is created and distributed. It is important to readers and listeners, even though they may only be interested in knowing about wage or price rises, house buying or currency exchange rates.

### Basic Principles

Although at first sight it may seem a very complicated area - full of theories, rules and numbers - you can report it well as long as you remember some simple principles.

### Understand the Basics

Like any specialist area, there is a basic core of knowledge which you must understand before you can write competently. You do not need to know every aspect of economic theory or possess a degree in business studies, but it is not possible to be a competent journalist without the ability to understand a simple balance sheet or explain profit and loss. Once you understand the basics, you can ask other people to fill in details. Then you can explain what happens in the financial world in a way your readers or listeners can understand.

## Report the Human Face

Because economics is about human actions, it should be possible to tell all economic news stories in human terms. If it is not possible, you must question whether you should really use the story at all.

| Good | Bad |
|---|---|
| • The price of sugar could rise by as much as 20 cents a kilo from next week.<br><br>• The Government wants to increase the duty on imported refined sugar by 15 percent, to protect local industry. | • The Government is to increase the duty on imported sugar by 15 percent.<br><br>• The increase is an attempt to protect local growers from cheap imported sugar. |

For example, a story about an increase in import duty should not be written in terms of financial policy, but in terms of what it will mean to your readers or listeners who buy imported goods.

Of course, simplification should not be taken too far. There are some economic issues which affect society as a whole and need serious treatment. It would be an over-simplification to view a plunge in the exchange rate of your currency only as if it will make travellers' cheques more expensive. There would be much greater consequences, both good and bad, such as a rise in the cost of imports and a boost to export industries.

Even these more serious effects should be put in human terms. The travellers' cheques aspect is a very minor side effect. The cost of imported goods on shelves and in showrooms is the right angle.

## Give the Local Angle

Economics is often expressed in terms of cooperation or competition between nations. Economic stories on the major international wire services are usually written from the viewpoint of the major developed nations (and figures are usually quoted in United States Dollars). You have to avoid presenting the issues through the eyes of foreigners.

Your readers or listeners will usually be interested in the economic effect on their own country. Imagine that you are a journalist in Fiji, and have been given a wire service story about a new fishing agreement with New Zealand. While your Fijian audience might be interested in economic stories about New Zealand, they will be more interested in the Fijian side of the deal. So you should research the story with the Fijian government, then write it from the Fijian angle:

| Good | Bad |
|---|---|
| • Fiji is to be a major partner in an expansion of New Zealand's fishing industry.<br><br>• The project will be worth $F10 million to Fijian companies and could mean an extra 500 jobs locally.<br><br>• The World Bank is to give New Zealand US$200 million ($F300 million) to expand etc. | • New Zealand is to receive US$200 million dollars from the World Bank to expand its fishing industry.<br><br>• The money will be used to buy boats and build processing factories in New Zealand and overseas.<br><br>• Processing plants will be established in Vanuatu, the Solomon Islands and Fiji. Each country will get etc. |

In this example, we also converted US Dollars (US$) into Fijian Dollars ($F). You must always convert foreign currencies into your country's currency, which your readers or listeners can understand. In some cases you may need to give both the original currency and the conversion in brackets.

## Do not overload with Numbers

Many economic concepts are quite complicated. You should lead your readers or listeners gently but firmly through your explanation. Your job will not be helped if you scatter numbers through the story like rocks on the path. Your readers or listeners will be held up whenever they stumble over a difficult number.

We suggested that two or three concepts (ideas) were the most that readers or listeners can handle in each sentence. Each number in an economics story must be regarded as an extra concept because the readers or listeners have to think about it separately before continuing their understanding of the sentence.

Your task is to select only those numbers which are most important (i.e. those which tell the story best) and then spread them throughout the story. Do not pile them like a barrier of rocks across the first paragraph.

| Good | Bad |
|---|---|
| • Teachers in the Cook Islands will get an average of $10 a week extra from next month.<br><br>• The rise is the first instalment of an agreement reached in November.<br><br>• Under the agreement, teachers will get a rise of 15 percent over the next year-and-a-half. | • Teachers in the Cook Islands are to get an average of $10 a week extra next month as the first instalment of a 15 percent wage rise spread over 18 months. |

Notice how much simpler the good version was, compared to the bad version which tried to crush four sets of figures into one sentence.

In radio especially, you should never give your audience complicated sums to do during news stories. They will either fail to do them and so miss an important aspect of the story, or they will be so busy doing mental arithmetic that they miss the rest of the bulletin.

You should have the figures in front of you as you write the story. Do the sums before you present the information? Money figures and fractions are usually easier to grasp than percentages. Remember that rounded figures are much easier to understand than long strings of numbers. Almost two thousand is easier to grasp than 1,963.

Instead of saying "wages will be cut by 50 percent", say "wages will be cut in half". Instead of "the price of Gurgles beer is to rise by five percent on June the first", say "Gurgles beer will rise by eight cents a can next month".

## Visualise what Numbers Mean

Whenever you deal in figures, try to visualise what each of the numbers means. This will help you gain a complete picture of the way the finances fit together. See if the numbers make sense by working them out into meaningful units. Spending $500,000 to build 120 houses may sound OK, but divide 500,000 by 120 and you have an average of just over $4,000 per house. Is that a likely price for a house? If we are talking about simple village houses, then perhaps it is; if we are talking about big fancy town houses, then it may not be. Perhaps someone has missed out or added a zero when typing the figures. One zero missed can mean a ten-fold increase or decrease.

Visualising the figures also helps you question people's claims. In our housing example, the politician who offers to spend $500,000 on public housing may seem to be promising a lot (half-a-million dollars), but if each house costs $40,000 to build, he'll only build 12 houses.

## Avoid Jargon

The world of commerce and economics, like politics and science, is full of specialist words we call jargon. These are phrases which mean a lot to those who use them every day. They do not, however, help your readers or listeners to understand what can already be complicated ideas.

Sometimes jargon is too long and can be easily shortened - "a medium of exchange" becomes "money". Sometimes jargon is shorthand for a longer concept and needs explaining in more detail - "hot money" becomes "money coming into the country to take advantage of high local interest rates".

If you get jargon in a press release, do not hesitate to go back to the source for an explanation. If you do not understand it, there is a good chance that many of your readers or listeners will also be confused.

## Investigative Journalism

Another of the main problems journalists face in reporting the world of commerce is that information may be hard to get. The people who have power over wealth often like to keep their knowledge as secret as they can. This is partly because they do not want competitors to know what they are doing, but also partly because many of them see wealth as a personal thing, not the concern of the rest of society. But if their power over wealth affects other people, particularly your ordinary readers or listeners, you have a duty to let them know what is happening in society. If people are employed or buy goods, they have a right to know what employers, manufacturers and retailers are doing.

If people in the world of commerce are doing things which are illegal or unethical, they should be exposed. Because many people in the financial world bend rules or take advantage of gaps in the law to make quick money, the field of investigative journalism is a rich one.

It is also a varied one. You may not be exposing financial wrongdoing. You may simply want to find out how much money a foreign company has invested in your country. Finding the information you need may be simple or difficult, depending on what you need to know, who you need to get it from and what they may have to hide (if anything).

## Finding Information

If you want some information about a company, the first place to look is in your own records or newsroom files. There may be previous stories which you can use. If you are investigating a foreign company, some public or college libraries have editions of overseas newspapers, often on micro-fiche.

You should ask the company itself for information. If they have nothing to hide, they may be willing to help.

However, if you are researching a story which could be critical of the company in any way, they may refuse to give the information you need. Sometimes they will plead the need to keep information from their competitors.

You should also try to get hold of the company's annual report. You may be able to get this direct from the company itself, from a good library or from the embassy or high commission concerned.

Finally, you can ask the Company Registrar's office (it may be called something like the Registrar General or Corporate Affairs Commission in your country). These offices keep records on registered companies and often investigate complaints of misconduct against companies. In some countries, they maintain records for public searches.

Usually all you need to do is go to the Company Registrar's office and ask to see the records of the particular company. You may have to pay a small search fee. You will not be allowed to take any files away, but may be allowed to make photocopies of relevant documents.

You may not be allowed to see all the company's files. Some are kept confidential for legitimate commercial reasons (for example, so that competitors cannot copy their ideas or see their pricing structures). However, with plenty of spare time and by cross-referring to other files, it is possible to construct a very accurate picture of a company's business links and activities from these public records.

You might, for example, want to trace how directors of one company are linked to other companies which are supposed to be competitors. You might find that politicians or public servants are directors of companies which are bidding for public contracts.

If your country has a Freedom of Information Act, you may be able to get copies of a company's records through a government department with which it does business. Unfortunately, many Freedom of Information Acts exclude public examination of commercial documents held by government departments.

Of course, investigative journalism is much more complicated than simply asking to be shown documents.

## Reading a Balance Sheet

Although the world of commerce seems full of documents containing figures, there is one kind of document which is at the heart of all business. It is called a balance sheet. As the name suggests, it shows how any organisation which deals in money balances the money coming in with the money going out. If more comes in than goes out, the organisation makes a profit; if more goes out than comes in, it makes a loss. If the loss is big enough, the organisation can die. It is essential, therefore, that you are able to read a balance sheet.

There should be nothing frightening about it. A balance sheet is not usually designed to hide figures, but to explain a mass of figures in a logical way.

Below we have provided a sample of a balance sheet showing government income and expenditure over three years. Following it there is an outline of how the individual totals relate to each other. Study the balance sheet and the outline until you can understand how all the figures fit together. There are a number of simple steps to follow whenever you are faced with a balance sheet:

- Read the title at the top of the sheet carefully. Make sure that the balance sheet is really what you thought it was. Many journalists have made the mistake of thinking that they were looking at the company's overall balance sheet when, in fact, they were simply looking at a balance sheet of one small aspect (for example, the capital account). There could be several balance sheets in an annual report, showing different aspects of the organisation's finances.

- The currency and units in which the figures will be expressed. Glance down at some to make sure you can work out whether the figures are in units of one, tens, hundreds, thousands or millions. There is normally an indication of the multiples used, either at the top of the sheet or at the top of each column.

- Look at the dates showing the periods under review. Simple end-of-year statements will usually have only two dates at the top - this year and last year. Some - like our example - may also have a budget estimate for the following year. Check whether the report periods are for a calendar year or - more usually – a financial year. Calendar years run from 1 January to 31 December. Financial years vary from country to country; in some countries it is the same as the calendar year, in others it may be from 1 July one year to 30 June the following year or from 1 April one year to 31 March the following year. If in doubt, ask someone who knows.

- The easiest way to come to grips with the table itself is first to try to see it as a whole and then break it down into smaller units. First of all, can you find the expenditure and income sections? In old balance sheets, these were put side by side, like the scales on either side of a measuring balance. In modern accounting they follow each other.

- Notice which lines of figures are sub-totals of each section, and which are totals. Do some quick mental arithmetic to check that you understand how all the figures relate to each other.

- Finally look at the bottom line of figures. Does this show the balance is in credit or deficit (profit or loss)? In some cases, the deficit is distinguished from profit by being inside brackets or having a minus sign in front of it. Occasionally on colour documents the negative amounts might printed be in red ink, which is the origin of the phrase "to be in the red" which means to be making a loss or in debt. On company balance sheets, the bottom totals usually balance (hence the term `balance sheet'), with the profit or loss shown as one element of a section higher up the sheet.

The profit/loss line is often the news angle, but you should search around for any unusual aspects. For example, are there any very large figures or any dramatic changes from one year to the next? Don't forget to read any notes at the foot of the balance sheets for explanations.

The following is an outline view of the balance sheet above. Take a few minutes to compare the two so you can see what the figures mean and how they relate to each other. While this is a simple form of balance sheet outline, most balance sheets will have similar features, even if they are more complex.

## Unions and Employers

The relationships between trade unions and employers play a very important part in the economic life of many countries. It is far too big a subject to discuss in detail here, although one or two facts are worth pointing out.

The first is that you must be fair in dealing with disputes. Unions traditionally exist to represent employees in negotiating with employers, whether these are companies, governments or individuals. In many countries they exist to fight for better wages and other working conditions, while in other countries they may exist only to keep workers informed of what their employers want. In whatever form, they are usually a means of airing complaints.

The essential point is that, wherever one group is arguing against another (such as union against employer) you must be fair to both sides. It is rare for one side in an industrial dispute to be totally right and the other totally wrong. There is usually some right and some wrong on both sides. It is not your job to judge. Simply report the facts, give comments from both sides, and leave your readers or listeners to judge for themselves.

Unions, where they exist, are useful for journalists because they provide identifiable people to comment regularly on industrial matters from the workers' point of view. Most companies or government departments have a boss or a person responsible for speaking to the media. It is more difficult to get comments on the workers' case unless there is an identifiable leader. Union leaders make useful contacts and may give you tip-offs about industrial disputes which the employers want to keep out of the media because of bad publicity. As in all cases of conflict, do not get too close to either side. Just as the company's press officer may try to feed you biased information from one side, so the union leader might try to feed you their propaganda. You will be able to deal with both sides fairly and also serve your readers or listeners if, every time they offer you new information, you ask yourself: "Is this news?"

Remember that unions and employers can both be powerful forces in society. In some countries, unions are affiliated to a Council of Trade Unions or a Trade Union Congress, which tries to agree common policies and co-ordinate industrial action such as strikes or boycotts. Employers also often join together in associations to defend their interests. The major employers' association is often called something like a "Confederation of Industry" or a "Federation of Employers", although at a lower level there may be such bodies as Chambers of Commerce, Chambers of Trade or a particular industrial federation. As with all powerful groups, whether unions or employers, you should not be afraid to report the truth if you work in a free press democracy.

## References

- News-reporting-definition-types-and-perquisites, journalism-mass-communication: studylecturenotes.com, Retrieved 22 February, 2019

- Sports-journalism: newworldencyclopedia.org, Retrieved 25 August, 2019

- Schwitzer G. (Jul 2014). "A guide to reading health care news stories". JAMA Intern. Med. 174 (7): 1183–6. doi:10.1001/jamainternmed.2014.1359. PMID 24796314

- Beat-reporting-education: newslab.org, Retrieved 5 March, 2019

- Kawamoto, Kevin (2003). Digital Journalism: Emerging Media and the Changing Horizons of Journalism. Rowman & Littlefield. p. 2. ISBN 9780742526815. Retrieved February 9, 2014

- Environmental-Reporting-Guideline: environment.govmu.org, Retrieved 7 June, 2019

# 6

# News Research

The work which is done in a systematic manner for increasing the quantum of knowledge on different topics is known as news research. Some of the key components of news research are determining the focus of the story and verifying the details. The chapter closely examines these major aspects of news research to provide an extensive understanding of the subject.

## Researching

Research comprises "creative work undertaken on a systematic basis in order to increase the stock of knowledge, including knowledge of humans, culture and society, and the use of this stock of knowledge to devise new applications." It is used to establish or confirm facts, reaffirm the results of previous work, solve new or existing problems, support theorems, or develop new theories. A research project may also be an expansion on past work in the field. To test the validity of instruments, procedures, or experiments, research may replicate elements of prior projects, or the project as a whole. The primary purposes of basic research (as opposed to applied research) are documentation, discovery, interpretation, or the research and development (R&D) of methods and systems for the advancement of human knowledge. Approaches to research depend on epistemologies, which vary considerably both within and between humanities and sciences. There are several forms of research: scientific, artistic, economic, social, business, marketing, practitioner research, life, technological etc.

A broad definition of research is given by Godwin Colibao – "In the broadest sense of the word, the definition of research includes any gathering of data, information and facts for the advancement of knowledge."

Another definition of research is given by John W. Creswell who states that – "Research is a process of steps used to collect and analyze information to increase our understanding of a topic or issue". It consists of three steps: Pose a question, collect data to answer the question, and present an answer to the question.

The Merriam-Webster Online Dictionary defines research in more detail as "a studious inquiry or examination; especially investigation or experimentation aimed at the discovery and interpretation of facts, revision of accepted theories or laws in the light of new facts, or practical application of such new or revised theories or laws"

### Importance of Research

Research is actually an act of studying something carefully and extensively in order to attain deep knowledge in the same. For being successful, research should be systematic, arranged, summarized and recorded properly. Research is not only a process that is limited to the field of science. It can, as well, cater to people and scholars from artistic, historic or any other field where an individual is willing to do extensive study to get relevant information. Research can be creative, exploring or just reassuring in nature. Each one of us does some or the other research in our lifetime for sure. Research can affect a subject both positively and negatively and can be constructive or destructive in nature. Some people believe that research is mostly destructive in nature. However, you need to understand that it's not the results from a research that determine its use; it's the people who handle the results. In the following lines, we have just tried to emphasize the importance of research.

## Significance of Research

### To Gather Necessary Information

Research provides you with all necessary information in field of your work, study or operation before you begin working on it. For example, most companies do research before beginning a project in order to get a basic idea about the things they will need to do for the project. Research also helps them get acquainted with the processes and resources involved and reception from the market. This information helps in the successful outcome of the project.

### To Make Changes

Sometimes, there are in-built problems in a process or a project that is hard to discover. Research helps us find the root cause and associated elements of a process. The end result of such a research invokes a demand for change and sometimes is successful in producing changes as well. For example, many U.N researches have paved way for changes in environmental policies.

### Improving Standard of Living

Only through research can new inventions and discoveries come into life. It was C.V Raman's research that prompted invention of radio communication. Imagine how you would have communicated had Graham Bell not come out with the first ever practical telephone! Forget telephones, what would have happened if Martin Cooper did not present the world the concept of mobile phones! Addicted as we are to mobile phones, we need to understand that all the luxuries and the amenities that are now available to us are the result of research done by someone. And with the world facing more and crisis each day, we need researchers to find new solutions to tackle them.

### For a Safer Life

Research has made ground breaking discoveries and development in the field of health, nutrition, food technology and medicine. These things have improved the life expectancy and health conditions of human race in all parts of the world and helped eradicate diseases like polio, smallpox completely. Diseases that were untreatable are now history, as new and new inventions and research in the field of medicine have led to the advent of drugs that not only treat the once-incurable diseases, but also prevent them from recurring.

## To Know the Truth

It has been proved time and again that many of established facts and known truths are just cover ups or blatant lies or rumors. Research is needed to investigate and expose these and bring out the truth. Research form an important aspect in any profession. As per the dictionary meaning Research is a systematic investigation into and study of materials and sources in order to establish facts and reach new conclusions.

The primary purpose of any research is of discovering, interpretation and analysis of information so to enhance human knowledge.

Research in Mass Communication and Journalism forms a core aspect in decision making, expressing and analyzing of news, views and information. Media is a very sensitive area as it is connected to the masses therefore care should be taken in the delivery of the message to the masses.

Accuracy and Objectivity is must in news reporting. A story should always be well researched before publishing or airing on TV. In Broadcast Media different programs are produced to run 24 hours news channels for that knowing audience behavior. Audience behavioral research can give an idea to a researcher. A good program is always a well-researched program.

Media practitioner can do their job more effectively if they get to know about the target audience which can help them in planning and executing programs. Media research is also used in conducting surveys, public opinion polls, Advertising and Public Relations campaigns which helps in providing perspective to a report.

## Top 5 Major objectives of Social Research

### Manipulation of Things, Concepts and Symbols

While, dealing with things the scientist remains at the concrete level. He is able to purposefully handle things for experimentation. But at this level his results are at best limited to the particular thing in a specific situation and none else. Therefore the concepts symbolizing the things and their properties are also dealt with, so as to make much sense to conduct controlled inquiries through abstract notions. Use of concepts or symbols in the process of manipulation not only reduces the content and load of the things but also provides the scientist with greater facility and effect.

### Generalization

The sole purpose with which manipulation of things, concepts or symbols is undertaken is to arrive at statements of generality. It implies that the findings of controlled investigation should be a conclusion which will enable us to expect that under certain class of conditions influencing a class of things, something will happen in a generalized manner, notwithstanding its degree.

But in any case the absence is generality cannot characterize science. Therefore the propositions derived on the basis of observations and through manipulation of things, concepts or symbols may vary in their levels of generality, may maintain a high or low degree but should never reach the null point.

Otherwise those will move beyond the framework of science. In this regard, Slesinger and Stepheson have given the example of a physician or automobile mechanic as playing the role of a researcher. Whereas the automobile mechanic endeavors to generalize about the automobiles, the physician attempts to make ailments for a given class of patients.

## Verification of Old Facts

A major purpose of social research is verification of conclusions which have already been accepted as established facts. Since there is no place for complacency in the arena of science, the established system of knowledge always warrant frequentative scrutiny so as to confirm whether or not the observations are in accordance with the predictions made on the basis of the established corpus of knowledge. In case it is confirmed, the empirical observation strengthens the established system of knowledge. Otherwise in the light of the research outcome, the system of established corpus of knowledge calls for revision or even rejection.

## Extension of Knowledge

As a sequel to generalization the seemingly inconsistencies in the existing corpus of knowledge are brought into light and attempts are made to reconcile these inconsistencies. The new general proposition, established as an outcome of research also identifies gaps in the established system of knowledge. A gap in knowledge implies the inadequacy of the theory as well as the failure of a conceptual scheme to explain and account for certain aspects of a social phenomenon.

The gap is bridged up in the light of the new empirical observations. Thus knowledge gets expanded. The expansion of systematic knowledge occurs at least in a couple of ways. First in cognizing certain aspects of phenomena which were not examined in these terms prior to the advent of the new general proposition.

Secondly in the light of new observation, the phenomena under investigation may be incorporated in a comparatively large class of phenomena, so as to be governed by a uniform law. As a result, the new system of knowledge not only accumulates more units under its conceptual scheme, but also appreciates greater depth of understanding and bettering of predictions.

## Knowledge may be used for Theory Building or Practical Application

By seeking to explain the unexplained social phenomena, clarifying the doubtful one and correcting the misconceived facts relating to it, social research provides the scope to use the fruits of research in two possible ways:

(a) Theory building

(b) Practical application.

In its basic or pure form social research gathers knowledge for the sake of it, for building a theory in order to explain human behavior in its totality, only for the satisfaction of knowing. For construction of theoretic models, the researcher organizes knowledge into propositions and then meaningfully articulated those propositions to constitute a more abstract conceptual system pertaining to a class of phenomena, influenced by a certain class of conditions.

In its practical or applied form, social research gathers information regarding the betterment of quality of life in social settings. The findings of social research are used as the means to an end, not construed just as an end in itself From its utilitarian point of view the results of social research provide decision makers with proper guidelines for policy making, social welfare, amelioration of practical problems, mitigation or resolution of social conflict and tensions as well as rectification and removal of social evils.

## Research in Mass Communication

During the early part of the twentieth century, there was no interest in the size of an audience or in the types of people who make up the audience. Since then, mass media operators have come to rely on research results for nearly every major decision they make. The increased demand for information has created a need for more researchers, both public and private. In addition, within the research field are many specializations. Research directors plan and supervise studies and act as liaisons to management; methodological specialists provide statistical support; research analysts design and interpret studies; and computer specialists provide hardware and software support in data analysis.

Research in mass media is used to verify or refute opinions or intuitions for decision makers. Although common sense is some- times accurate, media decision makers need additional objective information to evaluate problems, especially when they make decisions that involve large sums of money. The past 60 years have witnessed the evolution of a decision-making approach that com bines research and intuition to produce a higher probability of success.

Research is not limited only to decision- making situations. It is also widely used in theoretical areas to attempt to describe the media, to analyze media effects on consumers, to understand audience behavior, and so on. Every day there are references in the media to audience surveys, public opinion polls, growth projections, status reports of one medium or another, or advertising or public relations campaigns. As philosopher Suzanne Langer said, "Most new discoveries are suddenly-seen things that were always there." Mass media researchers have a great deal to see and virtually everyone is exposed to this information every day.

## Origins and Growth of Mass Media Research

At least four major events or social forces have encouraged the growth of mass media research. The first was World War I, which prompted a need to understand the nature of propaganda. Researchers working from a stimulus-response point of view attempted to uncover the effects of the media on people. The media at that time were thought to exert a powerful influence over their audiences, and several assumptions were made about what the media could and could not do. One theory of mass media, later named the hypodermic needle model of communication, suggested that mass communicators need only "shoot" messages at an audience and those messages would produce preplanned and al- most universal effects. The belief then was that all people behave in similar ways when they encounter media messages. We know now that individual differences among people rule out this overly simplistic view.

These assumptions may not have been explicitly formulated at the time, but they were drawn from fairly elaborate theories of human nature, as well as the nature of the social order. It was these theories that guided the thinking of those who saw the media as powerful.

A second contributor to the development of mass media research was the realization by advertisers in the 1950s and 1960s that research data are useful in developing ways to persuade potential customers to buy products and services. Consequently, advertisers encouraged studies of message effectiveness, audience demographics and size, placement of advertising to achieve the highest level of exposure (efficiency), frequency of advertising necessary to persuade potential customers, and selection of the medium that offered the best chance of reaching the target audience.

A third contributing social force was the increasing interest of citizens in the effects of the media on the public, especially on children. The direct result was an interest in research related to violence and sexual content in television programs and in commercials aired during children's programs. Researchers have expanded their focus to include the positive (prosocial) as well as the negative (antisocial) effects of television. Investigating violence on television is still an important endeavor, and new research is published every year.

Increased competition among the media for advertising dollars was a fourth contributor to the growth of research. Most media managers are now sophisticated and use managers are now sophisticated and use and an increasing dependency on data to support the decisions they make. Even program producers seek relevant research data, a task usually assigned to the creative side of program development. In addition, the mass media now focus on audience fragmentation, which means that the mass of people is divided into small groups, or niches (technically referred to as the "demassification" of the mass media). Researchers need information about these smaller groups of people.

The competition among the media for audiences and advertising dollars continues to reach new levels of complexity. The media "survival kit" today includes information about consumers' changing values and tastes, shifts in demographic patterns, and developing trends in lifestyles. Audience fragmentation increases the need for trend studies (fads, new behavior patterns), image studies (people's perceptions of the media and their environment), and segmentation studies (explanations of behavior by types or groups of people). Large research organizations, consultants, and media owners and operators conduct research that was previously considered the sole property of the marketing, psychology, and sociology disciplines. With the advent of increased competition and audience fragmentation media managers more frequently use marketing strategies in an attempt to discover their position in the marketplace. When this position is identified, the medium is packaged as an "image" rather than a product. (Similarly, the producers of consumer goods such as soap and toothpaste try to sell the "image" of these products because the products themselves are similar, if not the same, from company to company).

This packaging strategy involves deter mining what the members of the audience think, how they use language, how they spend their spare time, and so on. Information on these ideas and behaviors is then used in the merchandising effort to make the medium seem to be part of the audience Positioning thus involves taking information from the audience and interpreting the data to use in marketing the medium.

Much of the media research before the early 1960s originated in psychology and sociology departments at colleges and universities. Researchers with backgrounds in the media were rare because the mass media were young. But this situation has changed. Media departments in colleges and universities grew rapidly in the 1960s, and media researchers entered the scene. Today mass media researchers dominate the mass media research field, and now the trend is to encourage cross-disciplinary studies in which media researchers invite participation from sociologists, psychologists, and political scientists. Because of the pervasiveness of the media, researchers from all areas of science are now actively involved in attempting to answer media-related questions.

Modern mass media research includes a variety of psychological and sociological investigations, such as physiological and emotional responses to television programs, commercials, or music played on radio stations. In addition, computer modeling and other sophisticated computer analyses are now commonplace in media research to determine such things as the potential success of television programs (network or syndicated). Once considered eccentric by some, mass media research is now a legitimate and esteemed field.

Thorough research helps reporters get to the bottom of a story and it also ensures all the information is accurate. Journalists need to be confident about their facts, and good research helps them when they go out to report.

There are lots of different ways you can research a news story and here are a few handy hints to help you get started.

## Ask the Right Questions to the Right People

Speaking to people who can give you an insight into your story is a great way to carry out your research.

Talking to people is a great way to research.

This might take the form of an interview with someone you want to use in your report, or it might be speaking to someone who is not directly involved with the story but who can give you some expert advice and information. Think about what it is you want to get out of the person you are speaking to, and what questions you need to ask to get that information or viewpoint from them.

The best kind of questions to ask is usually open ones. These are the kind of questions where you get a fuller answer, not just a yes or a no. So ask "what do you think of the new skyscraper?" rather than "do you like the new skyscraper?"

Open questions are usually used by journalists because they encourage people to give more information. There are times when closed questions might be appropriate, perhaps if there is a specific fact that you are trying to check or a particular statistic you want to know is accurate.

Sometimes you'll need to ask a lot of questions to get the information you want. And if someone isn't able to answer your questions, they may be able to suggest someone else who can. Good reporters will usually speak to several people, rather than relying on just one source.

## The Internet

Most people are well accustomed to conducting internet searches, but there is so much information available on the internet that it can sometimes seem overwhelming. This is when it becomes helpful to narrow your search.

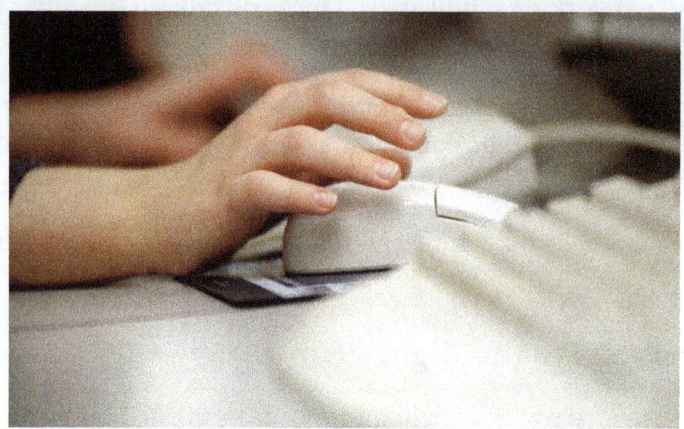

Don't believe everything you read on the internet.

When using a search engine, remember to use quotation marks around a person's name, such as "David Beckham" or "Usain Bolt". This will help narrow down your search results.

Bookmark you're most interesting and relevant results so you can return to them again. If you don't know how to do this, ask your teacher.

Another top tip for web searches is to use multiple words. For example entering just the word "turkey" will returns hits on the country and the bird. But if you type in "turkey christmas stuffing roast how long", your top hits will be for stuffed turkey.

Also, just as not every person you speak to is 100% reliable, not every story or report you find on the web will be completely accurate. It is also important to remember that just because you have read it on the internet, it doesn't mean it is true, so always check your facts. Websites like Wikipedia can be useful starting points, but you should try to corroborate important facts with other sources.

News websites like the BBC's can also be a useful reference point. You can search through old stories using key words to get some background to a story.

## Social Media Tools

Lots of journalists now use Twitter as a newsgathering tool. It can be a great way to search for contributors, case studies and information on a story. However, if you want to use Twitter as part of your journalistic research during the course of School Report you should think very carefully about safety issues and the age restrictions in place on the micro-blogging site.

Just like websites such as YouTube and Facebook, Twitter is aimed at people who are aged 13 and over. Within Twitter's pages on privacy is a section on their policy "towards children" which points out that" our services are not directed to persons under 13 we do not knowingly collect personal information from children under 13".

Twitter is aimed at people who are over 13.

Any use of Twitter or social media for School Report purposes should comply with your school's social media policy, and we strongly recommend it is done in a supervised capacity.

You can choose which other Twitter accounts you would like to follow. Depending on the stories you are working on, you might want to follow, for example, your local newspaper, your local council, your local football club or journalists who tend to cover these type of stories.

You can also create lists in Twitter to group together related accounts which can be a really useful way to manage lots of information coming in. Here are some step-by-step instructions to create lists.

You can search Twitter in a similar way to searching Google, Yahoo or other search engines and this can help you find out crucial information and even potential interviewees.

An advanced search can be a really good way of narrowing down the information that's coming in on a particular topic.

People often use hashtags to help their tweets get found by other Twitter users with an interest in a particular topic or event. So, for instance, during Prime Minister's Questions, journalists may compose a tweet about the exchanges and end with #pmqs which other people can then search for to bring all the tweets mentioning #pmqs together. It's vital that you treat Twitter just the same as any other source: just because something's on Twitter doesn't mean it's true.

Hoax accounts are common, and sometimes a Twitter user will pretend to be a famous person for the purposes of trying to arrange a face-to-face meeting. This is obviously dangerous and you should not allow yourself to be talked into a meeting with someone you do not know. Twitter uses blue ticks in profiles to verify many official accounts.

## Don't Forget Libraries

The internet is an amazing tool, but don't forget there's a wealth of information in books as well.

Get to know your subject inside out by reading up before you interview someone. Looking through recent and old newspapers or magazines can also be useful, and you can see how other journalists have covered the same or similar stories. Librarians can help point you in the right direction and help you figure out the best tools to carry out your research.

Libraries can help you get to know your subject.

## Focus of the Story

We know the basic questions that journalists strive to answer when chasing a news story — questions starting with "who," "what," "where," when," "why" and "how."

Even if you're on deadline, try having a 10-minute conversation guided by these questions. As an editor, the coaching you provide on the front-end can often save you time revising the story after the fact.

How would you tell this story to a friend? We're good at considering the news value of a story, but we're not always as good pondering the "Why should the reader care?" part. Having the writer imagine telling the story to a friend can help him or her think about why we should care. This approach can also help the writer move away from any jargon and bring a conversational tone to the piece.

What would an early headline be for this story, knowing that the headline is not set in stone? This is a variation on the question, "What is this story really about?" Boiling the premise down to five or six words can help the writer sharpen the story's focus. In my newsroom, we're asking reporters and line editors to write early Web headlines and short summaries on top of their stories. This is largely for production reasons, but the added benefit is that we're encouraging writers and editors to get at the heart of the story earlier in the process.

What surprised you? Asking about "surprise" can help the writer shed his or her journalistic mantle, at least for a moment, and just react to the story's events as a human being. Who were the quirky personalities you met? What was a jarring quote you heard? What did you not see coming? What interesting details and anecdotes do you have in your notebook that you left out of the story, and how do we get one or two of them back in?

What are the unanswered questions? As journalists, we're not always good at spelling out what we don't know in a story, especially if it's a breaking story. Oftentimes, we try to write around the holes. Better to be clear and 'fess up in the story about what remains to be explained and clarified. This question also prompts the writer and editor to compile a list of questions for any follow-up stories.

How do we bring something new to this story? Your best reporters want to be challenged. And chances are, if they are veterans, they have tackled a story similar to the one they are tackling now. What better way to challenge them than to ask them to come up with a fresh approach to the story? The approach could involve words, but it could also involve photography, graphics and online elements. This question will also help writers think about collaborating with visual journalists across the newsroom.

What's the glimpse of wisdom we can offer? The best stories for me are those that not only tell readers something they don't know, but also resonate with readers because they touch upon a universal theme. They offer readers a "glimpse of wisdom" — an important lesson that the people we're writing about have learned — whether it's about love or loyalty, betrayal or resilience. Those are the most satisfying stories for me. Equipped with cable TV, laptops, tablets and smart phones, our readers are lost in a sea of information. They are hungry for context and meaning. The "glimpse of wisdom" is one of the most important things we can offer them.

## Verifying the Details

Stop a journalist on the street and ask her to list the fundamentals of the job and you're almost certain to hear mention of accuracy. In "The Elements of Journalism," Bill Kovach and Tom Rosenstein wrote that journalism's "essence is a discipline of verification."

But how do journalists actually go about verifying information in their everyday work? What does it look like in practice, and how does it vary from one reporter to the next? Fundamental questions, and yet there's little academic research to answer them.

"While there is a long tradition of measuring news reports' accuracy post hoc substantially less work has examined the processes by which journalists seek to attain accuracy," write Canadian journalism researchers Ivor Shapiro, Colette Brin, Isabelle Bédard-Brûlé and Kasia Mychajlowycz in their newly published paper, "Verification As A Strategic Ritual: How journalists retrospectively describe processes for ensuring accuracy."

It's perhaps the first paper to offer a look at how working journalists view and practice verification. The researchers found that verification is widely seen as essential and core to a journalist's work. But at the same time, the methods for achieving accuracy vary from one journalist to the next. There is no single standard for verification, and not every fact is treated the same.

"A small, easily checkable fact needs to be checked; a larger but greyer assertion, not so much — unless it is defamatory," they write. "Thus, verification for a journalist is a rather different animal from verification in scientific method, which would hold every piece of data subject to a consistent standard of observation and replication."

### Method

To gather data, the researchers interviewed 28 Canadian journalists (men and women; French and English), half of whom had recently won an award for a piece of work; the other half were selected after the authors chose "14 stories semi-randomly from a constructed population of texts commensurate in length with the set of award-winning stories."

They met with the journalists and spoke about the verification practices used to produce the stories. Like good researchers, they noted one weakness to this approach.

"We were relying entirely on the subject journalists' own accounts of their work, with no available means to verify (!) The truth of those accounts," they write. "Apart from the possibility of the subjects varnishing their verification efforts, we also were limited by the capacity of their memories."

## Variations in Verification

One theme in the paper is that different journalists practice verification in different ways — though they all agree it's hugely important.

"There's no point in being a journalist if you're not going to relay accurate, correct factual information to the public," one interviewee said.

Shapiro told me by email that, "while journalists see the norm of verification as quite pivotal to their professional identity, the recognition of this norm is not quite matched by the kind of methodological discipline that Kovach and Rosenstiel speak of."

Rosenstiel, a member of Poynter's National Advisory Board, contributor to Poynter.org, and the executive director of the American Press Institute, disagrees with Shapiro's assessment of how the findings relate to the treatment of verification in "The Elements of Journalism."

"Far from challenging what we found in Elements, the study reinforces it," he told me. "We conclude, as they do from their 28 interviews, that journalists aspire to accuracy and being truth tellers but lack standard routines or sufficient intellectual training for seriously doing it. We note that these routines are highly individualized and idiosyncratic. We also outlined some of those individual routines as a way to suggest how to make this discipline more conscious and more serious. That, indeed, is the point. Elements is a call for journalists to live up to their aspirations with more rigor, not a celebration of current practice."

So why are journalists unable to systematize their aspirations of accuracy? In that regard, the paper shared an important fact: there's little specific guidance for verification offered in journalism textbooks.

Many journalism textbooks are devoid of references to verification or fact-checking; Harris and Spark or confine themselves to only the briefest references to the importance of double-checking basic facts such as names, ages and locations, and the necessity for more than one source where a charge of misconduct is made.

"Columbia [University's journalism school] has a course called 'evidence and inference'; Ryerson has a course called 'Exactly so', and I am sure many schools try to teach verification strategies and critical thinking, but textbooks are another matter," he said. "There are probably some great ones out there that do a good job of tackling this question, but I haven't seen them yet."

This partly explains the varying ways journalists practice verification: They come into the profession having been taught in different ways, or perhaps not much at all. And yet, we place accuracy on a pedestal.

"We actually found the interviews journalists' passion for accuracy often inspiring," Shapiro told me. Journalists "have to juggle competing priorities in delivering products that their employers can sell. Not one of our 28 interviewees gave us any reason to think that s/he does not take the responsibility for accuracy very seriously."

"They are professionals, but they are artists, not scientists – and, mostly, artists on a deadline," Shapiro added.

One positive trend I've seen in recent years, which wasn't part of this specific research, is that the increasing use of user-generated content by newsrooms has resulted in organizations creating a defined verification process. This is encouraging, particularly as new technologies and media continue to transform newsgathering and fact finding at a rapid pace.

## How Journalists Verify

"There's no hard and fast rule about any of this stuff," one interviewee told the authors. "You have to exercise your judgment all the time."

"To me, verification is much more rooted in the actual reporting process, step by step and looping back in upon itself," said another. Among the interviewees there were those who applied a disciplined approach to verification.

"Some arrived for the interview armed with indexed binders full of source materials; some had clearly refreshed their memories of the reporting by reviewing their notes, and related articles, before their meetings with us; one checked additional facts and followed-up via email," the researchers write.

A commitment to verification may be shared across journalists, but this research suggests any shared norms are combined with variations in practice.

"Methods for ensuring accuracy varied greatly, with some factual statements relayed, with or without attribution, based on a single subject's word, while others were rigorously triangulated," the authors write. "Strongly idealistic statements about the need for verification were often made during the course of the same interview as were indications of methodological ambiguity."

In terms of specifics, here are a few findings from the research:

- On checking names: "An almost universal practice among participants is asking sources to spell their own name to ensure correct spelling, either at the beginning or the end of the interview." Some journalists also check names against official sources.

- On offering sources pre-publication review: "Despite some evidence in the literature that partial pre-publication review is not the taboo it used to be our subjects displayed a strong sense that it was a discouraged practice."

- On quotes: "methods for checking the accuracy of quotes vary greatly. Some reporters routinely record and transcribe interviews, while some record but rarely transcribe and others rarely use recorders at all. Some check quotes against tapes only if there is a specific concern, such as difficulty hearing, or the threat of libel litigation."

- On a source's personal history: "Facts relating to a source's personal history are considered not to require verification or are simply not verified because there is no practical way to do so."

Rosenstiel told me, "the aspiration to vet the news is an essential goal of most journalists, but the processes for living up to that goal are not well-defined and not rigorous enough. And for journalism to survive, much more needs to be done to give the process of verification more throw weight."

## Sources of News

During the primitive times the command of the ruler used to be conveyed to the people through the beat of the drums. The similar method was used in conveying information pertaining to different matters. Verbal words also used to the spread to establish communication with the people. A stage came when with the spread of betray information used to be pasted on the walls. Later on the printing presses replaced all these news sources and information in the printed forms were conveyed to the people when the newspapers, started their publication they became the biggest source of news as they are today. The newspaper over a period of time has developed their own techniques and methods to carry information to their readers. Similar was the case with the news agencies that developed their own agencies that developed their own methods to carry information from their offices to the office of their subscribers that is news' papers. The news agencies also developed their links outside their own countries to secure news. The first known air link was established by the first news agency of the world known as Reuter. The relay of messages in the early period inside and outside the country was through pigeons. Mr. Writer, founder of the news agency trained the pigeons in such a manner that they first flew the information tied to their necks within the country and later on outside. The pigeous were subsequently replaced by tele-printer, wireless and cable as the systems of telecommunication developed.

### Some Best News Sources in Journalism

The major news sources for journalist are Radio T.V. newspapers and magazines, their own correspondents, press, interviews, press conferences, police stations, courts and handouts, press releases and press notes:

### Radio

Almost all newspapers in the country monitor news from the major foreign radio networks and publish the information. They also true in to listen to the national broadcast for news. The newspaper benefits them from the radio news because they are considered to be the latest. Moreover, it does not cost them anything by way of money. The authenticity of the news broadcast by a radio is generally taken for granted.

### Television

Another important source of news the newspapers listen to the news telecast by TV. The news telecast by T.V. is also carry the reputation of evening authentic. Besides supplying the news, the T.V.

reports give a pictorial view of an event. The T.V establishments generally enter into agreements for mutual exchange of film reports with one another. These reports when telecast give sufficient material to newspaper to convey information to the readers.

## Newspaper and Magazines

The newspapers and magazines, both in national and international contain good material for publication by the newspapers. Stories are published by a newspaper from interviews published in the magazines. The newspapers also themselves from the news published by the newspaper at other stations. Similarly the magazines and newspapers published abroad are also definite by the newspapers. The newspapers derive benefit from reports appearing in foreign press.

## Correspondents

The newspaper has their own correspondents based inside and outside the country. The correspondents keep in touch with their respective organization and reports events of their newspapers interest. The newspapers have a subdivision of different fields and reporters. The newspaper major specialized or general correspondents. They report their sources and correspondents to keep their organization informed about the latest news. The reporters are based in the same city whereas the correspondences are based outside the place of publication of the newspaper.

## Press Interviews

One yet another important source of the news for the newspaper. Interviews are secured to obtain information pertaining to different activities and fields. Men in the news are interviewed subject to the requirement of the newspapers for securing publicity material.

## Press Conferences

Newspapers give new coverage to the press conferences addressed by various personalities. The press conferences addressed are called or arranged by personalities who want to make some point known to the public. A statement is made at the start of the press conference explaining the precise reason for calling the press conference. Later on questions are invited from the newsmen to clear their doubts or for further elucidation of the points made in the press conference earlier.

## Police Stations

One of the major and bests sources of news is police stations. Almost every occurrence, every case and incident is reported in news reporter establish 'links with police stations to secure information. Every evening the reporter ring up the police stations for information on registration of new cases. On getting the due from the police stations the reporters precede further to get more information.

## Hospitals and Courts

Another big source is the hospitals from where news of cases regarding accidents etc., are known. A person can file a case against another, like the complaint against the police and this information can be had not from the reader out also from attendance in court.

## Handouts

All the documents containing information which are circulated for general information. They handouts may be issued by an organization to convey information to the public at large. The handouts now days are being issued contain material in respect of activities of the Govt., and government organization. They contain material in respect of the Govt. in various fields. The newspapers may or may not publish the information contained in the handout. The handout highlights the activities of the Govt., in different fields. They contain information about tours of minister and appointments of officers. Handouts are also issued by the agencies attached with the Govt. and the corporate bodies.

## Press Note

It is issued by the Govt. whenever some information in categorical terms or unambiguous terms is to be provided to the general public. They contain information on specific matters in which the Govts. firms stand is to be explained. They are to be published by the newspaper in the manner they are received by them. No change in the content or manner is to be affected in it by the newspaper. They are considered to be the last word on Govts. View point. They are not issued as frequently.by government as the handouts. They are issued whenever a need for high lighting government firm stand arises.

## Press Releases

Press Relations contains press releases information pertaining to the activities of different organizations and establishment. The press releases are issued whenever these organizations want to reach the public through the information media. They are issued on behalf of the organization. Concerned their office bearers on the spokesmen, they are always in the form of writing material meant for circulation to the press. They may contain ambiguous or categorical information in respect of their activities.

## Press Statements

Whenever someone in his individual or representative capacity. Lirses to make his point known through media, he reaches the press with a written statement and it is called a press statement. The statement must be issued by a person having some position in some organization or has attained distinction in one or the other. The statement is sent to the newspaper and it is used by them as subject to their interest in it.

## References

- Research-importance-research-aims-motives: masscommunicationtalk.com, Retrieved 9 February, 2019

- Schoolreport: bbc.co.uk, Retrieved 11 April, 2019

- 6-questions-that-can-help-journalists-find-a-focus-tell-better-stories, reporting-editing: poynter.org, Retrieved 18 July, 2019

- New-research-details-how-journalists-verify-information, reporting-editing: poynter.org, Retrieved 9 January, 2019

- Source-of-news-in-journalism-radio-tv-newspapers-magazines, journalism-mass-communication: studylecturenotes.com, Retrieved 10 March, 2019

# 7

# Interviewing

The process of asking questions and receiving answers is known as interviewing. There are numerous types of interviews such as hard news interview, informational interview, adversarial interview and personal interview. All the diverse principles of these types of interviews have been carefully analyzed in this chapter.

Interview refers to a formal, in-depth conversation between two or more persons, wherein exchange of information takes place, with a view of checking candidate's acceptability for the job.

## Objectives of Interview

- To evaluate applicant's suitability.
- To gain additional information from the candidate.
- To provide general information about the company to the applicant.
- To create a good image of the company, among applicants.

It is an effective tool for selection. It is a two way communication between interviewer and interviewee, wherein the former seeks information, by way of questions and the latter provides the same, through his/her verbal responses. However, the information flows in both directions.

- Structured Interview: The interview in which pre-set standardised questions are used by the interviewer, which are asked to all the candidates. It is also known as a patterned or guided interview.

- Unstructured Interview: The unstructured interview is one that does not follow any formal rules and procedures. The discussion is free flowing, and questions are made up during the interview.

- Mixed Interview: It is a combination of structured and unstructured interview, wherein a blend of predetermined and spontaneous questions is asked by the interviewer to the job seeker. It follows a realistic approach which allows the employer to make a comparison between answers and get in-depth insights too.

- Behavioural Interview: It is concerned with a problem or a hypothetical situation, put before the candidate with an expectation to solve. It aims at revealing the job seeker's ability to solve the problem presented.

- Stress Interview: The employer commonly uses stress interview for those jobs which are more stress prone. A number of harsh, rapid fire questions are put to the interviewee with intent to upset him. It seeks to know, how the applicant will respond to pressure.

- One to one Interview: The most common interview type, in which there are only two participants – the interviewer (usually the representative of the company) and interviewee, taking part in the face to face discussion, in order to transfer information.

- Panel Interview: Panel interview is one, in which there is a panel of interviewers, i.e. two or more interviewers, but limited to 15. All the members of the panel are different representatives of the company.

- Telephonic Interview: Telephonic interview is one that is conducted over telephone. It is the most economical and less time consuming, which focuses on asking and answering questions.

- Video Interview: An interview, in which video conference is being employed, to judge or evaluate the candidate. Due to its flexibility, rapidity and inexpensiveness, it is used increasingly.

## Halo Effect

Halo effect refers to cognitive bias, wherein the interviewer makes a judgement about the applicant's overall potential for the performance of the job, considering a single characteristic, like the way he/she talks, sits, dresses, etc.

Interviews also have several shortcomings, such as lack of reliability, i.e. no two interviewers give similar points to an applicant after the interview. Further, lack of validity and biases of interviewers may also trouble interview.

## Types of Interviews

Broadly speaking there are twelve different types of interview:

- Hard news interview

- Informational interview

- Investigative interview

- Adversarial interview

- Interpretative interview

- Personal interview

- Emotional interview

- Entertainment interview

- Actuality

- Telephone or remote interview

- Vox pop

- Grabbed interview.

## Hard News Interview

The hard news interview is normally short, to the point, and to illustrate a bulletin or news item. It deals only with important facts, or comments and reactions to those facts. The hard news interview, as a matter of fact, aims at getting answers to five Ws and one H.

In case a building is set on fire, the reporter will conduct interviews of those figures who can give him exactor almost exact information about the incident.

Following questions may be asked:

- When did it happen?

- What about the direct affected?

- What is the amount of damage?

- Where are the injured ones taken to?

## Informational Interview

The informational interview is similar to hard news interview, but not necessarily be restricted to main stories. An informational interview can be about an event, something that is happening or about to happen. It can also provide background.

Informational interview goes beyond the main point to seek an explanation of the HOWs and WHYs of the story. They intend to get bit more detailed than short bulletin items.

## Investigative Interview

The investigative interview aims at getting behind the facts to discover what really caused the happening of the events and sometimes what could be done to prevent a repeat of that incident, to get behind the facts to dig out the actual reasons of the accident/train collision/air crash/the reasons of the reconciliation between two arch rivals.

Investigative interview might be developed about stories and issues:

- Why the team showed poor performance in the match despite having been provided the best facilities and trained by the best coach?

- Why the minister resigned from his office?

- Why is our film industry not getting up to its feet?

- Why the fire brigade wasn't reaches the spot in time?

- Why the tank of the fire brigade ran short of water while putting out the fire?

## Adversarial Interview

A kind of interview in which the interviewer gets into a war of words with the interviewee to get his question answered. This approach should never be seen to be a head on clash between the interviewer and the interviewee. Though the interviewer is representing the audience or speaking up on the behalf of the public opinion, even then he needs not to be impolite or rude while asking questions.

## Precautions

A verbal assault on an interviewee might result in allegations of victimization and bias, and if it happens the public opinion about the reporter may get changed and the interviewee may get sympathies of the listeners.

Adversarial interview may expose the interviewer to the libel suit and the interviewee may drag him to the corridors of the court. So it is pertinent that the reporter think well before he speaks while he is conducting an interview.

- Get direct but avoid a head-on clash with the interviewee.

- The impression of victimization of the interviewee must be avoided.

- The impression of biasness must be avoided.

## Interpretative Interview

There are two types of interpretative interviews:

- A reaction story it is a response either for or against what has happened.

- Explanatory story this story provides details of a news story. So the interview that is conducted to get the details of an event, accident or incident is called interpretative interview.

For instance, if a train is derailed causing severe injuries and damage to the passengers the following questions may be asked from any representative of the railways:

- How will this accident affect public confidence in train traveling?·

- What measures will the ministry take to restore the public trust?

## Personal Interviews

The personal interview might be a short interview with an important figure of a society about his/her likes and dislikes, hobbies, pastimes, habits, or a detailed interview exposing personality profile.

In personality interview following areas are normally focused while putting questions:

- Family background

- Education (Place & degree)

- Why not further study
- Likes and dislikes
- Favorite dish, Book, Personality, Cologne, Game, Movie, Singer
- Hobbies -leisure-spending
- Any interesting incident, event.

## Entertainment Interview

It is a kind of interview in which light things are asked from the interviewee. The only purpose is to entertain listeners. The person to be interviewed may be an actor making parody of any famous personality or any real one whose profession is to entertain people.

## Emotional Interview

In this kind of interview an attempt is made to lay bare someone's feelings. Emotional interview lets the person who was the victim or one of the victims of an accident or event share the personal tragedy with the listeners.

A heart-stricken women having been saved from earth quake will be asked the question like the following ones:

- What were you doing at the time of earth quake?
- What about your kids?
- Were they school going, infants or toddlers?
- When did you first realize that the quake was going to be horrible?
- Were you able to save anyone? How did you manage to save yourself?

## Actuality Interview

It is a kind of interview in which the reporter's voice is not included in the final production and only interviewee's voice is made to be heard by the listeners. This kind of interview is made a part of documentary or feature.

While conducting actuality interviews following instructions must be followed by the reporter, the questions must be:

- Clear not vague
- Subjective not objective.

Subjective questions: Questions that start with Question words i.e., what, when, which, where, who, how. Objective questions that start with helping verbs like is, are, am, will, would, shall, should, etc. For instance, observe the following questions:

- Which areas in Pakistan is child labor more than the others and why?

- How many types of child labor are found in Pakistan? What are the government's efforts to curb child labor?

### Remote Interviews (Interviews on Telephone)

The personality to be interviewed is not in the city or country and is interviewed on telephone. While recording remote interview the telephone lines must be checked whether they are clear or not. If there is a noise problem in the line, try to change the line or wait until it is clear.

### Vox Pop Interviews

Vox pop is an abbreviation of the Latin expression vox populi that means `voice of the people'. It is conducted to obtain diversified public opinion on certain issue. The questions are asked from different people representing different age groups, races, classes etc.

### Grabbed Interviews

It means to interview a person who does not intend to give an interview but the reporter is determined to take. Normally it is a very short interview and sometimes the potential interviewee comes up with "no comments". In this case though the interviewee refuses to say anything about the issue but his saying "no comments" suggests the listeners to get the meaning.

## Interviewing for Newspaper

Interviews may be conversational, but they are not casual conversations. Organization is essential, as is attention to detail and a firm will. The process also begins well before you talk with the other person, be it face to face, on the telephone or over the Internet. The intensity of your preparations may vary depending on the gravity and importance of the interview.

The first thing to determine is your goals- Do you want to obtain specific information? If so, what? Even if you're working on a long-term project and are just interested in "learning more," do your best to determine what you'd like to learn. Based on your goals, compile a list of questions you'd like to ask. They can be highly specific ("What were you doing at noon on June 12, 2003?") or general in nature ("Tell me about your work"), as required. Err on the side of more questions rather than fewer, and prioritize them as you go.

Ensure that your list also includes the most basic questions: Is the interview on the record? Even if you know the subject's name (and presumably you do), you should always ask and confirm the spelling; if appropriate, get the name of his or her organization and title. If there's any other basic information you need for the article — say, if it's on young entrepreneurs born in your state, you'll need to ask his or her birthplace and age — make sure those questions are on the list.

Once you've got your list of targeted questions ready, turn them into a list of general topics that you will have in front of you for the interview. Ultimately, it's better to work with a topics list rather than a series of carefully worded questions. You should strive to create a natural, though purposeful, conversation.

Gather the tools of the trade: voice or video recorder (make sure it's fully charged and tested; if you're really cautious, you can bring a backup unit), reporter's notebook, pen or pencil (always carry a backup), laptop. If the interview is taking place in person and you have business cards, bring some with you.

If you're having to deal with press officers or public relations people to arrange the interview, they may ask you for a list of topics you want to cover. While you can give them a general sense of topics, resist agreeing that you will stick only to those topics and definitely don't send the questions you've compiled. Reserve your right to ask any question that you deem relevant during the interview itself.

Do not let anyone get you to agree to have quotations approved before they are used in your story; it is not good journalistic practice and does not serve your audience in an honest way. This has become a important ethical issue in contemporary American journalism.

## Good Practices during the Interview

First off, regardless of the situation, state that you are a journalist. It is unethical to fool or mislead people. You should also indicate that you are planning to publish or broadcast material from the interview, even if you are freelance and don't yet know where or how it will be published. (For student journalists, if you are going to put the article anywhere — including a blog — you should explain that it may be seen publicly).

If at all possible, arrange to conduct the interview at the subject's home or workplace (whichever is more appropriate). That places them in a target-rich environment, which greatly increases the chances that you will be able to meet people and see things that you would never get otherwise. In any case, find a quiet location to talk. Ask permission to record the interview and be sure to mute your mobile phone, particularly if you're using it as your recording device. Leave it up to the person you're interviewing to do the same.

If you are recording the interview, remember that some people may not say as much on tape — especially if it's the first time you've sat down together. Also, public officials may ask to be able to speak "on background" (meaning you can use the information, but without specific attribution) or even "off the record" (information that cannot be used). Establish the rules at the beginning of the interview. If you agree that an interview is all on the record, do not let the subject declare afterwards that something is off the record. At the same time, understand that you may be in a negotiation, and keep in mind what best serves the public interest.

When the time comes to record, start your device and put it on the table closer to your source than you (it's his or her words that are important, after all) but ideally in a position that allows you to see the timer.

First get the basic information (name, title and so on), then begin your list of questions. All people are different, of course, and some will talk without end while others barely speak. It can help to start with open-ended questions ("So, tell me about your childhood") rather than ones to which the subject can give a yes/no answer ("Was your childhood happy?"). Allowing your subject to talk a length early can help put them at ease and open up mutual communication.

As things continue, remember that as a journalist, it's your job to control the flow of the interview, asking the questions and keeping things on track. That doesn't mean you can't let the topic of discussion move in unexpected ways — indeed, this can sometimes be to your advantage — but make sure you get what you came for. If an important question is sidestepped, ask again. If the interviewee seems to become angry or upset, stay calm and ask the question in another way. If responses go off track or go on too long, gently steer the subject back in the right direction. Be polite and respectful, but also firm.

As the interview proceeds, take careful notes, but don't allow it to become distracting. If something is said of particular interest, it's helpful to jot down the time in the interview when it occurred — this will greatly speed finding and verifying the quote after the fact. If your source mentions the name of a person, organization or place, ask for confirmation of the spelling.

At the conclusion of the interview, thank the interviewee for his or her time and ask if you can be in contact again if there are additional questions; ask for a cell phone number and direct email if you don't already have them, as they can provide a quicker path to a response. Also ask for access to photos and any other documents or objects that have come up. It will be much harder to do this hours or days later.

## Maximizing your Material

Now that you have the interview, what you do with it depends on how it's going to be used. If you only need a few quotes, you can jump to those points in the recording based on the times you jotted down. If you're doing an extended printed Q&A — your questions and their responses — it's best to do a complete transcription and edit that down (of course making clear to your audience if it has been edited for brevity and clarity).

In editing the interview, remember that people rarely speak in perfect, well-formed sentences. There will be many an "uh" and "ah" that can be safely omitted, assuming that this does not distort meaning. While you can trim the beginning or end of responses without having to indicate with ellipses, if you cut out a sentence or phrase in the middle, they should be used. Similarly, if you insert text for clarity, use brackets.

If you have interviewed a public official, do not, under any circumstances, allow him or her to modify answers that are already on the record. But some reporters will read back sections of stories and ask if there's anything he or she might like to add. However, it's a reporter's role to decide whether or not to use additional information, not the person interviewed. When dealing with private citizens, take particular care in cases where identities, locations and other identifying elements may be sensitive and could expose persons to danger or unneeded distress. Use your judgment about how a sensitive quotation from a private citizen — particularly those who have no media sophistication — needs to be used, and what information and context best serves the public interest.

## The Need for more Homework

If the interviewee is someone whom you are seeking out because of his or her particular position or authoritative knowledge of a situation (the deputy transportation commissioner, the CFO of a company, etc.), you need to put in sufficient time researching previous news articles written about that person and other relevant background. Come informed — in many ways, a journalist is the one person in the community who represents only the public interest and whose job it is to give voice to collective concerns. It may be the only time an official has to be accountable for certain things, and it is in this way that journalists play a special role — with special responsibilities and burdens — in a democracy.

Another special case is experts whose views you seek to deepen a story. The same rule applies there: Prepare, prepare, prepare. The following are key things to keep in mind for these two special classes of sources:

## Academics and Experts

For research experts, don't just show up or call to "get a quote"; do enough reading of his or her materials that you show respect and can speak a little of the expert's professional language. Don't waste someone's time with factual questions that you should really know yourself. An example of a sub-par question would be asking a political scientist: "How many electoral votes does our state have?" An example of a good question might be: "What factors might influence the vote in our state?" That doesn't mean you can't ask simple, direct questions; just ensure they aren't things you could learn on your own perfectly easily.

Though it is not good professional practice to give questions in advance to sources such as public officials, with experts you may want to email some general questions before speaking on the phone or in person. Help them educate you. Most experts' Web pages feature links to their work; for academics, also search Google Scholar and other databases. Try to read any primary articles and research he or she has authored (at least be familiar with the subjects and extent) that directly relate to your subject of interest. For academic papers, try to at least read the introduction and conclusion, even if the methods section is heavily statistical. Know that most papers, at their root, are simply trying to figure out the logical relationship between several variables and test a hypothesis — try not to be intimidated. If the research is what you're interested in, email other academics cited in the paper and ask them what they think of the findings.

Greg Ip, the U.S. economics editor at The Economist, has this to say about interacting with experts: "If I don't have a lot of experience in the area, I'll ask, 'Can you point me to some other things so I can get a better grounding before we can begin the interview?' I find that academics are incredibly helpful and patient; they like to talk about their work, because they're excited by it and publicity is usually good. But one thing that I have learned about academics is that — even when they are not partisan or biased in the direction the research goes — I think it's the nature of the discipline that academia rewards people who develop very strong views on often narrow subjects."

Remember that many experts can be skeptical of journalists because of the media's general tendency to oversimplify. Show them you know the subject matter and care enough to read in depth. By doing so, you may earn a trusted source that can help you in the future. You will almost certainly get better answers and fresh angles for further stories.

## Public Officials and Newsmakers

When interviewing public officials and people in the news, know the job that he or she does — what their powers, limits and constraints are. Also come to the interview with a sense of his or her agenda. Is the person simply a good public servant? Running for higher office? Wants to clear the record on some specific point? Good interviews with public officials are directed but conversational. Remember, too, that one reason people want to have a conversation with a reporter is to learn things they may not know. As a reporter, you talk to people in the community that officials and newsmakers don't. Many good interviews involve a two-way exchange in which both parties learn something. Don't give up your professional objectivity, but recognize that you are dealing with human beings who are often just as curious as you are.

Above all, educate yourself so that you do not walk into an interview unaware of some previous controversial public issue or high-profile accomplishment or failure that serves as important context. Once an official realizes your ignorance, it would be very easy for him or she to sidestep questions or give easy answers, if that's what he or she wants to do. You may want to do some advance background interviews with others — especially those who may disagree with your primary interview subject — about key areas of concern.

Review related coverage in your own publication's archives and those of other sources. Also dig through Lexis-Nexis or Factiva; each differs in the kinds of articles and transcripts available, so try them all. If you need to search historical news, a good choice is Proust. If you don't have access to these, contact your local libraries and ask for access to similar databases, such as those through News Bank. Note that a Google News search only yields recent articles; to see older related content, go to the drop-down menu on the right of the search bar, and select "in archive" for the "Date added to Google News" option.

High-level persons typically have limited time in their schedule, so you'll want to plan your interview questions very carefully. Remember that you can ask for things to be put on the record at the end of the interview or later on; and you can always ask if there is another way you can confirm information, such as a public record that says the same thing. As mentioned, some of the most useful things that you can come away with are documents, so ask if there are reports, spread sheets, papers, transcripts, etc. that you can take or photocopy that might help your story. In the heat of an interview, it is not always easy to figure out what is important; but documents can be analyzed and studied afterward, when you have time to think.

If you are planning to ask difficult and uncomfortable questions, structure your questions so that the tougher ones come last, knowing that, sometimes, you may be asked to leave. And prepare to follow up even if things get tense. Maintain your composure. Frame the question so that it does not become a debate and consider triangulating so it does not become personal: For example, use the phrasing "Your critics have said- What do you say?"

Pulitzer Prize-winning investigative journalist Ron Suskind advises reporters about interviews as follows: "Be honest; and always say, 'Please explain this to me in words so I can understand it.' People live inside a lexicon. Lexicons often carry with them judgments. We're very tribal- Tribes develop language, and I am always wary of that. When I say, 'Explain that to me in terms I can understand,' then sources start to get more fundamental and elemental."

## Interviewing for Television

A TV interview can be as simple as asking questions of people on the street, or it can be as involved as a one-on-one, sit-down discussion with the president. Getting good answers in a TV interview can make a news story come to life and build your reputation as a probing journalist. Build your skills so that you can lead the people you interview into giving you the information you want with simple TV interview tips every news media professional can use.

### Decide the TV Interview Focus

Sometimes, all you want from an interview are some facts. If you're talking to the fire chief on the scene of a huge fire, you want to know the typical "who, what, when, where, why and how." As long as you get answers to these basic questions, your needs are satisfied. But that's not the kind of TV interview that can help you win media awards or help you build a job-winning resume tape or DVD. You need to demonstrate that your skills go beyond asking simple questions.

If you are interviewing a man whose wife was killed in a tornado, you want to prepare your questioning to draw out as much emotion as possible. Instead of asking something like, "What time did the tornado hit?", you'll get more by asking, "What will your life be like without your wife by your side?" Notice that's an open-ended question that will give you a meatier answer than something like, "Are you sad your wife is gone?" which could only produce a simple, "Yes." For investigative work, you may need to ask preliminary questions to get your subject to relax before you hit her with the question you really want to ask. It's tough to start an interview with a highly-charged question such as, "Do you feel your boss sexually harassed you?" unless the person has already filed a lawsuit.

## Learn something about the Topic

If you're assigned to cover the Libertarian Party's presidential candidate, asking the candidate "What's the Libertarian Party?" is a giveaway that you didn't come to the interview prepared. If you find yourself in that situation, it's better to camouflage your lack of knowledge by asking, "For people who don't understand what the Libertarian Party is all about, how would you put it into words?"

Better still is to know that answer before the interview so that you can ask smarter questions. The goal is to find out answers to questions that viewers would want to know.

Some interviewers go overboard to ask the most complicated, technical question they can find to demonstrate their own personal grasp of a subject. While that may inflate their ego, it's wasted effort if the answer doesn't interest the people watching the news report.

## Listen Closely during the Interview

Amazingly, this is one of the most common mistakes interviewers make. They are so wrapped up in planning their next question that it's obvious that they're not even listening to the conversation.

Here's an example of that: The mayor says, "I have failed my city and have decided that I must resign from office. I apologize for my poor performance in office and ask all residents to forgive me." The interviewer: "So when's the next city council meeting?"

An interview is a conversation; you just happen to have a microphone, camera, and notepad. Concentrating too much on the mechanics will prevent you from getting the most out of the discussion.

One aspect of listening is to not immediately jump in with your next question the moment the person stops talking. If you wait for a second or two, while maintaining eye contact, often the person will keep talking. That is useful if you are asking a question that is difficult to answer.

The person will sense that the pause means you're not satisfied with what you've heard and are waiting for more. If you seek to get the person to admit to something, that pause can be the trick that throws the person off-balance enough to get him to say what you want.

## Ask Follow-up Questions during the Interview

If you're listening during the interview and are not content with the answers you're getting, ask follow-up questions to get the information you want. Otherwise, you'll return to the newsroom and discover that while you recorded a ten-minute interview with your U.S. senator, you didn't get any information.

Politicians are masters of what some call the "non-answer answer." You ask, "Will you support raising taxes?" and the answer you get is that the economy is bad, people don't like paying taxes, yet that's the money required to build schools and roads. You need to follow that idle chatter with, "But are you voting for a tax increase?" to let the senator know that you expect a direct answer and will keep asking until you get it.

Asking follow-up questions requires not just listening, but flexibility. You may have your list of ten questions on your notepad, but if the conversation veers into an unplanned direction, you need to have something to ask. While planning is important, so is reacting to what you are hearing.

Sometimes follow-up questions have to challenge someone's answer. Other times, you may find follow-ups help you better understand a complicated answer. If you're not sure what someone means, it's better to say, "Explain it to me," than it is to get back to the newsroom and realize you can't write your story because you didn't understand what the person was talking about.

### Allow the Person to Speak Freely

Another useful technique when wrapping up an interview is to ask, "Is there anything else you'd like to say?" Sometimes, you've simply forgotten to ask the most basic question. This is the person's opportunity to answer it or say something else of value.

A person who might have been afraid of being interviewed and gave you nothing but timid answers could use this time to open up. "I'd just like to add that if it weren't for the fire-fighters who saved my life, I wouldn't be here. I'll be forever grateful for their bravery," is a comment that could go into your story even though you didn't ask for it directly.

Barbara Walters and Larry King are two people who made careers of mastering the TV interview. While you may be interested in other aspects of television that just conducting interviews, sharpening your skills will set you apart from the masses in the industry.

## Interviewing for Radio

As a simple definition, an interview should aim at getting from the interviewee, in their own words, facts, opinions or reasons on a particular subject so listeners can form their own opinion. Know what to get out of the interview. An important assets of the interviewer is the ability to listen.

1.  The informational interview aims at providing information for the listener. The interviewer is seeking the facts. The briefing will be detailed to define the angle of the interview, so that the interviewee can well prepare herself.

2.  In the interpretative interview the interviewee is asked to explain or to comment. Since the interpretive interview aims to get an opinion or reaction from the interviewee, the less explanation beforehand, the better. The briefing just includes the basic information.

3.  The emotional interview is the most sensitive kind of interview. The interviewer must use the utmost tact, respect, and be sensitive to the feelings of people at a time of grief. Define

in the briefing what areas will be discussed and what should not be touched. If needed protect the identity of the interviewee.

4. "Vox pops" or "vox populi" means the "voice of the people". Basically, you decide on a question, and ask a number of people the same question, and edit the answers together.

5. Studio - The advantage: sound proof best recording quality. The disadvantage the interviewees might be intimidated by all the equipment. Make the interviewee feel comfortable and at ease in the studio.

6. On Site - at the home or workplace of the interviewee, your interviewee will feel more relaxed. But there might be unwanted sound and distraction on site. So make sure you got a quiet corner.

7. The telephone Interview is quick and bridges distances. But is impersonal and the sound quality is bad. Try to keep telephone interviews short, 3 - 5 minutes.

8. Preparation: Research the topic and define what exactly you want to find out. Identify the best person to interview. Look for a woman interviewee who cares how the topic affects women. Set date, time, and location for the interview. This first contact with the resource person can be helpful to research the topic. Brief the resource person before the interview with what you expect and all relevant information.

9. How to interview people who are used to be interviewed? Politicians, celebrities, spokespersons, etc. Don't let them 'waffle' or avoid answering the questions. Be alert to keep control over the interview.

10. How about people who don't want to be interviewed? Anyone has the right NOT to be interviewed. Explain why it is in their best interest to inform the public. Be courteous at all times. You can also mention over the radio that a certain person did not want to give an interview on this topic.

11. How to interview the person in the street or community? These persons might be intimidated by the microphones. Give them the feeling that their opinion is important. You might begin the interview with a "throwaway question". Make sure you get women's voices.

12. How to interview a friends or people we work together with? Be careful that the interview does not sound boring. Don't use insider language. Ask critical questions or raise arguments of the opposition.

## Check list for your Interview

## Before the Interview

1. What do you want to know after the interview.

2. How long should the interview be?

## Prepare the Interview

- Research the topic and possible interviewees.
- Contact the interviewees, set date and time and place for the interview.

## Questions

- Clear and short questions
- Use the 5 W and 1 H
- No yes/no questions
- No double barrelled questions
- No either/or questions
- No non-question questions
- Act as devil's advocate.

## Equipment

- Check equipment before leaving
- Bring headphone and microphone
- Bring extra tape, extra batteries
- Make a sound check in the location before starting the interview
- Label your tape, MD or MP3 track.

## Location

- Disturbing noises, other interruptions and disturbances
- Telephone interviews good quality line and keep it short.

## Prepare the Interviewee

- Clarify Name, organisation and position of interviewee
- Agree on language of the interview
- Explain length and context of the interview
- Depending on the type of interview discuss the questions for the informative interview
- Discuss what can and what cannot be discussed in the emotional interview.

## The Interview Proper

- Sound interested
- Don't make excuses for asking a question

- Dare to interrupt but do it at the first and only attempt
- Hold on to the microphone and the question paper
- No yes, mmh or other affirmative sounds
- Use nonverbal communications
- Watch the time of the interview.

## Winding up the Interview

- Announce the end with a "last" question
- Repeat the person's name position, organisation and the topic of the interview.

## After the interview

- Check if the interview is recorded in radio quality.

## References

- Interview: businessjargons.com, Retrieved 21 May, 2019
- Types-of-interview-hard-news-interview-informational-interview-radio-news-reporting-and-production: zee-pedia.com, Retrieved 27 January, 2019
- Interviewing-a-source, reporting, tip-sheets: journalistsresource.org, Retrieved 7 March, 2019
- Tv-interview-tips-for-news-media-professionals-2315424: thebalancecareers.com, Retrieved 14 June, 2019
- The-radio-interview: isiswomen.org, Retrieved 9 August, 2019

# 8

# Broadcast Journalism

The distribution of video and audio content to a widely dispersed audience through any of the mediums of mass communication is known as broadcasting. Content can be broadcasted over a variety of mediums such as TV, radio and internet. The topics elaborated in this chapter will help in gaining a better perspective about these diverse types of broadcasting.

Broadcasting is the distribution of audio and video signals (programs) to a number of recipients ("listeners" or "viewers") that belong to a large group. This group may be the public in general, or a relatively large audience within the public. Thus, an Internet channel may distribute text or music worldwide, while a public address system in a workplace may broadcast very limited ad hoc "sound bites" to a small population within its range. Broadcasting may involve auditory information only, as in radio, or visual, or a combination, as in television. As technology has advanced, so too have the forms of broadcasting. Historically, the term broadcasting usually has referred to the radio and television industries. Broadcasting was previously synonymous with "over the air" broadcasts, where the radio frequency spectrum is limited and thus regulated; but with the advent of direct (satellite) radio broadcasting and especially cable television, channels (and programming variety) are far more numerous (digital cable television can support hundreds of different channels) and are subscriber-based. The concept and ability of broadcasting to convey the same information, whether announcements of current events, educational material or simply entertainment, to a worldwide audience simultaneously, is a great advance in allowing humankind to overcome long-standing barriers.

The term broadcast was coined by early radio engineers from the mid-western United States to distinguish electronic transmissions that are intended for general public reception, as distinguished from private signals that are directed to specific receivers. Broadcasting forms a very large segment of the mass media. Television and radio programs are distributed through radio broadcasting or cable, often both simultaneously. By coding signals and having decoding equipment in homes, cable also enables subscription-based channels and pay-per-view services.

A broadcasting organization may broadcast several programs at the same time, through several channels (frequencies); for example, the BBC broadcasts BBC One and BBC Two. On the other hand, two or more organizations may share a channel and each use it during a fixed part of the day. Digital radio and digital television may also transmit multiplexed programming, with several channels compressed into one ensemble. When broadcasting is done via the Internet, the term "webcasting" is often used.

Defining exactly when broadcasting first began is difficult. Very early radio transmissions only carried the dots and dashes of wireless telegraphy. Broadcasting in its familiar sense, sending signals to inform and entertain large numbers of people, began in the early twentieth century. Countries in which notable advances were made in the early decades of the twentieth century include the United States, Britain, Germany, and Sri Lanka.

## Broadcasting around the World

### United States

One of the first signals of significant power that carried voice and music was accomplished, in 1906, by Reginald Fessenden when he made a Christmas Eve broadcast to ships at sea from Massachusetts. He played "O Holy Night" on his violin and read passages from the Bible. However, his financial backers lost interest in the project, leaving others to take the next steps. Early on, the concept of broadcasting was new and unusual—with telegraphs, communication had been one-to-one, not one-to-many. Sending out one-way messages to multiple receivers did not appear to have much practical use.

Charles Herrold of California sent out broadcasts as early as April 1909 from his Herrold School electronics institute in downtown San Jose, using the identification San Jose Calling, and then a variety of different "call signs" as the Department of Commerce first began to regulate radio. The son of a farmer who patented a seed spreader, Herrold coined the terms "broadcasting" and "narrowcasting," based on the ideas of spreading crop seed far and wide, rather than only in rows. While Herrold never claimed the invention of radio itself, he did claim the invention of broadcasting to a wide audience, through the use of antennas designed to radiate signals in all directions.

By 1912, the United States government began requiring radio operators to obtain licenses to send out signals. Herrold received licenses for 6XF and 6XE (a mobile transmitter) and had been on the air daily for nearly a decade when World War I interrupted operations. A few organizations were allowed to keep working on radio during the war. The Westinghouse Electric Corporation was the most well-known of these. Frank Conrad, a Westinghouse engineer, had been making transmissions from 8XK since 1916 that included music programming.

Following the war, Herrold and other radio pioneers across the country resumed transmissions. The early stations gained new call signs. Conrad's 8XK became KDKA in 1920. Herrold received a license for KQW in 1921, later to become KCBS a CBS-owned station in San Francisco.

The National Broadcasting Company (NBC) began regular broadcasting in 1926, with telephone links between New York City and other eastern cities. NBC became the dominant radio network, splitting into Red and Blue networks. The Columbia Broadcasting System (CBS) began in 1927, under the guidance of William S. Paley. Several independent stations formed the Mutual Broadcasting System to exchange syndicated programming.

A Federal Communications Commission decision in 1939 required NBC to divest itself of its "Blue Network." That decision was sustained by the Supreme Court in a 1943 decision, National Broadcasting Co. v. United States, which established the framework that the "scarcity" of radio-frequency meant that broadcasting was subject to greater regulation than other media. This Blue Network became the American Broadcasting Company (ABC). Around 1946, ABC, NBC, and CBS began regular television broadcasts. Another network, the DuMont Television Network, founded earlier, was disbanded in 1956.

### Britain

The first experimental broadcasts, from Marconi's factory in Chelmsford, England, began in 1920.

Two years later, a consortium of radio manufacturers formed the British Broadcasting Company, later becoming the British Broadcasting Corporation (BBC), a non-commercial organization.

Lord John Reith took a formative role in developing the BBC, especially in radio. Working as its first general manager, he promoted the philosophy of "public service broadcasting," firmly grounded in the moral benefits of education and of uplifting entertainment, eschewing commercial influence, and maintaining a maximum of independence from political control.

Commercial stations such as Radio Normandie and Radio Luxembourg broadcast into the UK from European countries, providing a very popular alternative to the rather austere BBC. These stations were closed during World War II, and only Radio Luxembourg returned afterward.

## Germany

Before the Nazi assumption of power in 1933, German radio broadcasting was supervised by the Post Office. A listening fee for each receiver paid most subsidies.

Immediately following Hitler's assumption of power, Joseph Goebbels became head of the Ministry for Propaganda and Public Enlightenment. Non-Nazis were removed from broadcasting and editorial positions. Jews were fired from all positions. German broadcasting began to decline in popularity as the theme of Kampfzeit was continually played. Germany was easily served by a number of European medium wave stations, including the BBC and domestic stations in France, Denmark, Sweden, and Poland. It became illegal for Germans, with the exception of foreign correspondents and key officials, to listen to foreign broadcasts.

During the war, German stations broadcast not only war propaganda and entertainment for German forces dispersed throughout Europe and the Atlantic, but also provided air raid alerts.

Germany experimented with television broadcasting before the Second World War. German propaganda claimed their system was superior to the British scanning system, but this was disputed by persons who saw the broadcasts.

## The 1950s and 1960s

In the 1950s, television began to replace radio as the chief source of revenue for broadcasting networks. Although many radio programs continued through this decade, including *Gunsmoke* and *The Guiding Light,* by 1960, radio networks had ceased producing entertainment programs.

As radio stopped producing formal 15-minute to hourly programs, a new format developed—Top 40. "Top 40" was based on a continuous rotation of short pop songs presented by a "disc jockey." Top 40 playlists were theoretically based on record sales; however, record companies began to bribe disc jockeys to play selected artists.

Shortwave broadcasting played an important part in fighting the Cold War with Voice of America and the BBC World Service, augmented with Radio Free Europe and Radio Liberty transmitting through the "Iron Curtain." Radio Moscow and others broadcasted back, jamming (transmitting to cause intentional interference) the voices of the West.

In the 1950s, American television networks introduced broadcasts in color. The Federal Communications Commission approved the world's first monochrome-compatible color television standard in December 1953. The first network colorcast followed on January 1, 1954, with NBC transmitting the annual Tournament of Roses Parade in Pasadena, California, to over 20 stations across the country.

In 1952, an educational television network, National Educational Television (NET), predecessor to PBS, was founded.

## The 1970s, 1980s and 1990s

The growth of FM (frequency modulated) radio in the 1970s changed the habits of younger listeners. Many stations such as WNEW-FM in New York City began to play whole sides of record albums, as opposed to the "Top 40" model of two decades earlier.

AM (amplitude modulated) radio declined throughout the 1970s and 1980s, due to various reasons including the lower cost of FM receivers, narrow AM audio bandwidth, poor sound in the AM section of automobile receivers, and increased radio noise in homes caused by fluorescent lighting and the introduction of electronic devices. IS radio's decline flattened out in the mid-1990s due to the introduction of niche formats and over-commercialization of many FM stations.

## The 2000s

The 2000s saw the introduction of digital radio and direct broadcasting by satellite (DBS). Digital radios began to be sold in the United Kingdom in 1998.

Digital radio services, except in the United States, were allocated a new frequency band in the range of 1,400 MHz. In the United States, this band was deemed to be vital to national defense, so an alternate band in the range of 2,300 MHz was introduced for satellite broadcasting. American companies introduced DBS systems, which are funded by direct subscription, like cable television. European and Australian stations also began digital broadcasting (Digital Audio Broadcast).

## Distribution Methods

A broadcast may be distributed through several physical means. If coming directly from the studio at a single broadcast station, it is simply sent through the air chain to the transmitter. Programming may also come through a communications satellite, played either live or recorded for later transmission. Networks of stations may simulcast the same programming at the same time.

Distribution to stations or networks may also be through physical media, such as analog or digital videotape, CD, DVD, or other format. Usually these are included in another broadcast, such as when electronic news gathering returns a story to the station for inclusion on a news program.

The final leg of broadcast distribution is how the signal reaches the listener or viewer. It may come over the air as with a radio station or TV station to an antenna and receiver, or may come through cable TV or cable radio. The Internet may also bring either radio or TV to the recipient, especially with multicasting, allowing the signal and bandwidth to be shared.

The term "broadcast network" is often used to distinguish networks that broadcast an over-the-air television signal that can be received using a television antenna from so-called networks that are broadcast only via cable or satellite television. The term "broadcast television" can refer to the programming of such networks. In the U.S., examples of broadcast networks that transmit programming to member stations are ABC, CBS, NBC, and Fox.

## Recorded Versus Live Broadcasting

Broadcasting may be recorded or live. The former allows correcting errors, and removing superfluous or undesired material, rearranging it, applying slow-motion and repetitions, and other techniques to enhance the program. However, some live events like sports telecasts may include some of the features of recorded shows, such as slow-motion clips of important features of the game, in between the live action.

American radio network broadcasters habitually forbade pre-recorded broadcasts in the 1930s and 1940s, requiring radio programs played for the eastern and central time zones to be repeated three hours later for the Pacific time zone. This restriction was dropped for special occasions, as in the case of the German dirigible airship *Hindenburg* at Lakehurst, New Jersey in 1937. During World War II, pre-recorded broadcasts from war correspondents were allowed on U.S. radio. In addition, American radio programs were recorded for playback by Armed Forces Radio stations around the world.

A disadvantage of recording is that the public may know the outcome of an event from another source before the recording is broadcast. An advantage of recording is that it prevents announcers from deviating from an officially approved script, as occurred with propaganda broadcasts from Germany in the 1940s and with Radio Moscow in the 1980s.

Many events are advertised as being live, although they are often "recorded live." This is particularly true of performances of musical artists on radio when they visit for an in-studio concert performance. This intentional blurring of the distinction between live and recorded media is viewed with chagrin among many music lovers. Similar situations may appear in television, when a show is recorded in front of a live studio audience, and perhaps broadcast a few hours later (such as late-night variety shows).

## Business Models of Broadcasting

There are several dominant business models of broadcasting. Each differs in the method by which stations are funded:

- Individually donated time and energy.
- Direct government payments or operation.
- Indirect government payments, such as radio and television licenses.
- Grants from foundations or business entities.
- Selling advertising or sponsorship.
- Public subscription or membership.

- Fees charged to all owners of TV sets or radios, regardless of whether they intend to receive that program or not.

Broadcasters may rely on a combination of these business models. For example, National Public Radio (NPR), a non-commercial network within the United States, receives grants from the Corporation for Public Broadcasting, (which in turn receives funding from the U.S. government), by public membership, and by selling "extended credits" to corporations. Member NPR stations regularly fundraise over-the-air to augment subsidies.

## Broadcasting as Art

Aside from usually being profit-making, broadcasting is a tremendous medium for art. Those who work with the spoken word, film, or in music, are able to utilize broadcasting to convey their work to more people simultaneously than could ever fit in an assembly or concert hall. Broadcasting also allows for art to spread over vast expanses of terrain quicker than moving in person.

The new media of television and radio led to the creation of entirely new methods to best suit them. Radio personalities develop personas unique unto themselves that allow for the best connection with their audience. Television has led to a spur of technological and art advances as producers, actors, and directors had the freedom of working in a shorter format than full length feature films.

Television allows for the direct control of images and sounds to be seen by the audience, creating an entirely engrossing experience. This type of experience, although without actual physical presence, engenders a greater sense of intimacy between speaker or performer and audience than a public stage.

Though broadcasting represents great opportunity, perfecting the new media has been difficult. Modern audiences looking back on historical performances can see the advances made in stories, pacing, direction, and performance.

## The Broadcast Audience

Broadcasting has somewhat removed the communal aspect of performances as people watch or listen to broadcasts in their homes rather than in public places such as movie theatres or concert halls. This may contribute to the weakening of social ties, as it takes away another opportunity for socializing. The importance of this removal of social ties was made clear in the work of Emile Durkheim, who wrote of the phenomenon known as anomie, which describes a state of normlessness brought about by lack of human contact and belonging.

The anonymous nature of the broadcast market now, however, allows for the refinement and expression of exact tastes, as audience members do not have to defend or publicize their viewing or listening to any type of program as it is in the privacy of their home.

While the viewer may remain anonymous, the content of the material that enters homes has significant impact on human lives. Although there are constraints on the information allowed to be broadcast, many of the scenes in television programs showing news, current affairs, or interviews with celebrities, may shock viewers and change their outlook on life, either of those within their own country or in distant parts of the world. Disasters, such as the Indian Ocean tsunami of 2004, which took over 200,000 lives, and Hurricane Katrina, which devastated New Orleans in 2005, were reported instantly around the world. This led to greater awareness of the victims' suffering and outpourings of disaster relief efforts. The phenomenon of "embedded reporters" during the 2003 invasion of Iraq allowed live scenes of military action to be broadcast continuously on television. The broadcast images shown on television channels such as CNN, which included the bodies of slain Iraqis, literally brought home the reality of war to many households. Such experiences put a face on the otherwise anonymous victims of natural and man-made disasters.

## Broadcasting Ethics

There are a number of standards to which broadcasters around the world must adhere. In America, the body that decides these standards is the Federal Communications Commission (FCC), which in part lays out standards of decency. The FCC defines the amount of public service programming each broadcaster must provide, rules of ownership, and what is appropriate for public viewing at certain hours. The FCC levies fines against broadcasters that air material considered to be obscene. The FCC has been criticized as too strict in light of rulings over the broadcast of the film *Saving Private Ryan* and the Janet Jackson wardrobe "mishap" during the 2004 Super Bowl.

There also exist a number of private watchdog groups that monitor and critique decency and accuracy in radio, film, and television. These groups include Fairness & Accuracy In Media (FAIR) and Accuracy in Media (AIM).

## Broadcasting for TV

Almost everyone in the United States watches television. About 99 percent of homes have at least one television set, and, on average, the set stays on for slightly more than seven hours each day. Most viewers have favorite television programs, and they may even have favorite channels. What most viewers may not think about is how the channels and programs get to the set.

Television broadcasting is still the most prevalent form of television in the United States—compared to cable television, for example, which reaches around 70 percent of U.S. homes. Broadcasters also transmit the television programs that reach the largest audiences. Even though their share of the television audience has been decreasing since the 1980s, broadcasters still stand at the center of the television industry.

### The Television Broadcasting System

About fifteen hundred television stations make up the core of the television broadcasting system. Each is licensed by the Federal Communications Commission (FCC), a U.S. government agency, to operate in a particular area. The FCC gives out licenses to operate on frequencies in one of two bands of the electromagnetic spectrum: the very-high frequency (VHF) band and the ultrahigh frequency (UHF) band. VHF stations are more valuable than UHF stations because they have a greater geographical reach and thus can be seen and heard by more people.

It is quite possible for a television station to scramble its signal so that only members of the public who pay the broadcaster for a descrambler will be able to view it. This way of getting revenue is not how television broadcasting developed in the United States. Anyone who owns a television set and lives within range of a broadcast transmitter can receive its signals without charge. As a result, stations must make money through other means.

Most stations make money by selling time on their airwaves to advertisers; these broadcasters are called "commercial" stations. "Non-commercial" stations receive support in other ways, such as viewer donations as well as donations from private foundations, government agencies, and commercial firms in return for mentions at the start and end of programs.

More than 80 percent of the local stations link up with television networks for at least part of their broadcast day. A television network is an organization that distributes programs, typically by satellite and microwave relay, to all of its linked stations so that the programs can be broadcast at the same time. The American Broadcasting Company (ABC), the Columbia Broadcasting System (CBS), the National Broadcasting Company (NBC), and Fox are the broadcast networks that regularly reach the largest number of people. Known as the "big four," they are advertiser-sup-ported networks, as are three smaller networks, the Warner Brothers (WB) network, the United Paramount Network (UPN), and Planet. The Public Broadcasting Service (PBS) is the network for non-commercial stations.

The commercial networks, particularly the big four, are the giants of the broadcast television business, primarily because of their role in coordinating the distribution of shows to hundreds of local stations, which then transmit the shows to viewers' homes. However, ABC, CBS, Fox, and NBC, especially, are more than distributors. Each company is also involved in production of programs and their exhibition through broadcast stations. That is, the networks produce news, sports, situation comedies, dramas, and other types of programs for use on their networks. They also own stations (sometimes called "exhibition outlets") in the largest cities.

In the television industry, the local stations are called network O&Os (i.e., owned and operated). The federal government regulates the number of O&Os that a broadcast network can own. It does this primarily by prohibiting a network from owning stations that in total reach more than 35 percent of the U.S. population. The aim of the rule is to hinder networks from gaining too much power over the entire broadcast system. Federal rules also prohibit a company from owning more than one broadcast network. In 2000, executives from the newly merged Viacom-CBS were hoping to convince lawmakers to eliminate or modify this rule, because it would force them to sell UPN. NBC, which has a station management agreement with Paxnet, was also lobbying for the law's death. Both corporations argued that strong competition from cable and the weak state of UPN and Paxnet justified their ownership of two networks.

Local stations that are not owned by broadcast networks and yet transmit the network signals are called network affiliates. A network affiliate transmits the network's program feed on a daily basis. Traditionally, the network has agreed to return the favor by giving the affiliate a portion of the revenues that are received from advertisers that buy time on the network. Many affiliates are part of station groups, which are companies that own several local television stations. In the wealthiest of the groups, such as Allbritton Communications, each station is an affiliate of one of the major networks. A broadcast station that is not affiliated with one of the big four networks is called an independent. (Industry executives often consider WB, UPN, and Paxnet affiliates to be independent because they air relatively few hours of network programming per week.) Practically speaking, independents must find all (or almost all) of their programming themselves. Actually, even network affiliates and O&Os must look to sources other than ABC, CBS, Fox, and NBC for some programming because the big four do not distribute enough shows to fill a full period of twenty-four hours. Fortunately for the local stations, the broadcast industry has no shortage of companies that produce programming to sell to the independents, affiliates, and O&Os.

Advertisers are another set of key industry players. With the help of advertising agencies, advertisers pay for time between programs and segments of programs. In return, broadcasters allow advertisers to air commercials, which call attention to their products. A lot of money changes hands in this activity. In 1998, advertisers spent approximately $37 billion on television broadcast advertising.

Unlike cable or satellite television, viewers of broadcast television do not have to pay to receive the programming. As a result, there are few non-advertising revenue sources for television broadcasters. This situation suits local stations, because they are doing quite well with four sources of advertising money: their share of national network advertising, their sale of advertising time during their own programming (mostly local news), their sale of advertising time during programming that they purchase from non-network sources (e.g., reruns of Seinfeld or new episodes of Oprah Winfrey), and their sale of local commercials during some pauses in network programming.

Broadcast networks have only one source of advertising revenue, national commercials. Although that source yields a lot of money—approximately $14 billion in 1998—the expenses of running a network are such that only one or two broadcast networks have typically been profitable. A major reason for this is that the cost of the programming exceeds the advertising money that the networks are able to get when they air the shows. In an important sense, then, broadcast networks have been "loss leaders" for their O&Os. That is, although they operate at a loss, they provide their company's O&Os with programming and shared advertising monies so that the stations (which do not pay for the network programming) can make huge profit margins from their four commercial revenue streams.

Network executives do not enjoy operating at a loss, however, and they have been searching for new sources of revenue. They have tried three major ways. One involves owning more of the programming that they distribute. A second involves trying to change the standard affiliate agreement, asking affiliates to share some of the network programming costs. The third involves branching into new distribution venues, most notably cable television and the Internet.

## Production

From the standpoint of a broadcast executive, the word "production" actually has two meanings. Perhaps the most obvious is the creation of individual programs. The other, equally important, meaning is the creation of a line-up of programs to be aired on a broadcast channel or network.

The task of producing a channel is huge. Imagine having twenty-four hours of air time to fill every day of the year. How can it be accomplished in a way that will make money for the owners of the channel? That is the challenge that confronts programmers, the people who are in charge of operations as different as WWOR (Channel 9) in New York, an independent station; Channel 4 in Los Angeles, an NBC O&O; and the NBC-TV network.

The most basic challenge that confronts a local or network programming executive is to choose programming that attracts the intended audience. In some cities, where the FCC added several UHF stations and increased audience competition, a few stations have decided to pursue Spanish-speaking viewers or non-English-speaking viewers generally, to maximize their profits. Because they reach virtually everyone in their area, however, broadcast stations do not generally aim at the narrow audience slices that cable or satellite networks often try to attract. They typically try to create schedules that reach large population segments that interest advertisers—men and/or women who are between eighteen and forty-nine years of age—because they tend to have families and spend a lot of money.

In the television industry, audits of people's viewing behavior (i.e., ratings) help to determine where much of the advertising money goes. The size of a program's audience helps to determine the amount of money a station or network can charge an advertiser for time during that program. Ratings are consequently always on the minds of the programmers who produce schedules for their stations or networks. Many programmers break down their work into creating discrete schedules for different parts of the day. The most prominent of these day-parts is 8 P.M. TO 11 P.M. eastern standard time, when the largest numbers of people are viewing. These are the prime-time hours when the major broadcast networks put on their most expensive programs and charge advertisers the most money for commercial time.

The building block of a television schedule is a series. A series is a set of programs that revolve around the same ideas or characters. Series are useful to programmers because they lend predictability to a schedule. Programmers can schedule a series in a particular time slot with the hope that it will solve the problem of attracting viewers to that slot on a regular basis.

Programmers generally aim to bring viewers to more than just one show on their station or network. Keeping people tuned to more than one series also means keeping them around for the commercials between the series. In television-industry lingo, the challenge is to maximize the audience flow across programs in the day-part. Over the decades, programmers have developed a number of tactics with which they try to do that.

The key to audience carryover involves finding shows that attract the desired audience in large numbers. Every spring, network programming executives meet with creators from several production companies. Based on these meetings, the executives choose a large number of program ideas that they like. These ideas are then submitted in polls to see which ones the "audiences" are most interested in seeing. Once an idea passes the polling stage, a pilot (or sample) program is created. All of the pilots are then shown to sample audiences to get reactions. The pilots that get the strongest reactions are given a place on the next season's schedule. Once this has happened, the network executives typically sign contracts with the respective production companies to create thirteen episodes of each series. The contract— called a "license"—gives the network permission to air each episode a certain number of times.

One might think that with such a deal in hand, the executives of the production companies would be ecstatic, sure that the show will enrich the company. This is not necessarily the case. For one thing, the show may not last long because of low ratings. In addition, network licensing agreements typically do not agree to pay the full costs of each episode. A production company may find itself millions of dollars in debt as a result of producing thirteen episodes of a series.

Why would any company want to create shows while losing money? The answer is that production companies see network broadcasts as only the first step of a series of television domains in which they can make money from their series. They can make it from local stations, from cable networks, and from broadcasters outside the United States.

## Distribution

As suggested earlier, not all television programs are distributed through networks. The reason is that not all broadcast television stations affiliate with networks and these independents need to get their programming from somewhere. Another reason is that even network stations do not broadcast the network feed all of the time. Certain hours in the morning, afternoon, earlier evening, and late night belong to the stations. Therefore, they can take for themselves all the advertising revenue that they bring in during those periods. However, they must first find programs that attract an audience at a reasonable price.

Many non-network distributors are very willing to help local stations find attractive shows. Their business, syndication, involves licensing programs to individual outlets on a market-by-market basis. One way to attract audiences "off network" is with programs that are newly created for syndication. Examples include the talk show Oprah Winfrey, the entertainment news program Entertainment Tonight, the game show Wheel of Fortune, and the action-adventure series Xenia, Warrior Princess. Another major method through which stations get programming is off-network syndication. In off-network syndication, a distributor takes a program that has already been shown on network television and rents episodes to television stations for local airing. Off-network syndication enables the distributor to make back money that it lost when it delivered the program to the network at a deficit.

If producers fail to place their reruns on local stations, there are other venues. Cable and satellite networks have become voracious users of programs that have already been seen on broadcast networks. This interest results in part because such programs are less expensive than new shows and in part because they have shown (in their network run) that they can reliably attract certain categories of viewers. Foreign countries have also been useful markets for certain types of reruns. Broadcasters around the world purchase U.S.-made series as components for their schedules, though in most cases home-grown programming gets better ratings than the U.S. material.

Broadcast network executives, suffering from monetary losses even when the license fees they pay do not fully cover the costs of program production, have been looking at these post-broadcast network distribution venues with envy. From 1970 to 1996, federal law prohibited broadcast networks from owning or distributing most of the programming that they aired. Government regulators feared that allowing them to both own and distribute programming would give them too much power over the television system. With the rise of a new spectrum of program distribution routes beginning the 1980s—cable, satellite, videocassette recorders, and even the Internet—the broadcast networks were able to convince the U.S. Congress that the prohibition had outlived its usefulness.

The new right to own and syndicate the programs that they air has meant that broadcast network executives have placed great emphasis on trying to improve their bottom line by making money through more than advertising. By licensing their own made-for-broadcast series and their own made-for-television movies to local stations, cable networks, and foreign television firms, executives hope to make their broadcast networks more predictably profitable. Another part of their plan for increasing revenues goes beyond new sources of distribution to new ideas about exhibition.

## Exhibition

Local stations act as exhibitors when they broadcast material directly to viewers. However, the broadcast television exhibition system is in the midst of a major upheaval. Local broadcasters, the bedrock of the medium since its commercial introduction in the late 1940s, face ever-escalating competition from cable, satellite, and even telephone businesses. Local stations still make money, but observers wonder how the situation will change in the twenty-first century, as hundreds of channels race into American homes.

For the near term, network executives would like Congress to change the rule that prevents them from reaching 35 percent of U.S. homes. They reason that more revenues from local stations would flow back to their companies, rather than to affiliates that they do not own, thus better justifying the expenses of program creation. At the same time, the broadcast affiliates that are not owned and operated by the networks have begun to worry that the networks may at times be acting against their interests. Local television executives are concerned about the strong, increasing participation that the networks have in the cable, satellite, and Internet worlds. Disney-owned ABC, for example, controls cable/satellite networks ESPN, ESPN2, The Disney Channel, Lifetime, and A&E. NBC participates in MSNBC and CNBC, as well as other channels. Viacom-CBS runs MTV, Nickelodeon, Country Music Television, and The Nashville Network. Local broadcast affiliates worry that these channels chip away at the audiences that might otherwise be viewing their stations.

Some local station executives also worry that huge growth in the number of video channels in cable or broadband Internet will encourage the networks to send their feeds directly to homes, instead of, or in addition to, local stations. Or, even if they continue to send local stations the daily feed, the networks will give people the opportunity to view (for a small fee) previous network programming that they missed on their local stations. That might still lead substantial numbers of viewers away from local stations.

Another impending change in exhibition involves the conversion to digital television. This conversion essentially will give every network and broadcast station the capability of sending out either one high-definition television signal or a number of regular-definition signals. What will the stations broadcast on the extra channels if they choose to go the regular-definition route? Will some of the channels require a decoder to allow the local stations to tap into subscription as well as advertising revenue? What will be the relationship between local and network broadcasters in this environment? Only time will tell. What seems clear, though, is that the broadcast television system will change dramatically in the twenty-first century.

# Broadcasting for Radio

The radio broadcasting industry is the oldest form of electronic communication. At the beginning of the twentieth century, radio was purely an experimental medium, as innovators struggled with ways to transmit Morse code via the new wireless technology. Over time, the transmission of dots and dashes would give way to the broadcasting of voice and music. By the conclusion of the twentieth century, radio had developed into a multiple-lion-dollar entertainment and information industry used by individuals around the globe.

Radio is a business, linking advertisers with audiences attracted to a variety of programming formats. Radio has the ability to attract different demographic groups with its programming, making it an ideal medium for advertisers to target different messages. Programming is dominated by music on the FM (frequency modulation) band and by talk and information on the AM (amplitude modulation) band.

The radio industry consists of two distinct markets: the local market and the national market. Most listeners identify with the local market for radio programming, which consists of those stations licensed to a specific geographical area. The local market contains a mix of both AM and FM stations. Larger markets, such as New York, Los Angeles, and Chicago, each have more than sixty to seventy licensed stations. Smaller markets may only have three or four stations.

There are more than 10,300 commercial radio stations in operation in the United States. In addition, there are approximately 1,900 non-commercial radio stations, consisting of stations licensed to schools, colleges and universities, and religious/non-profit organizations. Non-commercial stations operate on the FM band, assigned to the range of frequencies between 88.1 to 91.9 megahertz.

Stations in local markets attract different listeners by offering a variety of different music formats. There are numerous variations of radio formats across the country. The most popular formats are country, adult contemporary, news-talk-sports, religious, oldies, classic rock, and Spanish.

At the national level, radio networks provide syndicated programming to local stations in the form of talk shows (e.g., Rush Limbaugh, Art Bell) and news and specials (e.g., concerts, interview programs). Programming is also available twenty-four hours a day in a variety of satellite-delivered formats, each targeting different demographic groups with various types of music. There are also regional networks in radio, most of which are geared to the broadcasting of collegiate and professional sporting events.

## Major Companies in the Radio Industry

In terms of ownership, the radio industry is best characterized as a two-tiered structure. On one tier are several large conglomerates that together own hundreds of radio stations. The major radio owners include Clear Channel Communications, CBS/Infinity, Entercom Communications, Cox, and ABC Radio (Disney). The other tier consists of numerous owners that perhaps own a single AM-FM combination or a small number of stations.

Prior to the passage of the Telecommunications Act of 1996, groups and individuals were limited to a certain number of stations that they could own in each class of stations. The 1996 act, however, removed all national ownership limits, instead placing caps on the number of stations that a single owner could control in a local market, depending on the total number of stations in the market. For example, in the largest radio markets (those with forty-five or more signals), the maximum number of stations that a single owner could own would be eight, with no more than five stations in a single class (i.e., AM or FM). Freed from ownership restrictions, the radio industry experienced rapid consolidation, especially in the financially lucrative major markets.

By 1998, more than seventy-five different companies had merged into one of four major group owners: AMFM Inc. (formerly Chancellor Media), CBS/Infinity, Clear Channel, and Jacor Communications. Clear Channel acquired both Jacor and AMFM in separate transactions in 1999, becoming the largest radio owner in the world with more than eight hundred stations in its portfolio. Industry consolidation, involving stations in medium and smaller markets, is expected to continue, but at a slower pace.

## The Products of Radio

The radio industry is a dual-product industry, in that it offers distinct products to consumers in the form of entertainment and information, and access to audiences for radio advertisers. In terms of targeting consumers, stations provide entertainment and information in the form of different music formats that appeal to different demographic groups. Stations deliver music that is provided by the recording industry and geared to the format of the station. The recording industry uses the exposure provided by radio to help sell recordings along with music videos, publications, and other promotional vehicles (such as concert tours).

In terms of information, the radio industry offers talk, news, sports, and feature programming that is produced by a number of different sources. Information may be local in nature, such as news, sports, and features, or may be syndicated in the form of national news and talk programs. Talk programming became increasingly popular during the 1990s on AM stations, helping to rejuvenate the medium that, over the years, had lost audience share to FM stations. Sports-talk stations began to flourish as well, especially in large markets that were home to a mix of professional and collegiate teams.

Advertisers purchase radio time in order to reach audiences in cars, at home, or at work or school. Radio is an efficient medium for many advertisers, complementing the use of print and television to reach target audiences. Radio advertising is broken into three categories: local, national spot, and network. Local advertising is the most important area for the radio industry, reflecting the fact that radio is a locally driven medium. National spot refers to national advertising by major advertisers who buy radio time on stations in specific markets. National spot is primarily found in the top twenty-five radio markets. Network advertising, which consists of advertising that is sold for syndicated and network programs, represents the smallest category of advertising revenue.

Radio advertising experienced strong growth during the 1990s. According to the Radio Advertising Bureau, total radio advertising revenues to taled $8.8 billion in 1990, but by 1998, revenue topped $15 billion for the first time. From 1990 to 1998, the radio industry generated approximately 79 percent of its advertising revenue at the local level, with national spot advertising drawing about 15 percent, and network advertising drawing between 5 percent and 6 percent.

When it comes to audiences and advertisers, radio faces competition from a number of other media and an array of new audio-related technologies (e.g., Internet radio and digital satellite radio services). Economically, the radio industry has never been stronger, but the competitive challenges that face the industry are great. Aggressive marketing and branding remains the best strategy for radio to maintain its competitive edge and awareness among consumers and advertisers.

## Industry Evolution

The radio industry showed remarkable resiliency during its first century of existence. As mentioned above, radio evolved as a result of a series of contributions by many different innovators, which led from being able to transmit dots and dashes to being able to broadcast voices and music. By the 1920s, radio had become an industry that was designed not to deliver programming but to sell radio receivers. Over time, radio became an important companion for Americans, a trusted friend during the Great Depression and World War II.

Radio historians refer to the 1930s and 1940s as the "golden age" of radio—a period when the popularity of the medium flourished. In a pre-television world, audiences tuned to radio for the latest news and entertainment programming, especially during the evening or prime-time hours. Amos and Andy, Bob Hope, and Bing Crosby were just as popular with listeners as were Edward R. Murrow, H. V. Kaltenborn, and President Franklin D. Roosevelt (with his fireside chats). Radio networks (e.g., NBC Red, NBC Blue, CBS, Mutual) distributed content on a national basis to affiliate stations around the country. Advertisers used radio to reach mass audiences with a single message, selling all types of products.

The 1950s forever changed the radio industry, as the advent of television in post-war America led to radio's loss of both entertainers and advertisers to the new visual medium. Networks de-empha-sized their commitment to radio. Radio recast itself as a purely local medium, emphasizing different music formats to attract listeners. The FM medium began to emerge as an alternative to standard or AM broadcasting. FM provided a clearer signal, and during the 1960s, it would add the ability to transmit in stereo. FM growth was also fueled by the introduction of AM-FM radios in new automobiles in the mid-1960s.

The year 1973 marked the first time that more listeners tuned in to FM stations than to AM stations. FM radio became more suited for different types of music formats thanks to its higher fidelity and superior sound quality. As a result, AM radio began to lose audiences in significant numbers. An effort to revitalize AM radio with the introduction of AM stereo during the 1980s was a disaster. The Federal Communications Commission (FCC) refused to set a technical standard for AM stereo, which resulted in confusion among broadcasters and the public. Less than 10 percent of all AM stations adopted AM stereo.

During the 1980s, program consultants took on an increasing role in advising radio station owners how to program their stations. Formula radio was introduced and was quickly copied by other stations. "Formula radio" was a term to describe programming clusters of music separated by sets of commercials, leading to the perception of more music with fewer interruptions. Talk and information programming experienced a rebirth on AM stations, and shock radio, with personalities such as Don Imus, Howard Stern, and the Greaseman, both repelled and attracted audiences.

Most of the changes that the radio industry experienced during the 1990s involved revisions of ownership regulations. When the American economy suffered a recession in 1991-1992, many local radio stations experienced heavy losses as local advertising faced major cuts in their budgets. In 1991, three out of every four stations lost money. The FCC relaxed the duopoly rule in 1992, which previously limited ownership to only one AM-FM combination in a market. But it was the Telecommunications Act of 1996 that revolutionized radio ownership, eliminating all ownership restrictions at the national level and leading to the creation of several radio conglomerates. The strong revenue potential of radio, and the opportunity to cluster operations in many markets, led to increasing industry consolidation by the end of the 1990s.

## Radio in the Twenty-first Century

Continuing evolution is expected to occur in the radio industry. A number of new technological innovations have the potential to affect the radio industry in both positive and negative ways. Digital audio radio services (DARS), such as Sirius and XM Satellite Radio, will offer high-quality subscription radio services to consumers. Because these services are subscription-based, their effect on terrestrial radio may be minimal in economic terms. However, they may help to siphon away radio audiences, especially among commuters using automobiles and public transportation. Digital audio broadcasting is now technically possible, but the expense to convert analog transmitters and millions of radio receivers to digital technology means digital audio will continue to be limited to technologies outside of radio.

The Internet has the potential to affect music listening habits. Hundreds of Internet-only radio stations have gone online, providing an alternative method of listening to music and information beyond a radio receiver. Internet-only stations face significant challenges in their ability to attract advertisers, but the costs to operate an Internet-only station are very modest compared to a traditional terrestrial station.

Another innovation in Internet-related broadcasting is the development of "personal" radio. The personal radio service uses digital music stored on a server. In a personal radio system, the user establishes a listener profile through an existing service. The user enters his or her music preferences, selecting a genre of music and, if preferred, individual artists. By adding a zip code, the listener can also access local weather. Eventually, access to other forms of local news and information will be possible.

Consumers can also build their own music collections by downloading MP3 audio files from the Internet and then record those files onto blank CD-ROM media. There are many issues, involving copyright and intellectual property, that are associated with MP3 technology. Recording companies are most affected by MP3, but radio stations could be affected as well if the recording industry adopts the Internet as the primary means to distribute music to consumers, thus bypassing radio. Furthermore, audience use of MP3 may mean less time spent with radio, which, over time, could have a cumulative effect on the ability of the industry to attract advertising.

The FCC established a new low-power FM (LPFM) service on January 20, 2000, to create new broadcasting opportunities for locally based organizations to serve their communities. LPFM stations will serve an area with a radius of approximately 3.5 miles, will have a maximum power of

100 watts, and will have non-commercial status. The commission began accepting applications for the new service in January 2001.

Although competition from new technologies is growing, traditional radio in the form of AM and FM broadcasting remains in a very strong economic condition. Furthermore, radio audiences remained stable throughout the 1990s, which in turn helped to increase radio advertising revenues. Consolidation has helped to make radio a more competitive medium for local advertising dollars, outpacing both television and newspapers.

# Webcasting

Webcasting is the real-time transmission to the public in a digital format of audio and audio visual works. Webcasting over the Internet is similar to broadcasting but uses special technology to reduce the size of the digital files being sent. Webcasts are widely available to anyone with a computer connected to the Internet. Webcasting opens new opportunities for authors and performers to expose and market their works to new audiences, and for the public to enrich their understanding and appreciation of cultures from around the world.

The world of broadcasting, as we have known it, is about to change with the leading broadcasting organizations ready to jump on the Internet bandwagon. Webcasting has a promise of presenting content which fits the slogan of 'anything, anytime, anywhere'. In view of the growing importance and widening reach of webcasting and increasing incidents of piracy involving webcasting, it has become extremely important for national laws and international conventions to address this phenomenon which till now has been ignored. In this light this unit examines the issues of:

- How the world of broadcasting is undergoing changes with the emergence of the digital and information technologies?

- Should Internet broadcasting/webcasting be accorded legal protection and if yes, how?

## Content Distribution on the Internet

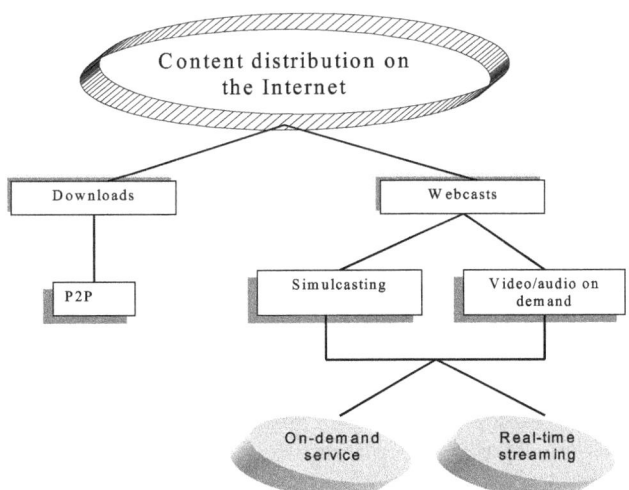

From a technical perspective, there are two principal methods for users to access sound and images (or a combination of both) over the Internet. The first are downloads, whereby a file on a server is accessed by a remote user, transmitted over the Internet in the form of "packets" to the user's machine and saved there locally (in most cases on the hard drive).

The second is streaming, which has been defined as an "Internet data transfer technique that allows users to see and hear audio and video files without lengthy download times. The host or source 'streams' small packets of information over the Internet to the user, who can access the content as it is received. The stream may be a real time (live) transmission or it may be an archived file". The common underlying feature of all different types of streaming, which distinguishes this method of transmission from downloads, is that, in the case of streaming, files are not saved locally on the user's machine.

## Emergence of Webcasting

Webcasting is the real-time transmission to the public in a digital format of audio and audio-visual works. The practice of webcasing is also described as netcasting or Internet broadcasting or streaming. Webcasting is seen as a new model of content delivery on the Internet providing automated and, possibly, personalised delivery of services. In case of webcasting of audio, video and animation the user receives the content when it is transmitted, but without retaining a copy of it. Webcasting services function on the basis of "pull technology", which means that the content is delivered to the user upon request.

Webcasting could further be divided into (i) on-demand service (ii) real-time streaming. On-demand service refers to that webcasting which can be activated by an individual used at his place and at a time individually chosen by him. Whereas in case of real-time streaming content is streamed at a time chosen by the webcaster; anyone who is interested in listening/viewing may log on to the server of the webcaster at that time. The difference between the two lies in that in case of on-demand service users have the choice to log on any time which in real-time streaming users have to log on at a time chosen by the webcaster and content can be perceived only at the time when it is transmitted. The content originates from one or more servers that make it accessible via the Internet. Each recipient requests the program from the initial server and is issued a separate stream from the source to his or her address.

Webcasting is a "point-to-point" technical process. Even though the same program is transmitted to multiple recipients, it is transmitted via a point-to-point bi-directional communication, instigated by the user. In other words, there is an individual virtual connection per user, over which parallel point to point streaming to each of the individual subscribers take place. In other words, there is an individual connection between each user and the source of the streamed content (a host) and such point to point streaming to multiple individual users takes place in parallel.

Works broadcast over the Internet may appear in conjunction with on-screen text and graphics. The audio or audio-visual broadcast data comprise streams that generally are separable from the data that appear as text and graphics on-screen; when viewed together, the user is provided with a rich multimedia experience heretofore unavailable through traditional broadcast media. These text and graphics may provide additional information concerning the broadcast material, and may incorporate hypertext links from which the listener or viewer can access additional information concerning the events or works being broadcast, or can be linked to e-commerce Web sites where the listener or viewer can learn about and purchase of goods and services related to the broadcast.

A number of Internet broadcasters retransmit the signals of radio stations. Radio stations also retransmit their own signals via webcasting. This retransmission is referred to as simulcasting which means the process of disseminating the same broadcast over two different transmission systems, for example, when the sound of a TV program is also played over a radio station. The term is also used for the simultaneous broadcasting and streaming over the Internet of a broadcast. Broadcasting organizations often simulcast their broadcast program services via both analog and digital systems.

Webcasting opens new opportunities for authors and performers to expose and market their works to new audiences, and for the public to enrich their understanding and appreciation of cultures from around the world. Rather than creating a homogenisation of experience, webcasting emphasizes the importance of local culture. An Internet channel from India, Nigeria, USA or Australia, for example, will attract listeners/viewers from around the world primarily because it provides a window to local information, news, customs and arts. Thus, webcasting is a source for information, culture and commerce of all nations and cultures in a way that transcends the normal physical limitations of terrestrial communications, or the channel bandwidth restrictions of satellite broadcasting. Importantly, webcasting unleashes new opportunities for artists and performers to market their works on a global basis.

The world of broadcasting, as we have known it, is about to change with the leading broadcasting organizations ready to jump on the Internet bandwagon. Webcasting has a promise of presenting content which fits the slogan of 'anything, anytime, anywhere'. In view of the growing importance and widening reach of webcasting it has become extremely important for national laws and international conventions to address this phenomenon which till now has been ignored.

## Difference between Broadcasting and Webcasting

In the case of broadcasting, users can simply access the broadcast by switching on the receiver as the signal transmitted by the broadcasting station is direct and present, whereas, in webcasting, users must access a server and incite its facilities to transmit back the information.

Unless specific technological restrictions are applied, webcasts can be accessed from any point that has Internet access. Since Internet is available globally, webcasts can be accessed from almost any point on the planet earth. This is the major difference in term of geographical coverage from broadcasts, be it via satellite, cable or over the air which have an inherent limitation in their reach.

On the Internet, there are no restrictions on the number of programs offered. Capacity can be obtained at relatively short notice and allows for a flexible adaptation to the level of demand. Consequently, the initiators of streams face no significant initial barrier to entering the market. Webcasting activities can be initiated with modest investments, albeit with a limited capacity of simultaneous listeners or viewers. Streaming services can be adapted to the consumers' preferences, for example, distributing niche programs for groups of consumers or basing the contents, arrangement and presentation of the service on intelligence gathered during earlier visits by the consumers.

One of the main characteristics of webcasting is that the transmission is always interactive at the machine level. The transmitting server is in active contact with the receiving machine, verifying the success of the transmission, exchanging status reports. This is not the case with broadcasting, where the main transmission is only one way.

## Broadcasting Piracy on the Internet

As a result of the huge investments and costs involved in broadcasting and the enormous marketing revenues generated because of the massive appeal of television programs, not to mention the rise of new recording and transmission technology, broadcasting piracy has become a main problem.

The pirate could steal the signal and bundle it with its own advertising and transmit the same to the public via the Internet; thus competing with the original broadcaster. In the digital environment, piracy is a severe threat since a digital signal, once received, can be perfectly cloned and reproduced. Pirates are increasingly able to obtain perfect digital copies of broadcast programs from which multiple copies and Internet downloadable/stream able copies can be made and re-distributed. Transmission of original broadcast over the Internet i.e. webcasting is also vulnerable to piracy because of the ease with which contents can be accessed and copied. Large segments of the public have access to broadcasting services, and at the same time copying devices have become cheap and commonplace.

Broadcasting and webcasting organizations make use of encryption systems so that only the viewers they authorize could access the programming content. But piracy could affect the market for encrypted transmissions too.

The notion of "program-carrying signal" relates to the issue of "signal theft". The pre-broadcast program-carrying signal can be described as the electronic signal carrying program material which is sent via a telecommunications link to a broadcasting organization for use in its broadcasts. Such signals are intended not for reception by the public, but for use by broadcasting organizations in their broadcasts. Therefore, they are not broadcasting, but a point to point transmission by tele-communications links from the site of an event (sports, news or cultural) to one or more national and foreign broadcasting organizations for the purpose of enabling the latter's broadcasting of the event. A broadcasting network (or program syndicator) also sends such signals, for example, to its affiliated broadcast stations. Pirates can intercept the signals, with their content, either at the stage of the pre broadcast transmission, for example, off a satellite, or at the stage of the actual broadcast. Since pre-broadcast signals are often digital, pirates are able to obtain perfect digital clones of the program carrying signals and content from which multiple streams, copies, downloads or rebroadcasting can be made.

The practice of retransmission of terrestrial radio stations' over-the-air broadcasts via the Internet has also raised copyright concerns. In National Football League et al v. iCraveTV.com a case brought by United.

States and Canadian motion picture and broadcasting companies, the Court issued a permanent injunction to prevent iCraveTV.com, a Canadian website, from converting copyrighted television material from 17 North American television stations into digital Web broadcasts and streaming them over the Internet. The unauthorized re-transmission was found to be an infringement of the plaintiffs' exclusive right to perform and display their works in the United States.

Webcasting will be widespread and one can be sure that piracy will be equally pervasive. In the light of huge promises that webcasting offers, it is essential that clear rules as to the practice of webcasting are adopted in both national and international environment.

## Legal Protection of Webcasts

Broadcasting organizations have in the past been granted protection for the result of their investment, their entrepreneurial efforts and their contribution to the diffusion of culture and their public information service. The same interests that initially impelled protection of copyright and neighbouring rights for broadcasting now compel adoption of equivalent protections for webcasting. Even for works consisting of retransmissions of terrestrial radio or television broadcasts, it would be illogical and irrational not to offer protection, as piracy over the Internet is more widespread and commonplace.

But what should be the mechanism of protection? Should webcasts and webcasters be protected independent of broadcasting? Or should webcasting be assimilated to broadcasting in terms of protection? Different views have been expressed as to whether such new services should be assimilated to traditional broadcasting. Protection to webcasts is being considered around the world at national and international level. In view of convergence of various technologies and services, and considering the threat of piracy both by webcasts and of webcasts it is only appropriate to assimilate new activities of webcasting to traditional broadcasting.

## International Framework for Protection of Webcasting/Broadcasting

Until 1961, broadcasting rights were essentially granted at the national level, and not all countries provided for such protection. At the international level, the main rights granted to broadcasting organizations were laid down in the International Convention for the Protection of Performers, Producers of Phonograms and Broadcasting Organizations (the Rome Convention), which was adopted on October 26, 1961. The Rome Convention of 1961 reflects the technological development of the time when it was negotiated. It defines broadcasting as:'

"Broadcasting" means the transmission by wireless means for public reception of sounds, or of images and sounds.

This definition confines broadcasting to cover the air transmissions, excluding coverage for cable transmissions. Protection for cable transmissions has, however, in a number of countries been granted at the national level. Articles 13 of the Rome Convention lay down the minimum rights for broadcasting organizations and ensure the exclusive right to authorize or prohibit a number of activities in the realm of broadcasting. Broadcasting organizations shall enjoy the right to authorize or prohibit:

- The rebroadcasting of their broadcasts.

- The fixation of their broadcasts.

- The reproduction: of fixations, made without their consent, of their broadcasts; of fixations, made in accordance with the provisions of article 15, of their broadcasts, if the reproduction is made for purposes different from those referred to in those provisions.

- The communication to the public of their television broadcasts if such communication is made in places accessible to the public against payment of an entrance fee; it shall be a matter for the domestic law of the state where protection of this right is claimed to determine the conditions under which it may be exercised.

The Agreement on Trade-Related Aspects of Intellectual Property Rights (TRIPS Agreement) does not contain any definitions relating to broadcasting, but it vests in broadcasting organizations rights to prohibit certain acts relating to their broadcasts. These acts are: the fixation; the reproduction of fixations; and the rebroadcasting by wireless means of broadcasts; as well as the communication to the public of television broadcasts of the same. Where Members do not grant such rights to broadcasting organizations, they shall provide owners of copyright in the subject matter of broadcasts with the possibility of preventing the above acts, subject to the provisions of the Berne Convention.

Under international copyright and related rights treaties the word "broadcasting" generally has been understood as transmission via Hertzian waves. A certain number of national copyright laws give providers of cable-originated programs, who do not merely distribute broadcasts simultaneously and unchanged, rights similar to those granted to broadcasting organizations, insofar as they are considered organizations which are analogous to broadcasting organizations, that is, offering program services for reception by the public at large.

## Types of Broadcasting Programmes

In broadcasting, a programme is seen as a broadcast material created to meet certain specific needs or attain some set objectives and transmitted to some pre-determined target audience.

Duyile classified programmes under two general headings which includes:

- Spoken words broadcasting: They are; talks, discussions, educational broadcasting, programmes for special audiences (women, children, rural listeners), drama, documentary, magazines, news and current affairs programmes and religious broadcasting.

- Music includes programmes of cassette recording, live musical performance of all kinds and variety of entertainment.

He further went to break down the different types of Broadcast Programmes which fits into the above classifications:

- Talk Programmes: this is termed straightforward talk, the interview and discussion. A talk programme ranges from a one minute contribution, to a magazine programme, to one hour interview programme which are audience participatory in nature. The purpose of the talk programme may be to inform, to educate or simply to entertain. The best talk programme is a chat built on one subject.

- Educational Programme: of all the uses to which television and radio have been put, educational programmes have commanded more enthusiasm. No other means of transmitting knowledge broadly whether by text, the classroom lecture or discussion or magazine articles would seem nearly effective as television and radio, which allow a single teacher to address thousands of people. For educational programme, several unique characteristics make television and radio especially useful. Among these are easy communication, sense of reality, technical assets available through the media, timeliness and special motivation. However, a number of shortcomings have been identified in educational programmes. They include general lack of such ingredients as reciprocal relationship, flexibility, regularity and system as well as limitation in the physical senses.

- Entertainment Programmes: Not all broadcast programming is serious or of vital social concern. A great number of hours are set aside simply for entertainment and these are the hours, which build the popularity of broadcast media and win as well as hold the audience. Light entertainment is a rather loose term used by many stations to cover a wide field of programming, book and short story reading, serialized drama, particularly light and humorous drama; variety of programmes featuring light musical entertainment, comics, community singing, some types of listeners feedback programmes, quiz and panel games. The success of these programmes is largely dependent upon the amount of talent available.

- Children Programme: No area of television programming is more susceptible to public criticism than that of children programmes.

Eastman & Ferguson added that programmers must also consider several other factors specific to children's programming like; Federal Government rules, children's interest, and packaging that will attract the kids.

News programmes are essential part of programming for any radio or television station. The broadcast of news is an activity, in which practically every broadcasting organization engages. News operations range from large scale undertakings involving news editors, film crews and special reporters. Because of the great audience for news and the public faith in the reliability of broadcast news, it is essential that news broadcasters have a full sense of responsibility and are intellectually equipped professionals. News is very important to everybody because it keeps people informed as to what is happening in their community and other communities. News satisfies people's curiosity and concern and it provides basic facts, which enable people to make up their minds and so join the general discussion that leads to community discussion.

In summary, according to James and Ward Programmes on radio and television can be classified into four major categories namely:

- Public Affairs or programmes which are made up of News, Interviews programmes and Sports programmes, documentaries.

- Entertainment programmes which are drama, musicals and talk shows.

- Children's programmes which are moonlight tales, children drama, children educational programmes and cartoons.

- Enlightenment programmes, mostly sponsored by government and its agencies.

# Commercial Broadcasting

Commercial broadcasting (also called private broadcasting) is the broadcasting of television programs and radio programming by privately owned corporate media, as opposed to state sponsorship. It was the United States' first model of radio (and later television) during the 1920s, in contrast with the public television model in Europe during the 1930s, 1940s and 1950s which prevailed worldwide (except in the United States) until the 1980s.

The global corporate media giants are not obsessed with smashing public service broadcasting systems per se. They have learned to exist alongside them amicably enough. Indeed, as the cases of PBS and the BBC indicate, they often cooperate with them in commercial joint ventures. Moreover, and somewhat ironically, the commercial media firms can be allies of sorts to movements that wish to keep public broadcasting systems non-commercial - meaning free of advertising. Because the last thing U.S. media firms want is for PBS and NPR to begin to compete for their advertisers, especially in view of the public system's affluent, well-educated, upper-middle-class audience - the kind of audience many important advertisers fantasize about. But the commercial media giants (and the advertising industry) always demand and work for a broadcasting system where the commercial logic is central and public service remains on the margins, serving those audiences that the commercial interests do not find profitable enough to exploit themselves.

At the same time, the commercial broadcasting, media, and advertising industries direct a never ending publicity and political lobbying campaign to promote the merits and genius of a commercial media system and, correspondingly, to deny and denigrate the supposed merits of public service broadcasting. It is well understood that the most powerful cases on behalf of public service broadcasting, from Graham Spry and John Dewey to the present, are premised on the limitations and absurdity of a commercial system. To the extent the two systems both depend upon public support, legislation, and government regulation, and to the extent the logics of the two systems are in opposition, this conflict is unavoidable. The corporate media, with their great wealth and control of access to the mass of people, are notorious for the leverage they wield over politicians. It was no surprise, then, in September, 1997, when the *Wall Street Journal* declared that the U.S. commercial broadcasting industry could "claim the crown" as "the most powerful lobby in Washington." It has been this way for 60 years. And commercial media lobbies hold similar (though perhaps not quite so formidable) positions of power in nations all over the world. A key part of this political strength is reflected in the broadcasters' expert use of public relations. Indeed, the U.S. broadcast and advertising industries were arguably the two industries that first developed the art of "spin" in its modern form during the 1930s, as a way of smashing their opponents and gaining favorable legislation and regulation.

The naked political and economic muscle of the commercial broadcasting industry is of course elegantly draped in layers of velvety public relations, all of which highlight the benevolence of the existing order and the evil of any and all nonmarket alternatives. Some of the myths include the idea that the owners and advertisers are insignificant because professional journalists and producers make the key programming decisions, and that revolutionary new technologies eliminate any need for concern about concentrated ownership. In combination, these myths work to prevent, or at least marginalize or neutralize, any public examination of corporate media power.

The single most important myth is the notion of the magical free market which, despite all outward appearances will always produce the optimum social outcome. In media, the free market notion is expressed in the dictum that competitive pressures force the commercial broadcasters to "give the people what they want." I have written at length about the holes in this argument, but there is an element of truth in it that makes it all the more plausible.

In the United States, the notion that commercial broadcasting is the superior system because it embodies market principles is closely attached to the notion that the market is the only "democratic" regulatory mechanism, and that this democratic market is the essence of Americanism, patriotism, and all that is good and true in the world. These themes all come together in the incessant campaign by commercial broadcasters to wrap their interests in the First Amendment to the U.S. Constitution, the amendment that prevents Congress from abridging freedom of speech and of the press, among other things. On the one hand, this is an ideological battle, because the extent to which commercial broadcasters are seen as the guardians of the First Amendment is the extent to which government or public intervention in their affairs will be regarded as "censorship", and therefore unacceptable. On the other hand, this is an important legal battle, because the extent to which the federal courts deem the commercial broadcasters worthy of First Amendment protection (all newspaper publishers) is the extent to which their activities are immune to government regulation. In effect, commercial broadcasting is made part of the Constitution and becomes nearly off-limits to political attack. At present, this is a battle the commercial broadcasters have yet to win in the courts, where the public right to regulate the airwaves has been recognized as more important than the broadcasters' right to do whatever they please. But make no mistake: they are making inroads.

The argument of the commercial broadcasters goes something like this: The First Amendment means that any government intervention in the affairs of the media is prohibited, regardless of the social or political implications. Any government intervention will invariably produce anti-democratic outcomes, regardless of the intent. Even if the market does not produce especially desirable outcomes, the First Amendment demands that media be in the hands of the private sector to develop as it sees fit.

That broadcasting takes place on publicly owned airwaves is considered irrelevant. Newspapers must use publicly owned roads to be delivered, and nobody calls for their regulation. (And for that matter, broadcasting is a vastly more competitive industry than newspaper publishing.) So there is no justification for government regulation; let the market rule. Nor is this simply a U.S. matter. The commercial media have pushed for the U.S. government to advance this interpretation of the First Amendment as the only guarantor of a "free press" upon other nations since at least the 1940s, and in the 1990s this vision has underpaid the media principles implicit in trade deals such as NAFTA and GATT.

Although it goes unstated, the implicit belief among the commercial broadcast media is that it is ok for government to turn a scarce spectrum over to certain commercial broadcasters and effectively subsidize them; it only violates the First Amendment when governmental actions threaten the bottom line. Indeed, the commercial broadcasters' appropriation of the First Amendment is drenched in opportunism as much as any commitment to principle. During the early years of commercial broadcasting, say 1927-1934, when the government was aggressively commandeering the airwaves from non-profit users for commercial exploitation, the commercial lobby argued that the government needed carte blanche to regulate the airwaves in any way it desired. Once the commercial system was in place, however, the government was viewed as potentially more antagonistic, and any regulation of broadcasting suddenly violated the First Amendment.

More broadly, the corporate media today have an unprincipled relationship to state power. The media complain that any government activities that harm business are grotesque violations of the First Amendment and freedom in general; but government activities that assist corporate power, no matter how unseemly, barely rate comment. Thus the Central Intelligence Agency, the top secret, $30 billion-dollar-a year agency whose abuses of law are legendary, is virtually unreported in the commercial news media. But low-level fraud in the welfare office is considered a crucial public affairs story. And the media giants show scant interest in stopping the government from keeping its affairs secret - a process aided, ironically, by the supposedly "anti-government" right wing. The media giants use their political muscle not to battle for freedom of information but to protect their corporate privileges and subsidies.

In the hands of the commercial broadcasters, the First Amendment takes on an almost Orwellian cast. These semi-monopolistic broadcasters eschew any public service obligations and claim that public efforts to demand them violates their First Amendment rights, which in their view means their unimpeded ability to maximize profit regardless of the social consequences. Commercial broadcasters and their ideologues concede that this First Amendment may not seem pretty, but theirs is simply an "absolutist" interpretation. Any other interpretation, their argument goes, opens the door to government tyranny and the end of formal democracy. To make this interpretation more appealing, they dress it up in the metaphor of the "marketplace of ideas." By this, they mean to suggest that so long as there is no governmental interference, all manner of ideas will thrive under democracy's sun, with the truest ideas growing tallest and blooming fairest. The marketplace is assumed to be a neutral, value-free regulatory mechanism. In fact, a commercial "marketplace" of ideas has a strong bias toward rewarding ideas that support the status quo and marginalizing socially dissident views. In practice, the marketplace tends to reproduce social inequality economically, politically, and ideologically.

Given the importance of the First Amendment to the PR and political activities of the corporate media giants, their claims about the First Amendment deserve closer inspection.

The notion that the commercial broadcasters have the only plausible "absolutist" interpretation of the First Amendment - an interpretation held by the Founding Fathers and, who knows, perhaps handed down to them by Moses or the Big Guy himself - is self-serving nonsense. First Amendment absolutism is anything but absolute. Modern absolutism and civil libertarian groups like the American Civil Liberties Union were born in the tumultuous first decades of the 20th century, with their passionate commitments to the protection of dissident political opinion and labor activism from government harassment. Absolutism was inspired by the promise of democracy but, then, after defining what speech was necessary for democracy, it was absolutist in its rejection of any government regulation, regardless of the justification.

Hence absolutism - and arguably any theory of the First Amendment for than matter - has two components. The theory first determines what speech is protected and then, once that determination has been made, pronounces that it is protected absolutely. But even the most strident "absolutist" cannot avoid determining what speech qualifies for protection, or what constitutes speech. (Hence today's debate is over whether advertising, or food labeling, or campaign contributions are speech.) The first great wave of 20th century absolutists, including people like Alexander Meiklejohn, argued that the First Amendment protected any and all political speech under any and all circumstances. But they also argued that commercial speech (for example advertising) was protected not by the First Amendment but rather by the Fifth Amendment and its "freedom to contract" clause. Indeed, Meiklejohn argued that if commercial speech were given the same weight under the First Amendment as political speech, the First Amendment would lose its integrity and soon become primarily a tool for commercial interests who had no particular interest whatsoever in politics and public life per se.

Commercial speech, on the other hand, was never considered fair game for First Amendment protection by the first generation of absolutists, nor is it so considered by their most principled academic heirs today. When the U.S. Supreme Court considered in 1942 whether advertising should be protected by the First Amendment from government regulation, the Court, including absolutist Hugo Black, voted 9-0 against the proposition. But in the past 30 years, that has begun to change -- to no small extent because of the sheer commercialization of culture, as the market began its spread into every nook and cranny of social life. When commercialism penetrates everything, and when non-commercial public life diminishes or merges with commercialism, the capacity to distinguish between the two is compromised.

The commercialization of the press or the media was the critical factor that accentuated the problem of maintaining a strict line between political and commercial speech. Although discussions of the First Amendment protection of a "free press" often simply take discussions of individual speech and apply them to the press without qualification, there are important differences. It is one thing to assure individuals of their right to say whatever they please without fear of government regulation or worse. This is a right that can be enjoyed by every individual on a relatively equal basis, since everyone has a right to say what he likes on the proverbial street corner soapbox. It is quite another thing to say that every individual has the right to establish a newspaper or broadcast network with which to disseminate their free speech to a broader audience than what could be reached by the spoken word. Here the free speech analogy weakens. As a practical matter, this right is denied to almost everyone. Those who possess the wherewithal to establish their own vehicles for "free speech," whether a newspaper or a radio station, are in a position to determine who is empowered to disseminate their free speech to the great mass of citizens -- and who is not. Plainly, in this sphere, the doctrine of "free speech" accords special privileges to some citizens and effectively gives them the power to dominate public debate, thereby drowning out those who are unable to own newspapers and radio stations, or who are refused access to the media by those who own them.

The core debate for First Amendment theorists, then, is whether the First Amendment protects the rights of press owners absolutely, regardless of the implications for democracy, much as it protects the rights of individuals to free speech, regardless of the content of that speech.

The alternative is to view the First Amendment protection of a free press as a social right to a diverse and uncensored press. In this view, the right to a free press is a right enjoyed by all citizens equally, not just by press owners. Here the explanation for constitutional protection is implicitly linked to the necessity of a free press for the health of a functioning democracy. (If not, there would be no more need to guarantee free speech in the First Amendment than there would be for guaranteeing individuals the right to establish a bakery or a shoe repair service. As Meiklejohn correctly points out, such commercial rights are explicitly covered in the constitution in the Fifth Amendment).

In fact, few dispute the argument that the free press clause was inserted in the First Amendment to protect democracy. In colonial times, the press was explicitly connected to political parties and factions; such protection was necessary to protect minority political opinion from direct harassment by the dominant political party that controlled Congress and the government. Was this a legitimate concern? Absolutely, only a few years after the adoption of the First Amendment, the crisis surrounding the Alien and Sedition Acts emerged, in the course of which the dominant Federalist Party attempted to muzzle dissident Republican newspaper editors.

The conflict between the anti-democratic potential of a private press system and the needs of democracy was not an important debate for much of U.S. history. During the early days of the republic, the press system was highly partisan, often subsidized by government printing contracts or partisan contributions, politically motivated, and relatively non-commercial. In this period, even small political factions found it relatively easy to establish and maintain all shades of political organs. One need only consider the broad array of abolitionist and feminist newspapers in the first half of the 19th century to appreciate the capacity of the press system to accommodate a wide range of political opinion. Later, during much of the l9th century, the partisan press system was replaced by a highly competitive, yet still fairly political, commercial press system. But even in this system, there was still relative ease of entry to the market. A cursory glance at any city of moderate to large size would disclose a diverse press representing nearly every segment of the population. The press systems of the republic's first century were far from perfect, but they were by no means a primary barrier to political democracy.

All this began to change toward the end of the 19th century, when the press (and, later, the media generally) became an important capitalist industry, following the explicit logic of the commercial marketplace. Over time, the media system became vastly less competitive in the economic sense. Not only were most media industries concentrated in the hands of a small number of large firms, but barriers to entry made new competitive challenges almost impossible. Hence, the "ease of entry" to make free press protection in the First Amendment a near-universal right for citizens was effectively eliminated. As a consequence, virtually no new daily newspapers have been successfully launched in existing markets in the United States since World War I, despite their immense growth and profitability. Moreover, the logic of the marketplace has led to the conglomeration of media giants so that the largest firms like Time Warner and Disney have dominant holdings across nearly every major media sector.

And that's not all. The media have become increasingly dependent upon advertising revenue for support, which has distinct implications for the nature of media content. Modern advertising was an outgrowth of the arrival of corporate capitalism in the past century, and advertising is conducted disproportionately by the very largest corporations. (In the business press, the media are often referred to as simply a branch of the advertising industry.) This corporate media system has none of the intrinsic interest in politics or journalism that existed in the press of earlier times. At its worst, this commercial "marketplace of ideas" is a hideous parody of the free marketplace of ideas inspired by John Milton and John Stuart Mill. Truth is less something to be respected and argued over than it is something to be auctioned off to the highest bidder. Truth, as such, loses its intrinsic meaning. The system's commercialized news fare, if anything, tends to promote depoliticization, and all evidence suggests that its fundamental political positions, such as they are, are closely linked to political and business elites. In view of the ownership and subsidy, anything else would be astonishing. To be fair, the formal right to establish a free press is exercised by dissidents on the margins; but the commercial system is such that these voices have no hope of expanding beyond their metaphorical house arrest.

In our time, the emergence of this gigantic, domineering corporate media system augurs a moment of truth for the First Amendment and its protection of a free press. Are corporations the same as people? Do shareholders and executives at corporations - clearly driven by law to maximize profit regardless of the social implications - possess the unconditional right to censor media content? Should investors be granted the First Amendment right to select and censor journalists when they have no more concern for the press per se than they have for any other potentially profitable investment? Is it right that this capacity to censor be restricted to the very wealthiest Americans, or their hired hands? How does one distinguish what speech is necessary for politics - and thereby absolutely protected by the First Amendment - when it seems that all speech is increasingly concerned only with commercial gain, and political democracy is not even a prerequisite for its existence? And if the First Amendment does in fact absolutely protect the corporate media, by what logic should it not also protect corporate advertisers, or food manufacturers, or commerce in general.

The implicit answers to these questions suggest that being a free speech absolutist for a commercial media system has precious little to do with democracy and a great deal to do with protecting a powerful industry (and the class that owns it) from the same public accountability faced by similar industries.

This conflict first emerged in the Progressive Era, when chain newspaper ownership, one newspaper towns, and commercial advertising had converted much of the U.S. press into blatant advocates for the status quo, while the nominal right to launch newspapers meant little to dissidents who could not survive commercially in a semi-monopolistic market. The material response to this crisis was the introduction of "professional" and "objective" journalism and formal university-level schools of journalism, usually at the urging of the largest newspaper publishers. By the logic of "professionalism," journalists would produce a neutral product that did not reflect the biases of the owners, the advertisers, or themselves. Hence, while the owners maintained control of the industry and enjoyed First Amendment protection, they would informally recognize the need for autonomous journalism with integrity that the public could trust. How successful or viable professionalism has been as a counterbalance to corporate commercial media control has been the subject of considerable debate over the years. Recently, however, most observers have conceded that journalistic autonomy has been diminished, or eliminated, by commercial pressures from corporate owners.

Some "Meiklejohnians" "most notably Jerome Barron" would eventually argue that a commitment to the spirit of the First Amendment required the government to intervene to ensure that semi-monopolistic newspapers provided the public with a diverse range of views. But for the most part, those in the Meiklejohnian tradition have shied away from this response to the anti-democratic implications of the corporate media market: the prospect of government intervention or censorship in the press is simply not acceptable under any circumstances. The experience of the media under fascist, stalinist, and other authoritarian media systems justifiably makes everyone leery of government regulation. And when the Supreme Court heard Barron's argument in *Miami Herald v. Tornillo* in 1974, it voted 9-0 against his position. Justice William O. Douglas, himself a famous liberal justice, displayed his utter contempt for Barron's position by reading a newspaper during his argument.

There are two other "Meiklejohnian" solutions to the crisis for democracy generated by a corporate-dominated, commercially marinated media system. The most radical is to eliminate commercial media for the most part and create a large non-profit, non-commercial media system accountable to the public. In the Progressive era, for example, John Dewey and others proposed that newspapers be established as non-profit and non-commercial enterprises, supported by endowments, and managed through direct public election (or election by the workers) of their officers. Even press magnate Joseph Pulitzer broached the idea of converting his newspapers into non-profit trusts to be run like universities. (He backed down, one suspects, when his heirs got wind of the idea.)

The less radical solution is to accept the existence of the corporate media giants, but to tax them (or use public monies) to establish a viable non-profit, non-commercial media system to serve the needs of the majority of citizens who lack the resources to own media corporations.

But proposals like these have met with significant corporate opposition. Even sympathizers have expressed their concern that such a revision would permit the government to control media to an unacceptable extent, no matter how the non-profit media system might be structured. From the Progressive Era to the present day, the corporate media giants have fanned the flames of this sentiment, using their immense resources to popularize the notion that a Gulag-style, "darkness at noon" media system was the only possible alternative to the corporate, commercial status quo. Piously, they have preached that any challenge to their power was a challenge to democracy.

Broadcasting, in particular, offered the most hope for those who wished to see a First Amendment committed to democratic media, since the limited number of possible channels meant that there was no escaping that the government would determine who would broadcast and who would not, and the terms under which they would broadcast. All Supreme Court decisions have affirmed the right of the government to regulate broadcasting in a manner that would be unconstitutional if applied to the print media. In broadcasting, at least, the First Amendment has formally been acknowledged to be the property of viewers and listeners more than of licensed broadcasters. Hence, even though the print media were off-limits here there was one area where the public could organize to demand a system that pursued the principles of public service.

Broadcasting proved to be the Waterloo of Meiklejohnian absolutism. In the 1930s, the ACLU, inspired by its mentor Meiklejohn and with the active encouragement of John Dewey, was so alarmed by the explicit and implicit censorship in corporate and advertiser control of radio - especially against labor and the left - that it argued that the very system of commercial broadcasting was a violation of the First Amendment. For most of the 1930s, the ACLU worked with the broadcast reform movement to have the government establish a non-profit, non-commercial radio system that would foster more coverage of social issues and public affairs, freer exchange of ideas, and greater diversity of opinion. The ACLU only backed off from this position when it became clear that the corporate power was entrenched and unchallengeable - not as the result of principled debate. After abandoning its commitment to structural reform, the ACLU went from being a proponent of an aggressive regulation of commercial broadcasters in the public interest to the ambiguous defender of the commercial broadcasters to do whatever they pleased to maximize profits without government interference. Eventually, many liberals and progressives connected to the ACLU and elsewhere began to concentrate on defending the First Amendment rights of commercial broadcasters to censor material as they saw fit.

Since then, absolutists and civil libertarians in general have shown increased willingness to include commercial activities under the rubric of the First Amendment, even if their relationship to political democracy is weak or non-existent. This position was fueled to some extent by the aggressive lobbying of media, advertising, and corporate interests. Those interests were ever eager to eliminate government regulation of their activities, and always quick to invoke high-minded principles to justify their self-interest. If not in the nation's law schools, at least in the popular mind these corporate interests and their think-tank ideologues have been among the leading definers and advocates of an "absolutist" version of the First Amendment. Eventually their efforts paid off. In the 1970s, for the first time, the courts began to include corporate activities under the First Amendment - thereby weakening or eliminating government regulation of commercial activities.

In my view, this softening stance toward non-political speech was less the result of a principled debate on the matter than it was simply a concession to the total domination of U.S. society by enormous corporations, commercial values, and aggregated capital in general. If the line between what is commercial and what is political is muddled - and it became increasingly muddled during the course of the 20th century - absolutists and civil libertarians have two options. One is to extend the First Amendment to include more commercial fare; the other is to narrow the First Amendment down so that it only covers non-commercial and perhaps even non-profit speech. The former course offends no one in power and comports to the existing social structure, hence requiring no social change. The latter course goes directly counter to the trajectory of the political economy, hence demanding an explicit commitment to sweeping institutional change in the media industries and placing one in direct conflict with dominant media and corporate power. The latter course regards the First Amendment as a fundamentally radical statement, not a fundamentally conservative one. This was in fact the logical trajectory of Meiklejohnian absolutism, and its decline mirrors the general decline of the democratic left in the United States.

But as impractical as Meiklejohnian absolutism seems today, Meiklejohn's analysis hit the bullseye. As he feared, we are losing our capacity to distinguish public life from the commercial realm, with public life suffering as a consequence. It is a primary factor in the rampant depoliticization and atomization of social life. Indeed this is a theme that resounds in some of the most penetrating contemporary social criticism, from C. Wright Mills and Jürgen Habermas to Noam Chomsky and Robert Putnam. As one legal scholar has noted, in the 19th century the image of the market was used to expand the boundaries of free speech, whereas in the 20th century the image of free speech has been used to expand the power and scope of the market. It is a crisis that the proponents of extending the First Amendment to commercial broadcasters and to commercial speech are incapable of addressing. They therefore dismiss it as irrelevant.

And so, today, we have this irony: engraved over the entryways to the headquarters for many of the largest corporate media firms (and of the entryways to many of the journalism schools that dutifully train employees to serve these same corporations) are lofty quotations from John Stuart Mill, Thomas Jefferson, Abraham Lincoln, and other greats from the liberal pantheon -

all of them invoking the necessity of a free press to establish an informed citizenry and a viable democracy. And all the while, the corporate media, marching behind their "absolutist" commitment to the First Amendment, produce a media culture that makes a mockery of these democratic values. If ours was a world where honesty was not regarded as a nuisance, our media giants would remove those incised quotes and replace them with more appropriate visionaries of the current media system. Although I have never been approached by Rupert Murdoch or Michael Eisner or any other corporate media executive on this matter, if I were, I would tell them exactly who to designate as architect of the modern "free" press: Josef Goebbels, Minister of Propaganda in Nazi Germany.

Why Goebbels? Well, consider three of his most important maxims for Nazi media.

- First, Goebbels argued that the Nazi news media should be such that the more of it Germans consumed, the less they would know, and the more likely they would be to support Nazi policies unconditionally. Unfortunately this seems to be exactly the case with much of our contemporary corporate media fare. The most striking recent example, perhaps, was the survey from the Persian Gulf War that showed the more TV news coverage of the war people watched, the less they knew about the war, and the more they supported government policy.

- Second, Goebbels' first edict to the German film industry was to avoid political themes and to concentrate on light entertainment and escapist fare. The current system seems to have accomplished that, too. The corporate film industry has virtually eliminated social commentary and serious drama from its output, and devotes the bulk of its resources to light comedy and action fare. Instead of *The Grapes of Wrath* or *Citizen Kane* we get *Dumb and Dumber*. Dr. Goebbels would be impressed.

- Third, Goebbels asserted that the media system should give the outward appearance of diversity, but underneath there should be a clear sameness to the messages being conveyed. What better describes a system with the potential for hundreds of cable channels, but which in fact airs only a handful of commercially marinated genres, and where each of the media giants apes the successful output of its competitors?

Now I admit that dwelling on Josef Goebbels as the appropriate symbol for contemporary media is not entirely fair. In the interest of accuracy, the corporate media giants and journalism schools should probably reserve a place over their entryways next for the words of another, even more famous German: the Führer himself, Adolf Hitler. Hitler's inclusion is especially appropriate when one considers how much the media, and especially commercial broadcasting, are part of the advertising industry. As the CEO of Westinghouse, owner of CBS Television and of the largest group of radio stations in the world, stated in 1997: "We're here to serve advertisers. That's our raison d'être." And when Hitler came to power, the U.S. advertising industry noted that, finally, one of their own had grabbed the brass ring. "Whatever Hitler has done," the trade publication *Printers' Ink* wrote in 1933, "he has depended almost entirely upon slogans made effective by reiteration, made general by American advertising methods. Hitler and his advertising man Goebbels issued slogans which the masses could grasp with their limited intelligence. Adolf has some good lines of present-day application to American advertisers."

Naturally, this sort of praise for Hitler died off after the war began. The industry shifted its position to arguing that propaganda was bad when governments did it, but perfectly acceptable when done by advertisers on behalf of corporate clients. After the war it wasn't even called propaganda anymore.

This private control and formal independence from the government is the genius of the current media system. Clearly, it is superior to, and more refined than, the flawed Goebbels model as an engine of social control. As Meiklejohn's mentor, Walter Hale Hamilton, put it in the 1930s: "Business succeeds rather better than the state in imposing restraints upon individuals, because its imperatives are disguised as choices." So it is, in the past decade, that the number of working journalists has been cut, that the foreign bureaus of U.S. media firms have been shut down, that the content of the media has been shaded to suit the needs of the owners, the advertisers, and the business community in general. Had these things occurred as the result of government edicts, it would have been regarded as a gross violation of the First Amendment, perhaps precipitating the worst constitutional crisis since the U.S. Civil War. Watergate, by comparison, would have looked like a day at the beach.

As it is, however, these developments happened through the organic workings of the commercial media market, receiving virtually no notice -- surprise, surprise! -- in the press or among the populace. Indeed, the First Amendment has been twisted to ensure that this process continues without recognition, debate, or interruption. Sad to say, the current corporate media machine makes Goebbels look like a small time hustler.

## Public Broadcasting

Public broadcasting in the United States is widely seen as an important component of the media culture of the nation. Its programming and the terms of public support for it are not without criticism; it has its detractors from both the right and the left, and it regularly is a subject of debate. On the whole, however, public broadcasting tends to be endorsed as a social good; American society is seen as being better off for having it because of its role in broadening the base of information, education, cultural experience, and political discourse.

However, U.S. public broadcasting is much different from its counterparts abroad. By comparison with other major systems of public-service broadcasting (e.g., in Great Britain, Canada, Germany, Italy, Japan, and most other advanced "information societies"), the U.S. enterprise is not seen to be as central and as important to the overall national media culture. It is largely an afterthought, heavily rooted in a formal educational rationale and in some eyes serving principally as a palliative to the perceived shortcomings of the dominant commercial broadcasting system upon which it has been grafted.

Broadcasting began in the 1920s, and by the middle of the century, it had developed its various basic institutional structures and social roles throughout the world. In other industrialized, democratic nations, broadcasting typically began and grew around a model of itself as a cultural institution, as an extension of language, arts, and national identity. In contrast, U.S. broadcasting was considered at the outset to be principally a business enterprise, as a creature and promoter of commerce, and this has continued to be the prevailing view.

As in other countries, U.S. broadcasting has been subject to regulatory oversight. It is licensed under the assumptions of spectrum scarcity and related expectations about its public trustee obligations as a government sanctioned quasi-monopoly. In the United States, the fiduciary responsibilities of commercial broadcasting (to serve "the public interest, convenience, and necessity") were initially considered to be adequate to guarantee a broad range of services, such that no other major institutional alternative was seriously or widely contemplated. As a result, there was no commitment to a general model of a public-service broadcasting institution in the United States. The small, decentralized educational, non-commercial alternative that did emerge was considered to be only marginally necessary and was forced to begin life swimming upstream against the materialist currents of the dominant media structures and purposes.

Simultaneously, the modest educational broadcasting enterprise developed around a doctrine of localism and a resistance to the establishment of strong, national producing and programming entities. As such, it reflected the general public-policy structure for education in the United States, as well as the deeper constitutional debates about the structure of American government and politics.

During the latter third of the twentieth century, U.S. public broadcasting was given a new, seemingly firmer, public-policy mandate, plus public and private resources that were sufficient for it to build a system of local and national entities (i.e., stations, networks, and support agencies). That system was markedly larger and more stable than what had been imagined at the outset for non-commercial broadcasting. Nonetheless, at the beginning of the twenty-first century, it still remains a relatively small part of the overall broadcasting, media, and telecommunications nexus in the United States. Additionally, even as its existence seems more secure, it also is facing the substantial challenges of a new era of digital communications technology, marked by a widespread process of convergence and reconfiguration in media forms. Those developments are associated with increasingly rapid, broadband, multimedia and interactive forms of production and distribution, new business models, and changing regulatory assumptions.

## Public Policy and Funding Patterns

The strengths and weaknesses of U.S. public broadcasting are reflected in the structure and amounts of its funding and in the associated legislative and regulatory environment.

The principal strength of the system's funding pattern is its diversity. Public broadcasting abroad tends to be supported by a combination of annual taxes for the right to own and use television sets (i.e., license fees) and limited amounts of commercial advertising. By comparison, the U.S. system has a much wider variety of revenue sources. This pattern of multiple public and private funding tends to protect it from direct control by any single social institution, such as government or business.

The financial situation of U.S. public broadcasting improved considerably after the Public Broadcasting Act of 1967. By the year 2000, that growth had led to the establishment of nearly eleven hundred CPB-qualified radio and television stations, a sophisticated satellite distribution system, two full-time national networks, various other national and regional services, thousands of hours of original programming every year (with much of it having exceptionally high quality), and a professional cadre of more than sixteen thousand employees. The infusion of federal funds also helped strengthen the other public and private sources of support.

However, a major weakness of the funding system was the relatively small amount of actual funding that it provided. Total funding for public broadcasting had reached $2.0 billion by 1998, but that amount was only 2 percent of the total revenues for U.S. commercial broadcasting and cable, which were about $95.8 billion in 1998. In addition, the diversity of funding sources reflected ambivalence about responsibility for the institution. No single sector, public or private, had emerged to sponsor public broadcasting.

By the end of the twentieth century, the principal funding sources for public broadcasting could be divided into tax-based funding (which includes federal, state, and local funding) and private support (which includes sponsorship, underwriting, memberships, subscriptions, auctions, and special events).

## Tax-based Funding

Tax revenues for public television are provided at federal, state, and local levels, though the latter is small and insignificant. In virtually all instances, federal and state funding is appropriated from general treasury revenues.

Throughout the educational radio period and the early ETV years, there was no federal funding for public broadcasting. In the late 1950s and early 1960s, some federal support (e.g., the National Defense Education Act of 1958 and the Educational Television Facilities Act of 1962) began to emerge for instructional programming and the construction of non-commercial television facilities. However, such funding was modest and did not become significant and include support for programming and operations until after the Public Broadcasting Act of 1967 and the creation of CPB.

The total amount of federal support (for CPB, facilities, and special educational initiatives) grew from approximately $7 million in 1966 to approximately $400 million for 2001. The latter amount is still small when compared with funding for public broadcasting abroad. By the late 1990s, public broadcasting's per capita rate of federal support—the annual amount of national, tax-based public broadcasting revenue per citizen of the country—remained well below that of national government expenditures in all other advanced industrial, first-world nations (e.g., less than $1.20 in the United States versus $30 to $60 in Canada, Japan, and the United Kingdom). As a result, the U.S. public broadcasting program production rate, particularly in television, was far smaller than most other public-service broadcasting institutions around the world.

Additionally, federal funding has been consistently tenuous. The receiving-set license fees are widely employed in other countries and are relatively stable pools of funds, but in the United States, there are no special national funding mechanisms dedicated to public broadcasting. National task forces, study commissions, and leading political figures have at various times recommended the establishment of taxes on such things as the sales of receivers, the profits of commercial broadcasting and telecommunications, and the use or purchase of the spectrum. None of these ideas was ever implemented, and federal funding continued to come principally through appropriations from the general treasury.

There also have been serious limits on what is possible with regard to appropriations. Federal funding for public media has always been contentious in the United States. It lies at the heart of

American ideological debates over the state of the arts, education, and communication (i.e., the "culture wars") and First Amendment issues about the role of government in such matters. As a result, even as federal funding for public broadcasting tended to increase, it was periodically reduced and regularly subjected to serious threats of elimination altogether. Such episodes occurred in the early 1970s, the early 1980s, and again in the mid-1990s. Those crises also undermined efforts to maintain a firm policy of multiyear advanced authorizations and appropriations.

The costs of overcoming such problems have been significant. To generate the appropriations and to recover from the reduction episodes, public broadcasters and their supporters have had to engage in constant, intensive lobbying, thereby exposing themselves to regular political oversight, similar to the process that is required of any federal agency or program. Those efforts also have required public broadcasters to divert considerable energy and resources from other essential tasks, such as the core mission of program planning and production and the longer-term strategic planning needs for service development in a rapidly changing technological world.

Taken altogether, state and local government support for educational or public broadcasting has always been a larger source of capital and recurring revenue than has federal income. That support has been channeled primarily through university licensees and state educational and telecommunications authority station boards. Increased numbers of stations licensed to such institutions, as well as support for various state and local instructional programs, accounted for a considerable portion of the system growth in the 1960s and 1970s.

Steady increases in such support during the late 1970s and early 1980s, when state government budgets were otherwise widely leveling off or dropping, did much to offset the reductions in federal support. That growth has remained remarkably solid, even through the fluctuations in congressional support during the mid-1990s. However, while state and local support was significant and even increasing, its growth remained slow and modest enough to guarantee only minor continued increases in public broadcasting facilities and program services.

State government funding also varied widely in type and amount across the country; many states did not make public broadcasting a high priority. Even where such support was substantial, it was typically annual or, at most, biennial, its overall levels showed no dramatic increases, and its actual proportion of overall public broadcasting funding was still shrinking. Proportionately, it declined from about 50 percent of overall public broadcasting revenues in the early 1970s to about 30 percent in the late 1980s and through the 1990s. By the end of the twentieth century, state support remained a substantial pillar of U.S. public broadcasting, predicated largely on the traditional belief in its instructional and educational potential, enhanced by its more contemporary Internet, distance-learning, and web-based instructional efforts. A large majority of the states had even committed to special funding initiatives to help public broadcasting make the conversion to digital technology. Overall, however, it was unclear whether state support could become the basis for anything more significant, such as providing operating support for the large increase in the numbers of non-commercial public-service channels and program efforts implied in digital conversion.

## Private Support

In the absence of large amounts of federal and state funding, U.S. public broadcasting turned increasingly to private sources of support. In keeping with the pattern associated with other non-profit institutions in the arts, culture, education, and health, public broadcasting came to rely increasingly on membership subscriptions, foundation grants, commercial underwriting, and special fundraising events. Altogether, these various forms of private funding grew at substantial rates after the early 1970s. Accounting for only about one-fifth of all public broadcasting revenues in 1970, they amounted to more than one-third by 1980. They more than trebled during the 1980s, and they accounted for well over one-half throughout the 1990s.

Up through the late 1950s, memberships and subscriptions were little used outside of a few listener-supported radio stations and the new community corporation ETV licensees. In time, particularly with the emergence of the stronger Carnegie Commission notion of *public* broadcasting, stations of all sorts began soliciting membership subscriptions; eventually, even school and university licensees began to seek subscriptions. Such patronage practices were already common in the arts and other cultural and social activities, such as symphony orchestras, opera companies, museums, and hospitals. The adoption of patronage practices for non-commercial broadcasting reflected expectations that public radio and television might play comparable roles in communities around the country. By the late 1980s, membership solicitation came to provide more than 20 percent of the total income for public broadcasting. That statistic rose to nearly 25 percent in the late 1990s.

The membership phenomenon was an encouraging sign of public loyalty and commitment to public broadcasting, and it reflected the institution's increasing acceptance in U.S. culture. It also was a source of largely unrestricted support that provided an important margin of extra capacity and independence for the stations individually and for the system collectively.

On the other hand, only about 10 percent of the audience contributed in this way, and generating such revenues had certain material and opportunity costs. The regular, frequent practice of soliciting subscriptions in special membership drives (derogatorily referred to as "begathons") required a large investment of staff and board time, and it disrupted program schedules, diverting stations and the national services from their core production goals and threatening to alienate viewers and listeners. Also, memberships turned over a great deal (a process referred to as "churning"), and their retention and replacement came to depend to a large extent on the value of the premiums that were offered, which themselves represented a considerable cost to stations. There also were questions about the frequently commercialized forms of pledge programming that stations were using. Those developments reflected an increasingly "transactional," goods-for-support character to the membership and subscription process that in some respects seemed to be at odds with the normal nature and purposes of public broadcasting.

Public stations also became creative in developing special fundraising projects such as auctions and the sponsorship of performances and other events in the community. These devices were similar to the ancillary revenue efforts of other cultural and educational institutions. Many of them became the responsibility of volunteer ("friends") groups, and they provided additional revenues, publicity, new audiences, and community grounding for the stations. As with memberships, however, these alternate devices also required considerable investment of staff time and energy, as well as an investment in inventories of material goods—all of which raised questions about cost-benefit ratios and their relationship to mission.

As with government funding, industrial and corporate support for public broadcast programming and operations is highly sensitive. The practice of underwriting was never explicitly defined and authorized in early legislation, and in many quarters, it was initially looked down on as antithetical to the educational mission. Nonetheless, the practice of soliciting underwriting developed early in the history of community ETV licensees, where appeals to foundations and various other private interests had become, like individual membership subscriptions, a material necessity and a symbol of public broadcasting's legitimacy as a particular kind of cultural institution. In time, as public broadcasting's popularity grew and its evening and weekend audiences took on a somewhat disproportionately upper-level, educational, professional, and politically significant demographic character, many national and local corporate interests began to recognize that there could be important public relations and political benefits in reaching such audiences. At first, identification of underwriters was possible only in brief, strictly regulated credits, but those practices became increasingly liberalized as program costs rose, federal funding proved to be continuously problematic and corporate interests in reaching public broadcasting audiences grew.

Over time, federal policy actually began to encourage expansion of private, commercial support and even explicit sponsorship, particularly after the advertising experiments conducted under the auspices of the Temporary Commission on Alternative Financing in 1983. While that project did not lead all the way into the sort of limited spot-advertising provisions that exist for public broadcasting abroad, it did permit substantial movement in that direction by authorizing more liberalized sponsorship in the form of "enhanced underwriting." During the 1980s and 1990s, such support grew from less than 10 percent to approximately 15 percent of all public broadcasting revenues.

Public broadcasters, their friends, and their critics have remained sharply divided over this issue. There were strong concerns that any increasing commercialization of public broadcasting was unhealthy—that it was driving the institution ever closer to the programming and audience considerations that guide commercial broadcasting and against which it is assumed that public broadcasting must stand. At the very least, questions were asked about what programming efforts and voices went unheard when underwriting resources were unavailable. Another practical concern was that increased commercialization would seem to threaten all the other significant forms of revenue generation and raise costs for such things as copyright and talent without any guarantee that it would offer sufficient replacement funds.

Other observers, however, felt that none of the other forms of financial support would ever provide the extent of revenue necessary for public broadcasting to survive, let alone to grow and substantially increase its range of services and appeal. From this perspective, there were no realistic alternatives to increased commercial revenues, and, although there were dangers associated with them, it was thought that they could be managed well enough to ensure that the better, unique characteristics of public-service programming would persist and even prosper.

A related issue was that of attempting to recover some of the profits on the public investment in programs that developed aftermarkets and ancillary commercial products (e.g., toys, books). There were mutually incompatible criticisms of public broadcasting for, on the one hand, allegedly not adequately exploiting such opportunities and, on the other hand, for being precisely that commercial and exploitative, particularly of children. In the end, such "deals" were never as potentially large as frequently represented, but they reflected the continuing pressure on public broadcasting to develop external forms of revenue and the confusions of public policy in that regard.

## New Media and Digital Technology

As with all other media, the dramatic changes in telecommunications technology in the last quarter of the twentieth century had a substantial effect on the character and prospects for public broadcasting. Broadcasting had been built as an analog system of production and transmission, using open, "over-the-air" spectrum frequencies and serving generally as a mass medium. Beginning in the 1970s, the quickly spreading uses of and interactions among coaxial cable, fiber optics, satellite distribution, and computerization inaugurated a series of challenges to the conventional model and began to take broadcasting more explicitly into the complex welter of telecommunications. Those challenges became more significant with the rapid increase in the pace of digital technology development in the 1980s and 1990s, leading to a process of convergence and reconfiguration among media forms generally. By the end of the twentieth century, the very structure and associated industrial and service forms of traditional broadcasting were breaking down in the face of the much higher carrying and multimedia capacities of digital transmission, the Internet, and the World Wide Web. Public broadcasting was being challenged in similar ways.

Public broadcasting had been able to take creative advantage of the early phases of those changes, such as in its adoption of geostationary orbiting satellite services for distributing its national signals. In keeping with its ownership and fiscal base in the stations, it had been more open to the flexibility of that technology than had commercial broadcasting initially, where centralized network controls militated longer against such distribution options. It also had taken a leading role in the development of closed captioning for use by the hearing impaired.

In other respects, however, public broadcasting's reactions were more muted and uncertain. It had difficulty thinking through and effectively using all the multichannel capacity that was available to it in both conventional broadcast channels and the broader spectrum pipelines represented by coaxial and fiber-optic cable. In contrast, the commercial television responses of the broadcasting and cable industries to the newer program service opportunities seemed initially stronger, and by the mid-1980s, those industries were cooperating to develop new services that to many eyes resembled much of traditional public broadcasting.

Apart from certain limited efforts in its early days—the so-called golden years of radio (in the 1930s and 1940s) and television (in the 1950s)—commercial broadcasting had not demonstrated much of its educational and cultural service potential. The commercial marketplace seemed incapable of providing such programming on a continuing basis, and public broadcasting had come into existence largely in an effort to fill that need. However, the newer cable channels, such as Nickelodeon, the Discovery Channel, Arts & Entertainment, the History Channel, CNN, and C-SPAN, had much deeper funding resources than did public broadcasting, and they seemed to be providing much of the special educational, public affairs, and children's services that had been public broadcasting's traditional mandate. The true extent of the new channels' replication of the programming of public broadcasting remained debatable, and public broadcasters were quick to note that such services were available only on cable and direct broadcast satellite television, both of which involved a fee. These new channels were not free, over-the-air stations, and many of them were more commercialized than public-service models would permit. Nonetheless, their presence and persistence vexed the question of public broad-casting's special status as an institution deserving of continuing public funding by federal and state governments.

There also was the persistent problem of public broadcasting's small minority position in the overall structure of telecommunications and its concomitantly small audiences. Throughout the 1960s and 1970s, educational and public broadcasting stations constituted a minor but nonetheless noticeable share of the channel capacity of conventional broadcast radio and television (e.g., in television, the local ETV or public station was typically one of five or six locally receivable broadcast signals or of ten to twenty cable channels). By the 1990s, with the steady expansion of cable and direct broadcast satellite capacities, public broadcasting had not kept pace. The number of its stations continued to grow but at a much slower rate than had been the case during the late 1960s and early 1970s, and its relative share of the broadcast, cable, and satellite channel offerings had declined. In television, even with the development of new local stations, its presence amounted to no more than two or three signals in a sixty to one hundred cable-channel environment. Public broadcasting's audiences were likewise small, typically accounting for less than 5 percent of the viewers and listeners at any one time.

Despite proposals that it do so, public broadcasting had developed neither master plan nor any clear, longer-term goal for maintaining and building a larger share of the nation's telecommunications carrying capacity. Throughout the growth of the cable and satellite era, public broadcasting therefore tended to be restricted in its thinking about the alternative service models that were available to it with increased numbers of signals and channels. Federal policy throughout much of the 1980s and 1990s, as reflected in the programs of CPB, the National Telecommunications and Information Administration (NTIA, which is a division of the U.S. Department of Commerce), and the Public Telecommunications Facilities Program (PTFP, which is a program within NTIA), actually contributed to that restrictive thinking, bowing to pressures within Congress and even among public broadcasters themselves that "overlap" stations and more diversity of signal and voice should not be encouraged. For many years, public broadcasting had the technical capacity to provide multiple streams of complimentary programming nationally and in every community, but with its continuing fiscal uncertainties, perhaps most dramatically exposed in the congressional calls for "zeroing out" of federal funding in the mid-1990s, public broadcasting tended not to press forward in the multiple-channel arena.

By the late 1990s, that issue began to be put into a new perspective, due in part to the decision by the FCC to convert all broadcasting to digital technology and by the steady growth and public acceptance of Internet, web-based online and interactive communications. Together, those changes provided a whole new set of opportunities for public broadcasting to supplement and even compete with its traditional video services. It was becoming increasingly apparent that, if public broadcasting did not position itself to take advantage of those opportunities by expanding the range, volume, and even forms of its services, it risked remaining trapped in the straitjacket of an obsolete mass-media model.

At the same time, it was uncertain if national, state, and local public policy would support all the implications of these new opportunities. The digital conversion process was an "unfunded mandate," something the federal government was requiring of public broadcasting but for which adequate federal and state funding was in doubt. Likewise, it was unclear whether the federal government was willing to continue supporting the traditional reservations, set-aside and must-carry policies that had done so much to help public broadcasting find and keep a toehold in the U.S. telecommunications system. The cable television industry had always resisted the FCC's must-carry requirements. As it was beginning to implement digital cable services in the late 1990s, much of that resistance was continuing, and FCC support for must-carry appeared questionable. Similarly, the direct broadcast satellite industry was resisting implementation of a "local-into-local" station carriage requirement, an equivalent of must-carry. Although that policy had been written into law in 1999 as the Intellectual Property and Communications Omnibus Reform Act, it had been vigorously opposed by the direct broadcast satellite industry.

By the turn into the twenty-first century, the institutional structure of U.S. public broadcasting that had been built on the original educational broadcasting model and put into place in the late 1960s and early 1970s remained largely intact. Public radio and television were much larger and more secure entities than they had been twenty-five years earlier, with solid, measurable, albeit, by commercial standards, still small sets of audiences.

However, public broadcasting also continued to be laden with an organizational complexity that was difficult to explain and understand. Without a clear national consensus on its appropriate goals, size, and structure, that complexity had increased throughout the 1980s and 1990s, making it difficult to describe the institution and the various roles of its many organizations. For similar reasons, it also was struggling with a continuing base of funding that was small by comparison with public broadcasting elsewhere in the world, and it was facing the challenges and opportunities of new interactive, Internet, and web technologies, as well as the federally mandated conversion to digital broadcasting, all without clear sources of adequate capital and operating funding.

The old debates about how much public broadcasting should focus on being an institution of formal education versus a high-quality general-audience service remained, as did the tensions over the relative balance of control between and among the stations and the national entities. Likewise, there was an even more intense phase of the debate over the extent to which the commercial telecommunications marketplace, in its new broad-spectrum environment, could provide the diversity and quality of alternative programming services reflected in public broadcasting.

By the beginning of the twenty-first century, there were signs that the stations and national services were making significant plans for creative uses of their impending new digital and multimedia capacities, and it appeared that many of them would be notably different from those that the commercial industries were proposing to use. However, the costs of digital conversion and the development of sophisticated Internet provider (IP) services were substantial, and it appeared they could not be met by existing funding sources. Additionally, it was unclear whether federal policy would continue to support the reservation of educational, non-commercial channels and require their carriage on the newer digital cable and direct broadcast satellite environments.

During the late twentieth century, U.S. public broadcasting had worked its way up to a relatively stable plateau upon which it had built a diverse funding system, a large local station infrastructure, and an active set of programming services and support agencies. It had a large corps of dedicated and effective personnel and a strong, if small, base of membership and public support. It continued to be seen as a public and social good and as more necessary than not. It therefore did not appear to be in danger of disintegrating and fading away. However, without adequate public-policy support and resources to fulfill its basic mission, public broadcasting was going to have difficulty moving up to the next plateau. Public broadcasting remained an important, some would say indispensable, element of U.S. telecommunications and culture, but it was still far from being central to those institutions. Public broadcasting was still swimming upstream against a swift, dangerous set of commercial and political currents.

## Broadcasting Regulations

The system of broadcast regulation by the U.S. government evolved from the early twentieth century into an intricate web of influences that include government agencies, courts, citizen groups, and the industry itself. These entities work in concert to shape the regulation of broadcast content, networking, technology, advertising, ownership, public-interest obligations, community relations, and other aspects of the broadcast business.

### Entities Involved in Broadcast Regulation

Operating under the Communications Act of 1934 as amended by the Telecommunications Act of 1996, the Federal Communications Commission (FCC) is the major independent regulatory agency that sits in the heart of the regulatory web. The FCC is primarily responsible for issuing operating licenses, managing the use of the airwaves, and creating rules and regulations that all non-government broadcasters must follow, both commercial and non-commercial. The FCC holds rule-making proceedings and inquiries to gather information needed to create, change, or abolish regulations. It also enforces existing rules and regulations using such measures as consent orders, forfeitures (fines), conditional license renewal, denial or revocation of license, or letters and other "raised eyebrow" actions. However, despite its position as the main regulatory agency for the broadcast medium, it must listen to the demands of the U.S. Congress, the president of the United States, the courts, the broadcasting industry, the general public, and other regulatory agencies.

Because Congress was responsible for creating the FCC as part of the Communications Act of 1934, Congress holds substantial power over the agency, including appropriation of the budget, approval of the five FCC commissioners, and reauthorization every two years of the agency's very existence. Congress can also appoint special committees to investigate FCC decisions or operations if it so chooses. However, the greatest power that Congress has over the FCC is that Congress may amend the Communications Act of 1934 at any time, thereby changing the rules, regulations, or organization of the agency.

Like Congress, the president of the United States also has some control over the FCC. The president nominates each of the five FCC commissioners, although they must be approved by Congress. The president may select which commissioner will become the FCC chairman. Other powers of the president include control of the airwaves during wartime and assignment of frequencies for government use.

In order to keep abreast with telecommunication matters, the president must have telecommunication advisors. The National Telecommunications and Information Administration (NTIA) fills this capacity. The NTIA advises the president on domestic and international communication policy and competitiveness, conducts telecommunication research, and encourages the development of various educational and public services. In addition, the NTIA promotes presidential policy to the FCC, Congress, and the general public.

The Federal Trade Commission (FTC), another independent regulatory agency, enters the web of broadcast regulation as a watchdog for false advertising and antitrust violations. The FTC, for example, may declare an advertisement to be misrepresentative or deceptive, and then charge the respective broadcaster and advertising agency to either cease, alter, or correct the faulty ad.

The Equal Employment Opportunity Commission (EEOC) enforces federal discrimination laws as well as affirmative action for all businesses in the United States. The broadcasting industry is not exempt from scrutiny by the EEOC. Therefore, all broadcast stations, networks, and affiliated offices must follow the equal employment opportunity guidelines and record their compliance in public inspection files.

Whenever an FCC decision is appealed, that appeal is taken to the federal courts. The U.S. Court of Appeals for the District of Columbia usually hears FCC-related appeals, reviews the various FCC decisions in question, and declares its findings. In certain situations, the U.S. Supreme Court may review a lower court's decision. Depending on the outcomes of the court decisions, the FCC must take the appropriate action, whether it is to abandon an initiative or try again.

The general public gained some influence over broadcast regulation during the twentieth century. For example, citizen groups and public-interest organizations took broadcasters to court pressured local broadcast stations with petitions to deny license renewal, and negotiated settlements. Citizen groups also influenced the FCC directly by petitioning the agency to enforce its existing policies or to create new policies that would further broaden the scope of broadcast regulation.

## Broadcast Industry Self-regulation

In order to keep outside regulation at a minimum, the broadcasting industry undertakes measures of self-regulation, including voluntary programming ratings; voluntary screening of violent, indecent, and otherwise inappropriate program content; and refusal to accept advertising selling such items as cigarettes and hard liquor. These actions, like those taken under the Codes of Practice of the National Association of Broadcasters in the mid-1900s, have served to restrain the government from regulating what the industry has already been self-regulating.

## Rationales for Broadcast Regulation

Broadcast regulation, despite basic First Amendment protection for the press, grew and evolved as each succeeding act of legislation attempted to shape and control the burgeoning industry. Five rationales for regulating broadcasting introduced in the Radio Act of 1927 and carried forward in the Communications Act of 1934 have endured.

The first rationale for broadcast regulation is the notion that the public owns the airwaves. Therefore, the public, represented by its government, is entitled to demand that the airwaves be used in the public interest. The second rationale, consequently, is that a licensed broadcaster is merely a trustee of the publicly owned airwaves and therefore must act as the public's proxy while using the public resource.

The third rationale, scarcity of the airwaves, suggests that the government must regulate the assignment and use of the airwaves because there are a limited number of useable frequencies in the electromagnetic spectrum. From this, it follows that government has the right to deny or revoke a broadcaster's license to use a frequency, so long as that action is in the public interest.

Media uniqueness, the fourth rationale, claims that the broadcast media have a more "captive" audience than do print media. Behind this rationale is the assumption that users of broadcast media will be less likely to actively select and scrutinize the messages that are received via broadcasting. Therefore, it is important that the government ensure that these unique media are programming in the public interest.

The fifth rationale for broadcast regulation addresses the very nature of the airwaves. It states that the airwaves do not have the traditional physical boundaries that other, more tangible means of communication share. Consequently, because broadcast messages are more pervasive, their potential for social influence is great. It is this potential that allows the government to regulate broadcasting and limit, to some extent, its First Amendment protection.

## References

- Broadcasting: newworldencyclopedia.org, Retrieved 28 June, 2019

- Television-broadcasting, almanacs-transcripts-and-maps, media: encyclopedia.com, Retrieved 13 February, 2019

- Radio-broadcasting, almanacs-transcripts-and-maps, media: encyclopedia.com, Retrieved 3 April, 2019

- Commercial-broadcasting: definitions.net, Retrieved 2 July, 2019

- Public-broadcasting, film-and-television, literature-and-arts: encyclopedia.com, Retrieved 7 January, 2019

- Broadcasting-government-regulation, almanacs-transcripts-and-maps, media: encyclopedia.com, Retrieved 27 May, 2019

# 9

# Ethical Journalism

The ethics of journalism are a bunch of code of ethics which have common elements such as truthfulness, accuracy, objectivity and impartiality. This chapter discusses in detail the theories and concepts related to ethical journalism as well as qualities of a good journalist.

Ethical journalism strives to ensure the free exchange of information that is accurate, fair and thorough. An ethical journalist acts with integrity. The Society declares these four principles as the foundation of ethical journalism and encourages their use in its practice by all people in all media.

## Seek Truth and Report it

Ethical journalism should be accurate and fair. Journalists should be honest and courageous in gathering, reporting and interpreting information.

Journalists should:

- Take responsibility for the accuracy of their work. Verify information before releasing it. Use original sources whenever possible.

- Remember that neither speed nor format excuses inaccuracy.

- Provide context. Take special care not to misrepresent or oversimplify in promoting, previewing or summarizing a story.

- Gather, update and correct information throughout the life of a news story.

- Be cautious when making promises, but keep the promises they make.

- Identify sources clearly. The public is entitled to as much information as possible to judge the reliability and motivations of sources.

- Consider sources' motives before promising anonymity. Reserve anonymity for sources that may face danger, retribution or other harm, and have information that cannot be obtained elsewhere. Explain why anonymity was granted.

- Diligently seek subjects of news coverage to allow them to respond to criticism or allegations of wrongdoing.

- Avoid undercover or other surreptitious methods of gathering information unless traditional, open methods will not yield information vital to the public.

- Be vigilant and courageous about holding those with power accountable. Give voice to the voiceless.

- Support the open and civil exchange of views, even views they find repugnant.

- Recognize a special obligation to serve as watchdogs over public affairs and government. Seek to ensure that the public's business is conducted in the open, and that public records are open to all.

- Provide access to source material when it is relevant and appropriate.

- Boldly tell the story of the diversity and magnitude of the human experience. Seek sources whose voices we seldom hear.

- Avoid stereotyping. Journalists should examine the ways their values and experiences may shape their reporting.

- Label advocacy and commentary.

- Never deliberately distort facts or context, including visual information. Clearly label illustrations and re-enactments.

- Never plagiarize. Always attribute.

## Minimize Harm

Ethical journalism treats sources, subjects, colleagues and members of the public as human beings deserving of respect.

Journalists should:

- Balance the public's need for information against potential harm or discomfort. Pursuit of the news is not a license for arrogance or undue intrusiveness.

- Show compassion for those who may be affected by news coverage. Use heightened sensitivity when dealing with juveniles, victims of sex crimes, and sources or subjects who are inexperienced or unable to give consent. Consider cultural differences in approach and treatment.

- Recognize that legal access to information differs from an ethical justification to publish or broadcast.

- Realize that private people have a greater right to control information about themselves than public figures and others who seek power, influence or attention. Weigh the consequences of publishing or broadcasting personal information.

- Avoid pandering to lurid curiosity, even if others do.

- Balance a suspect's right to a fair trial with the public's right to know. Consider the implications of identifying criminal suspects before they face legal charges.

- Consider the long-term implications of the extended reach and permanence of publication. Provide updated and more complete information as appropriate.

## Act Independently

The highest and primary obligation of ethical journalism is to serve the public.

Journalists should:

- Avoid conflicts of interest, real or perceived. Disclose unavoidable conflicts.

- Refuse gifts, favors, fees, free travel and special treatment, and avoid political and other outside activities that may compromise integrity or impartiality, or may damage credibility.

- Be wary of sources offering information for favors or money; do not pay for access to news. Identify content provided by outside sources, whether paid or not.

- Deny favored treatment to advertisers, donors or any other special interests, and resist internal and external pressure to influence coverage.

- Distinguish news from advertising and shun hybrids that blur the lines between the two. Prominently label sponsored content.

## Be Accountable and Transparent

Ethical journalism means taking responsibility for one's work and explaining one's decisions to the public.

Journalists should:

- Explain ethical choices and processes to audiences. Encourage a civil dialogue with the public about journalistic practices, coverage and news content.

- Respond quickly to questions about accuracy, clarity and fairness.

- Acknowledge mistakes and correct them promptly and prominently. Explain corrections and clarifications carefully and clearly.

- Expose unethical conduct in journalism, including within their organizations.

- Abide by the same high standards they expect of others.

## Ethics of Journalism

Journalism ethics and standards comprise principles of ethics and of good practice as applicable to the specific challenges faced by journalists. This subset of media ethics is widely known to journalists as their professional "code of ethics" or the "canons of journalism". The basic codes and canons commonly appear in statements drafted by professional journalism associations and individual print, broadcast, and online news organizations.

While various existing codes have some differences, most share common elements including the principles of truthfulness, accuracy, objectivity, impartiality, fairness, and public accountability, as these apply to the acquisition of newsworthy information and its subsequent dissemination to the public.

Like many broader ethical systems, journalism ethics include the principle of "limitation of harm". This often involves the withholding of certain details from reports such as the names of minor children, crime victims' names or information not materially related to particular news reports release of which might, for example, harm someone's reputation.

Some journalistic codes of ethics, notably the European ones, also include a concern with discriminatory references in news based on race, religion, sexual orientation, and physical or mental disabilities. The Parliamentary Assembly of the Council of Europe approved Resolution 1003 on the Ethics of Journalism, which recommends that journalists respect the presumption of innocence, in particular in cases that are still sub judice.

## Evolution and Purpose of Codes of Journalism

The principles of journalistic codes of ethics are designed as guides through numerous difficulties, such as conflicts of interest, to assist journalists in dealing with ethical dilemmas. The codes and canons provide journalists with a framework for self-monitoring and self-correction. Journalism is guided by five important values. The first is honesty: a journalist should not make up news or share news that give off wrong impressions. The second is independence: a journalist should avoid topics they have an interest in. The third is fairness: a journalist should not tell the truth if it is with bad intentions. The fourth is productiveness: a journalist should work hard to try to gather all the facts. The last value is pride: a journalist needs to be able to accept all credit for their work, bad or good.

## Codes of Practice

While journalists in the United States and European countries have led the formulation and adoption of these standards, such codes can be found in news reporting organizations in most countries with freedom of the press. The written codes and practical standards vary somewhat from country to country and organization to organization, but there is substantial overlap between mainstream publications and societies. The International Federation of Journalists (IFJ) launched a global Ethical Journalism Initiative in 2008 aimed at strengthening awareness of these issues within professional bodies. In 2013 the Ethical Journalism Network was founded by former IFJ General Secretary Aidan White. This coalition of international and regional media associations and journalism support groups campaigns for ethics, good governance and self-regulation across all platforms of media.

One of the leading voices in the U.S. on the subject of journalistic standards and ethics is the Society of Professional Journalists. The Preamble to its Code of Ethics states: public enlightenment is the forerunner of justice and the foundation of democracy. The duty of the journalist is to further those ends by seeking truth and providing a fair and comprehensive account of events and issues. Conscientious journalists from all media and specialties strive to serve the public with thoroughness and honesty. Professional integrity is the cornerstone of a journalist's credibility.

The Radio Television Digital News Association, an organization exclusively centered on electronic journalism, maintains a code of ethics centering on public trust, truthfulness, fairness, integrity, independence, and accountability.

## Common Elements

The primary themes common to most codes of journalistic standards and ethics are the following:

### Accuracy and Standards for Factual Reporting

- Reporters are expected to be as accurate as possible given the time allotted to story preparation and the space available and to seek reliable sources.

- Events with a single eyewitness are reported with attribution. Events with two or more independent eyewitnesses may be reported as fact. Controversial facts are reported with attribution.

- Independent fact-checking by another employee of the publisher is desirable.

- Corrections are published when errors are discovered.

- Defendants at trial are treated only as having "allegedly" committed crimes, until conviction, when their crimes are generally reported as fact (unless, that is, there is serious controversy about wrongful conviction).

- Opinion surveys and statistical information deserve special treatment to communicate in precise terms any conclusions, to contextualize the results, and to specify accuracy, including estimated error and methodological criticism or flaws.

### Slander and Libel Considerations

- Reporting the truth is almost never libel, which makes accuracy very important.

- Private persons have privacy rights that must be balanced against the public interest in reporting information about them. Public figures have fewer privacy rights in U.S. law, where reporters are immune from a civil case if they have reported without malice. In Canada, there is no such immunity; reports on public figures must be backed by facts.

- Publishers vigorously defend libel lawsuits filed against their reporters, usually covered by libel insurance.

### Harm Limitation Principle

During the normal course of an assignment a reporter might go about gathering facts and details, conducting interviews, doing research and background checks, taking photos, and recording video and sound. Harm limitation deals with the questions of whether everything learned should be reported and, if so, how. This principle of limitation means that some weight needs to be given to the negative consequences of full disclosure, creating a practical and ethical dilemma. The Society of Professional Journalists' code of ethics offers the following advice, which is representative of the practical ideas of most professional journalists.

Quoting directly:

- Show compassion for those who may be affected adversely by news coverage. Use special sensitivity when dealing with children and inexperienced sources or subjects.

- Be sensitive when seeking or using interviews or photographs of those affected by tragedy or grief.

- Recognise that gathering and reporting information may cause harm or discomfort. Pursuit of the news is not a license for arrogance.

- Recognise that private people have a greater right to control information about themselves than do public officials and others who seek power, influence or attention. Only an overriding public need can justify intrusion into anyone's privacy.

- Show good taste. Avoid pandering to lurid curiosity.

- Be cautious about identifying juvenile suspects or victims of sex crimes.

- Be judicious about naming criminal suspects before the formal filing of charges.

- Balance a criminal suspect's fair trial rights with the public's right to be informed.

## Self-regulation

In addition to codes of ethics, many news organizations maintain an in-house ombudsman whose role is, in part, to keep news organizations honest and accountable to the public. The ombudsman is intended to mediate in conflicts stemming from internal or external pressures, to maintain accountability to the public for news reported, to foster self-criticism, and to encourage adherence to both codified and unmodified ethics and standards. This position may be the same or similar to the public editor, though public editors also act as a liaison with readers and do not generally become members of the Organisation of News Ombudsmen.

An alternative is a news council, an industry-wide self-regulation body, such as the Press Complaints Commission, set up by UK newspapers and magazines. Such a body is capable of applying fairly consistent standards and of dealing with a higher volume of complaints but may not escape criticisms of being toothless.

## Ethics and Standards in Practice

One of the most controversial issues in modern reporting is media bias, particularly on political issues, but also with regard to cultural and other issues. Another is the controversial issue of checkbook journalism, which is the practice of news reporters paying sources for their information. In the U.S. it is generally considered unethical, with most mainstream newspapers and news shows having a policy forbidding it. While tabloid newspapers and tabloid television shows, which rely more on sensationalism, regularly engage in the practice.

There are also some wider concerns, as the media continue to change, for example, that the brevity of news reports and use of soundbites has reduced fidelity to the truth, and may contribute to a lack of needed context for public understanding. From outside the profession, the rise of news management contributes to the real possibility that news media may be deliberately manipulated. Selective reporting (spiking, double standards) are very commonly alleged against newspapers, and by their nature are forms of bias not easy to establish, or guard against.

## Standards and Reputation

Among the leading news organizations that voluntarily adopt and attempt to uphold the common standards of journalism ethics described herein, adherence and general quality vary considerably. The professionalism, reliability, and public accountability of a news organization are three of its most valuable assets. An organization earns and maintains a strong reputation in part through the consistent implementation of ethical standards, which influence its position with the public and within the industry.

## Genres, Ethics and Standards

Advocacy journalists—a term of some debate even within the field of journalism—by definition tend to reject "objectivity", while at the same time maintaining many other common standards and ethics.

Civic journalism adopts a modified approach to objectivity; instead of being uninvolved spectators, the press is active in facilitating and encouraging public debate and examining claims and issues critically. This does not necessarily imply advocacy of a specific political party or position.

Creative nonfiction and literary journalism use the power of language and literary devices more akin to fiction to bring insight and depth into the often book-length treatment of the subjects about which they write. Such devices as dialogue, metaphor, digression and other such techniques offer the reader insights not usually found in standard news reportage. However, authors in this branch of journalism still maintain ethical criteria such as factual and historical accuracy as found in standard news reporting. They venture outside the boundaries of standard news reporting in offering richly detailed accounts. One widely regarded author in the genre is Joyce Carol Oates, as with her book on boxer Mike Tyson.

Investigative journalism often takes an implicit point of view on a particular public interest, by asking pointed questions and intensely probing certain questions. With outlets that otherwise strive for neutrality on political issues, the implied position is often uncontroversial—for example, that political corruption or abuse of children is wrong and perpetrators should be exposed and punished, that government money should be spent efficiently, or that the health of the public or workers or veterans should be protected. Advocacy journalists often use investigative journalism in support of a particular political position, or to expose facts that are only concerning to those with certain political opinions. Regardless of whether or not it is undertaken for a specific political faction, this genre usually puts a strong emphasis on factual accuracy, because the point of an in-depth investigation of an issue is to expose facts that spur change. Not all investigations seek to expose facts about a particular problem; some data-driven reporting does deep analysis and presents interesting results for the general edification of the audience which might be interpreted in different ways or which may contain a wealth of facts concerned with many different potential problems. A factually-constrained investigation with an implied public interest point of view may also find that the system under investigation is working well.

New Journalism and Gonzo journalism also reject some of the fundamental ethical traditions and will set aside the technical standards of journalistic prose in order to express themselves and reach a particular audience or market segment. These favor a subjective perspective and emphasize immersive experiences over objective facts.

Tabloid journalists are often accused of sacrificing accuracy and the personal privacy of their subjects in order to boost sales. The 2011 News International phone hacking scandal is an example of this. Supermarket tabloids are often focused on entertainment rather than news. A few have "news" stories that are so outrageous that they are widely read for entertainment purposes, not for information. Some tabloids do purport to maintain common journalistic standards but may fall far short in practice. Others make no such claims.

Some publications deliberately engage in satire, but give the publication the design elements of a newspaper, for example, The Onion, and it is not unheard of for other publications to offer the occasional, humorous articles appearing on April Fool's Day.

## Relationship with Freedom of the Press

In countries without freedom of the press, the majority of people who report the news may not follow the above-described standards of journalism. Non-free media are often prohibited from criticizing the national government, and in many cases are required to distribute propaganda as if it were news. Various other forms of censorship may restrict reporting on issues the government deems sensitive. In the United States, freedom of the press is protected under the First Amendment in the Bill of Rights. Under the First Amendment, the government is not allowed to censor the press. The government does not have the right to try to control what is published and cannot prevent certain things from being published by the press. Prior constraint is an attempt by the government to prevent the expression of ideas before they are published. Some countries that have freedom of the press are the U.S., Canada, Western Europe and Scandinavia, Australia, New Zealand, Japan, Taiwan and a handful of countries in South America.

## Variations, Violations and Controversies

There are a number of finer points of journalistic procedure that foster disagreements in principle and variation in practice among "mainstream" journalists in the free press. Laws concerning libel and slander vary from country to country, and local journalistic standards may be tailored to fit. For example, the United Kingdom has a broader definition of libel than does the United States.

Accuracy is important as a core value and to maintain credibility, but especially in broadcast media, audience share often gravitates toward outlets that are reporting new information first. Different organizations may balance speed and accuracy in different ways. The New York Times, for instance, tends to print longer, more detailed, less speculative, and more thoroughly verified pieces a day or two later than many other newspapers. 24-hour television news networks tend to place much more emphasis on getting the "scoop." Here, viewers may switch channels at a moment's notice; with fierce competition for ratings and a large amount of airtime to fill, fresh material is very valuable. Because of the fast turn-around, reporters for these networks may be under considerable time pressure, which reduces their ability to verify information.

Laws with regard to personal privacy, official secrets, and media disclosure of names and facts from criminal cases and civil lawsuits differ widely, and journalistic standards may vary accordingly. Different organizations may have different answers to questions about when it is journalistically acceptable to skirt, circumvent, or even break these regulations. Another example of differences surrounding harm reduction is the reporting of preliminary election results. In the United States, some news organizations feel that it is harmful to the democratic process to report exit poll results or preliminary returns while voting is still open. Such reports may influence people who vote later in the day, or who are in western time zones, in their decisions about how and whether or not to vote. There is also some concern that such preliminary results are often inaccurate and may be misleading to the public. Other outlets feel that this information is a vital part of the transparency of the election process, and see no harm (if not considerable benefit) in reporting it.

Objectivity as a journalistic standard varies to some degree depending on the industry and country. For example, the government-funded BBC in the United Kingdom places a strong emphasis on political neutrality, but British newspapers more often tend to adopt political affiliations or leanings in both coverage and audience, sometimes explicitly. In the United States, major newspapers usually explicitly claim objectivity as a goal in news coverage, though most have separate editorial boards that endorse specific candidates and publish opinions on specific issues. Adherence to a claimed standard of objectivity is a constant subject of debate. For example, mainstream national cable news channels in the United States claim political objectivity but to various degrees, Fox News has been accused of conservative bias and MSNBC accused of liberal bias. The degree to which these leanings influence cherry-picking of facts, factual accuracy, the predominance of non-news opinion and commentators, audience opinion of the issues and candidates covered, visual composition, tone and vocabulary of stories is hotly debated.

News value is generally used to select stories for print, broadcast, blogs, and web portals, including those that focus on a specific topic. To a large degree, news value depends on the target audience. For example, a minor story in the United States is more likely to appear on CNN than a minor story in the Middle East which might be more likely to appear on Al Jazeera simply due to the geographic distribution of the channels' respective audiences. It is a matter of debate whether this means that either network is less than objective, and that controversy is even more complicated when considering coverage of political stories for different audiences that have different political demographics.

Some digital media platforms can use criteria to choose stories which are different than traditional news value. For example, while the Google News portal essentially chooses stories based on news value (though indirectly, through the choices of large numbers of independent outlets), users can set Google Alerts on specific terms which define personal subjective interests. Search engines, news aggregators, and social network feeds sometimes change the presentation of content depending on the consumer's expressed or inferred preferences or leanings. This has both been cheered as bypassing traditional "gatekeepers" and whatever biases they may have in favor of audience-centric selection criteria, but criticized as creating a dangerous filter bubble which intentionally or unintentionally hides dissenting opinions and other content which might be important for the audience to see in order to avoid exposure bias and groupthink.

## Taste, Decency and Acceptability

Audiences have different reactions to depictions of violence, nudity, coarse language, or to people in any other situation that is unacceptable to or stigmatized by the local culture or laws (such as the consumption of alcohol, homosexuality, illegal drug use, scatological images, etc.) Even with similar audiences, different organizations and even individual reporters have different standards and practices. These decisions often revolve around what facts are necessary for the audience to know.

When certain distasteful or shocking material is considered important to the story, there are a variety of common methods for mitigating negative audience reaction. Advance warning of explicit or disturbing material may allow listeners or readers to avoid content they would rather not be exposed to. Offensive words may be partially obscured or bleeped. Potentially offensive images may be blurred or narrowly cropped. Descriptions may be substituted for pictures; graphic detail might be omitted. Disturbing content might be moved from a cover to an inside page, or from daytime to late evening when children are less likely to be watching.

There is often considerable controversy over these techniques, especially concern that obscuring or not reporting certain facts or details is self-censorship that compromises objectivity and fidelity to the truth, and which does not serve the public interest.

For example, images and graphic descriptions of war are often violent, bloody, shocking and profoundly tragic. This makes certain content disturbing to some audience members, but it is precisely these aspects of war that some consider to be the most important to convey. Some argue that "sanitizing" the depiction of war influences public opinion about the merits of continuing to fight, and about the policies or circumstances that precipitated the conflict. The amount of explicit violence and mutilation depicted in war coverage varies considerably from time to time, from organization to organization, and from country to country.

Reporters have also been accused of indecency in the process of collecting news, namely that they are overly intrusive in the name of journalistic insensitivity. War correspondent Edward Behr recounts the story of a reporter during the Congo Crisis who walked into a crowd of Belgian evacuees and shouted, "Anyone here been raped and speaks English."

## Campaigning in the Media

Many print publications take advantage of their wide readership and print persuasive pieces in the form of unsigned editorials that represent the official position of the organization. Despite the ostensible separation between editorial writing and news gathering, this practice may cause some people to doubt the political objectivity of the publication's news reporting. (Though usually unsigned editorials are accompanied by a diversity of signed opinions from other perspectives).

Other publications and many broadcast media only publish opinion pieces that are attributed to a particular individual (who may be an in-house analyst) or to an outside entity. One particularly controversial question is whether media organizations should endorse political candidates for office. Political endorsements create more opportunities to construe favoritism in reporting, and can create a perceived conflict of interest.

## Investigative Methods

Investigative journalism is largely an information-gathering exercise, looking for facts that are not easy to obtain by simple requests and searches, or are actively being concealed, suppressed or distorted. Where investigative work involves undercover journalism or use of whistleblowers, and even more if it resorts to covert methods more typical of private detectives or even spying, it brings a large extra burden on ethical standards.

Anonymous sources are double-edged—they often provide especially newsworthy information, such as classified or confidential information about current events, information about a previously unreported scandal, or the perspective of a particular group that may fear retribution for expressing certain opinions in the press. The downside is that the condition of anonymity may make it difficult or impossible for the reporter to verify the source's statements. Sometimes news sources hide their identities from the public because their statements would otherwise quickly be discredited. Thus, statements attributed to anonymous sources may carry more weight with the public than they might if they were attributed.

The Washington press has been criticized in recent years for excessive use of anonymous sources, in particular to report information that is later revealed to be unreliable. The use of anonymous sources increased markedly in the period before the 2003 invasion of Iraq.

## Examples of Ethical Dilemmas

One of the primary functions of journalism ethics is to aid journalists in dealing with many ethical dilemmas they may encounter. From highly sensitive issues of national security to everyday questions such as accepting a dinner from a source, putting a bumper sticker on one's car, publishing a personal opinion blog, a journalist must make decisions taking into account things such as the public's right to know, potential threats, reprisals and intimidations of all kinds, personal integrity, conflicts between editors, reporters and publishers or management, and many other such conundrum. The following are illustrations of some of those.

- The Pentagon Papers dealt with extremely difficult ethical dilemmas faced by journalists. Despite government intervention, The Washington Post, joined by The New York Times, felt the public interest was more compelling and both published reports. The cases went to the Supreme Court where they were merged and are known as New York Times Co. v. United States.

- The Washington Post also once published a story about a listening device that the United States had installed over an undersea Soviet cable during the height of the cold war. The device allowed the United States to learn where Soviet submarines were positioned. In that case, Post Executive Editor Ben Bradlee chose not to run the story on national security grounds. However, the Soviets subsequently discovered the device and, according to Bradlee, "It was no longer a matter of national security. It was a matter of national embarrassment." However, the U.S. government still wanted The Washington Post not to run the story on the basis of national security, yet, according to Bradlee, "We ran the story. And you know what, the sun rose the next day."

- The Center for International Media Ethics, an international non-profit organisation "offers platform for media professionals to follow current ethical dilemmas of the press" through its blog. Besides highlighting the ethical concerns of recent stories, journalists are encouraged to express their own opinion. The organisation "urges journalists to make their own judgments and identify their own strategies."

- The Ethics AdviceLine for Journalists, a joint venture, public service project of Chicago Headline Club Chapter of the Society of Professional Journalists and Loyola University Chicago's Center for Ethics and Social Justice, provides some examples of typical ethical dilemmas reported to their ethical dilemma hotline and are typical of the kinds of questions faced by many professional journalists.

A partial listing of questions received by the Ethics Advice Line:

- Is it ethical to make an appointment to interview an arsonist sought by police, without informing police in advance of the interview?

- Is lack of proper attribution plagiarism?

- Should a reporter write a story about a local priest who confessed to a sex crime if it will cost the newspaper readers and advertisers who are sympathetic to the priest?

- Is it ethical for a reporter to write a news piece on the same topic on which he or she has written an opinion piece in the same paper?

- Under what circumstances do you identify a person who was arrested as a relative of a public figure, such as a local sports star?

- Freelance journalists and photographers accept cash to write about, or take photos of, events with the promise of attempting to get their work on the AP or other news outlets, from which they also will be paid. Is that ethical?

- Can a journalist reveal a source of information after guaranteeing confidentiality if the source proves to be unreliable?

## Media Regulations

The U.S. federal government has long had its hand in media regulation. Media in all their forms have been under governmental jurisdiction since the early 1900s. Since that time, regulatory efforts have transformed as new forms of media have emerged and expanded their markets to larger audiences.

### Major Regulatory Agencies

Throughout the 20th century, three important U.S. regulatory agencies appeared. Under the auspices of the federal government, these agencies—the FTC, the Federal Radio Commission (FRC), and the FCC—have shaped American media and their interactions with both the government and audiences.

## Federal Trade Commission

The first stirrings of the FTC date from 1903, when President Theodore Roosevelt created the Bureau of Corporations to investigate the practices of increasingly larger American businesses. In time, authorities determined that an agency with more sweeping powers was necessary. Founded on September 26, 1914, the FTC came into being when President Woodrow Wilson signed the FTC Act into law, creating an agency designed to "prevent unfair methods of competition in commerce (Federal Trade Commission)." From the beginning, the FTC absorbed the work and staff of the Bureau of Corporations, operating in a similar manner, but with additional regulatory authorization.

Like the Bureau of Corporations, the FTC could conduct investigations, gather information, and publish reports. The early Commission reported on export trade, resale price maintenance, and other general issues, as well as meat packing and other specific industries. Unlike the Bureau, though, the Commission could challenge "unfair methods of competition" under Section 5 of the FTC Act, and it could enforce more specific prohibitions against certain price discriminations, vertical arrangements, interlocking directorships, and stock acquisitions (Federal Trade Commission).

Although its primary focus was on the prevention of anticompetitive business practices, in its early years, the FTC also provided oversight on wartime economic practices. During World War I, for example, President Wilson frequently turned to the FTC for advice on exports and trading with foreign nations, resulting in the Trading with the Enemy Act, which restricted trade with countries in conflict with the United States.

## Federal Radio Commission

First established with the passage of the Radio Act of 1927, the FRC was intended to "bring order to the chaotic situation that developed as a result of the breakdown of earlier wireless acts passed during the formative years of wireless radio communication (Messer)." The FRC comprised five employees who were authorized to grant and deny broadcasting licenses and assign frequency ranges and power levels to each radio station.

In its early years, the FRC struggled to find its role and responsibility in regulating the radio airwaves. With no clear breakdown of what could or could not be aired, nearly everything was allowed to play. As you learned in, the FRC lasted only until 1934, when it was absorbed by the FCC.

## Federal Communications Commission

President Franklin D. Roosevelt established the Federal Communications Commission in 1934 as part of the New Deal. FDR Presidential Library & Museum – 61-406 – CC BY 2.0.

Since its creation by the Communications Act in 1934, the FCC has been "charged with regulating interstate and international communications by radio, television, wire, satellite and cable (Federal Communications Commission)." Part of the New Deal—President Franklin D. Roosevelt's Great Depression—era suite of federal programs and agencies—the commission worked to establish "a rapid, efficient, Nation-wide, and world-wide wire and radio communication service (Museum of Broadcast Communications)."

The responsibilities of the FCC are broad, and throughout its long history the agency has enforced several laws that regulate media. A selection of these laws include the 1941 National TV Owner-ship Rule, which states that a broadcaster cannot own television stations that reach more than 35 percent of the nation's homes; the 1970 Radio/TV Cross-Ownership Restriction, which prohibits a broadcaster from owning a radio station and a TV station in the same market; and the 1975 News-paper/Broadcast Cross-Ownership Prohibition, which discourages ownership of a newspaper and a TV station in the same market.

## Regulation Today

Today, the FCC continues to hold the primary responsibility for regulating media outlets, with the FTC taking on a smaller role. Although each commission holds different roles and duties, the over-all purpose of governmental control remains to establish and bring order to the media industry while ensuring the promulgation of the public good.

## The Structure and Purposes of the FCC

The FCC contains three major divisions: broadcast, telegraph, and telephone. Within these branch-es, subdivisions allow the agency to more efficiently carry out its tasks. Presently, the FCC houses 7 operating bureaus and 10 staff offices. Although the bureaus and offices have varying specialties, the bureaus' general responsibilities include "processing applications for licenses and other filings; analyzing complaints; conducting investigations; developing and implementing regulatory pro-grams; and taking part in hearings (Federal Communications Commission)." Four key bureaus are the Media Bureau, the Wireline Competition Bureau, the Wireless Telecommunications Bureau, and the International Bureau.

The Media Bureau oversees licensing and regulation of broadcasting services. Specifically, the Me-dia Bureau "develops, recommends and administers the policy and licensing programs relating to electronic media, including cable television, broadcast television, and radio in the United States and its territories (Federal Communications Commission)." Because it aids the FCC in its deci-sions to grant or withhold licenses from broadcast stations, the Media Bureau plays a particularly important role within the organization. Such decisions are based on the "commission's own evalu-ation of whether the station has served in the public interest," and come primarily from the Media Bureau's recommendations. The Media Bureau has been central to rulings on children's program-ming and mandatory closed captioning.

The Wireline Competition Bureau (WCB) is primarily responsible for "rules and policies concern-ing telephone companies that provide interstate—and, under certain circumstances, intrastate—telecommunications services to the public through the use of wire-based transmission facilities (i.e. corded/cordless telephones) (Federal Communications Commission)." Despite the increasing market for wireless-based communications in the United States, the WCB maintains its large pres-ence in the FCC by "ensuring choice, opportunity, and fairness in the development of wireline tele-communications services and markets (Federal Communications Commission)." In addition to this primary goal, the bureau's objectives include "developing deregulatory initiatives; promoting economically efficient investment in wireline telecommunications services; and fostering economic growth (Federal Communications Commission)." The WCB recently ruled against Comcast regarding blocked online content to the public, causing many to question the amount of authority that the government has over the public and big businesses.

Another prominent bureau within the FCC is the Wireless Telecommunications Bureau (WTB). The rough counterpart of the WCB, this bureau oversees mobile phones, pagers, and two-way radios, handling "all FCC domestic wireless telecommunications programs and policies, except those involving public safety, satellite communications or broadcasting, including licensing, enforcement, and regulatory functions (Federal Communications Commission)." The WTB balances the expansion and limitation of wireless networks, registers antenna and broadband use, and manages the radio frequencies for airplane, ship, and land communication. As U.S. wireless communication continues to grow, this bureau seems likely to continue to increase in both scope and importance.

Finally, the International Bureau is responsible for representing the FCC in all satellite and international matters. A larger organization, the International Bureau's goal is to "connect the globe for the good of consumers through prompt authorizations, innovative spectrum management and responsible global leadership (Federal Communications Commission)." In an effort to avoid international interference, the International Bureau coordinates with partners around the globe regarding frequency allocation and orbital assignments. It also concerns itself with foreign investment in the United States, ruling that outside governments, individuals, or corporations cannot own more than 20 percent of stock in a U.S. broadcast, telephone, or radio company.

## The Structure and Purposes of the FTC

Although the FCC provides most of the nation's media regulations, the FTC also has a hand in the media industry. As previously discussed, the FTC primarily dedicates itself to eliminating unfair business practices; however, in the course of those duties it has limited contact with media outlets.

One example of the FTC's media regulatory responsibility is the National Do Not Call Registry. In 2004, the agency created this registry to prevent most telemarketing phone calls, exempting such groups as nonprofit charities and businesses with which a consumer has an existing relationship. Although originally intended for landline phones, the Do Not Call Registry allows individuals to register wireless telephones along with traditional wire-based numbers.

## Role of Antitrust Legislation

As discussed in, the federal government has long regulated companies' business practices. Over the years, several antitrust acts (law discouraging the formation of monopolies) have been passed into law.

During the 1880s, Standard Oil was the first company to form a trust (a unit of business made up of a board of trustees, formed to monopolize an industry), an "arrangement by which stockholders transferred their shares to a single set of trustees." With corporate trustees receiving profits from the component companies, Standard Oil functioned as a monopoly (a business that economically controls a product or a service). The Sherman Antitrust Act was put into place in 1890 to dissolve trusts such as these. The Act stated that any combination "in the form of trust or otherwise that was in restraint of trade or commerce among the several states, or with foreign nations" was illegal.

The Sherman Antitrust Act served as a precedent for future antitrust regulation. As discussed in , the 1914 Clayton Antitrust Act and the 1950 Celler-Kefauver Act expanded on the principles laid out in the Sherman Act. The Clayton Act helped establish the foundation for many of today's business and media competition regulatory practices. Although the Sherman Act established regulations in the United States, the Clayton Act further developed the rules surrounding antitrust, giving businesses a "fair warning" about the dangers of anticompetitive practice. Specifically, the Clayton Act prohibits actions that may "substantially lessen competition or tend to create a monopoly in any line of commerce."

The problem with the Clayton Act was that, while it prohibited mergers, it offered a loophole in that companies were allowed to buy individual assets of competitors (such as stocks or patents), which could still lead to monopolies. Established in 1950 and often referred to as the Antimerger Act, the Cellar-Kefauver Act closed that loophole by giving the government the power to stop vertical mergers. (Vertical mergers happen when two companies in the same business but on different levels—such as a tire company and a car company—combine.) The act also banned asset acquisitions that reduced competition (Financial Dictionary).

These laws reflected growing concerns in the early and mid-20th century that the trend toward monopolization could lead to the extinction of competition. Government regulation of businesses increased until the 1980s, when the United States experienced a shift in mind-set and citizens called for less governmental power. The U.S. government responded as deregulation became the norm.

## Move Toward Deregulation

Media deregulation actually began during the 1970s as the FCC shifted its approach to radio and television regulation. Begun as a way of clearing laws to make the FCC run more efficiently and cost effectively, deregulation truly took off with the arrival of the Reagan administration and its new FCC chairman, Mark Fowler, in 1981. The FCC began overturning existing rules and experienced "an overall reduction in FCC oversight of station and network operations (Museum of Broadcast Communications)." Between 1981 and 1985, lawmakers dramatically altered laws and regulation to give more power to media licensees and to reduce that of the FCC. Television licenses were expanded from 3 years to 5, and corporations were now allowed to own up to 12 separate TV stations.

The shift in regulatory control had a powerful effect on the media landscape. Whereas initially laws had prohibited companies from owning media entities in more than one medium, consolidation created large mass-media companies that increasingly dominated the U.S. media system. Before the increase in deregulation, eight major companies controlled phone services to different regions of the United States. Companies such as Viacom and Disney own television stations, record companies, and magazines. Bertelsmann alone owns more than 30 radio stations, 280 publishing outlets, and 15 record companies (Columbia Journalism Review). Due to this rapid consolidation, Congress grew concerned about the costs of deregulation, and by the late 1980s, it began to slow the FCC's release of control.

Today, deregulation remains a hotly debated topic. Some favor deregulation, believing that the public benefits from less governmental control. Others, however, argue that excessive consolidation of media ownership threatens the system of checks and balances.[2]Proponents on both sides of the argument are equally vocal, and it is likely that regulation of media will ebb and flow over the years, as it has since regulation first came into practice.

## Qualities of a Good Journalist

Journalistic content is as broad and far-reaching as global economics and as specific as the celebration of your neighbour's 110th birthday, but in any instance it will impart you with a particular impression of the world you live. This impression you are given is based on what is presented to you by journalists, whether it be good or bad, favourable or unsavoury, they have the power to tell the truth or impersonate it.

We have compiled a list with all the important qualities a good journalist should have. If you are planning on pursuing a career in journalism make sure you have these traits.

### A Good Journalist uses his Power to Influence Correctly

Since content is created by people and not some stoic, perfectly impartial, and unbiased entity, there will inevitably be those journalists that will act selfishly and impede the divulgence of the truth. Through this powerful platform these anti-journalistic pursuits can reach a wide number of people. With such an opportunity, some might use it to leverage human emotions that elicit strong reactions, for the purpose of benefitting themselves and their publication. And it's precisely because of the influential nature of journalism that we need good journalists.

As Edward Bernays –the "father of public relations" and a pioneer in the understanding and usage of advertising- has said:

"Small groups of persons can, and do, make the rest of us think what they please about a given subject." Possessing the power of influence can be a dangerous tool at the disposal of those with less than admirable intentions, or those who are simply ignorant and incompetent. Whichever the case, sensationalism, fear mongering, and other biases can be used to misinform, or rather more deviously, manipulate the public to accept an amended truth. Journalists work hard to uncover the truth but ultimately they make the decision to present it as such or not. Without good journalists the truth is only optional.

### A Good Journalist is a Watchdog

Though certain misguided journalists may divert from reality for selfishly prosperous reasons, those in powerful positions in society attempt to cover the truth also. As such we need good journalists that will act boldly as watchdogs, exposing injustice, corruption, and poor decision making on the part of leaders. Those who seek to take advantage of their position at the expense of those they directly impact will continue to do so until they are revealed.

Journalists have a unique perspective and method in addressing this issue. Since they collect information and investigate in a different way than other parties, it's important to have good journalists who will boldly step towards the truth and require from these individuals to answer to their actions. Whatever information is found, good journalists should present the truth in the findings in a neutral way.

## A Good Journalist Acknowledges his Responsibility to Citizens

Journalists give you information that you most likely wouldn't know otherwise. Because of this, there is a level of trust with those journalists, like that of a parent and child. A parent has viewed the world and experienced many things, but the way they react to them and pass on that perspective will influence the way the child perceives the information. In a similar fashion, journalists will pass on either accuracy or their interpretations, or purposely present an untruth or a vast extension of the truth to an audience as part of their agenda. As journalists are one of the very few, if not the only ones, who will disseminate this information as a complete story, whatever they choose to present is usually seen as the truth.

There is a need for bold journalists, unafraid to present the truth. Sometimes the truth is unsavoury or damaging, but despite that, the truth is still paramount. Nothing should be hidden because of self-interest or bias however unfortunate the information - there is a responsibility to the public to show transparency.

There are instances in which journalists need to make important ethical decisions about what they present to the public. For instance, Edward Snowden and journalist Glenn Greenwald worked together to propagate the truth about national security and privacy, which labelled Snowden as a traitor and spy.

Another instance involves Charlie Hebdo murders over the satirical depiction of a religious prophet. There was a debate as to whether such depictions should be shown by media outlets in the name of free speech or omitted entirely.

## A Good Journalist Promotes Public Discussion

The news is called news for a reason. When new, exciting or upsetting things occur people want to know about it to better understand and contribute to the world in which they live. For this reason, publications and the journalists that work for them need to provide a public forum regarding the important events and ideas to promote discussions at all levels.

However, it is not solely about talking. As many of us can attest to, people can talk and often do about the most mundane and inconsequential things, while ignoring the real issues. Journalists, being the presenters of this topical information, should be involved in pinpointing the important topics or aspects of those topics to engage people in relevant conversation about the state of society. This should be for the purpose of progressing society to a place we want it to be and not to achieve the highest number of habitual followers for a publication.

## A Good Journalist Provides Credibility and Expertise

In recent time there has been a disintegration of traditional media outlets and a rise of numerous smaller outlets in its place. There are so many loud voices yelling so many different things, what are viewers, listeners, and readers supposed to believe as truth and what will they ultimately believe as truth?

With so many new, smaller outlets appearing in place of what was once a massive network or newspaper, the credibility of the information may come into question as these outlets are not held to the same standards. We need good journalists to provide credibility and expertise.

With advancements in technology, the dissemination of information is instantaneous and coming from innumerable sources, some without much confirmation of credibility. We need good journalists in society to interpret the vast amounts of available information, understand the context and importance, and sift through the information to determine source integrity. We need good journalists to find the truth in the haystack.

Good journalists are needed to continue a precedent and make sure that in spite of the major changes that may lie ahead for journalism, the journalists' integrity and mission for truth will be untarnished.

By now it should be evident that a "good" journalist is someone who strives for the truth, boldly acts as a watchdog to expose injustice and corruption, creates and maintains public discussion, and someone who sorts through the world of data and puts the important topics into the spotlight.

Bottom line is that we want good journalists just like we want good police officers. They are at the front lines they make decisions that impact our lives as individuals and as members of a society. If we don't have journalists that remain impartial and fair we will live in a world that is even more selfish and confusing because even if we search for the information and desire to learn about our world it could end up all being a farce.

Recommended remedy? Good journalists. Journalists with integrity, intelligence, finger on the pulse of the world, and a desire to live in a transparent and honest society.

## Fake News

The usage and meaning of the term fake news has evolved over time. A Google Trends Analysis of the term reveals a sudden burst in popularity around the time of the 2016 US presidential election.2 Although originally used to reference false and often sensational information disseminated under the guise of news reporting, the term has evolved and become synonymous with the spread of false information. Fake news has generally been defined as "a news article that is intentionally and verifiably false" or "information presented as a news story that is factually incorrect and designed to deceive the consumer into believing it is true". However the existing definitions are narrow, restricted either by the type of information or the intent of deception, and do not capture the broader scope of the term based on its current usage. News article or message published and propagated through media, carrying false information regardless the means and motives behind it.

This definition allows us to capture the different types of fake news identified in which can be differentiated by the means employed to falsify information, such as fabricated content (completely false), misleading content (misleading use of information to frame an issue), imposter content (genuine sources impersonated with false sources), manipulated content (genuine information or imagery manipulated to deceive), false connection (headlines, visuals or captions that do not support the content), and false context (genuine content shared with false contextual information). The definition also allows us to include different types of fake news identified by their motive or intent, such as malicious intent (to hurt or disrepute), profit (for financial gain by increasing views), influence (to manipulate public opinion), sow discord (to create disorder and confusion), passion (to promote ideological biases), amusement (individual entertainment). We can also subdivide false information by intent as misinformation and disinformation. Misinformation refers to unintentionally spread false information which can be a result of misrepresentation or misunderstanding stemming from cognitive biases or lack of understanding or attention; and disinformation refers to false information created and spread specifically with the intention to deceive. Another type of information that might be closely connected to fake news is satire - satire presents stories as news that might be factually incorrect, but the intent is not to deceive but rather to call out, ridicule, or expose behavior that is shameful, corrupt, or otherwise "bad". The intent behind satire seems legitimate enough to exclude it from the definition, however, does include satire as a type of fake news when there is no intention to cause harm but it has potential to mislead or fool people. Also, mentions that there is a spectrum from fake to satirical news which they found to be exploited by many fake news sites, which used disclaimers at the bottom of their webpages to suggest they were "satirical" even when there was nothing satirical about their articles; to protect them from accusations about being fake. Thereby, our definition must include articles that are falsely posed as satire, as well as satirical articles that can potentially mislead, and exclude others that do not fall in this area. Additionally, we disambiguate the terms hoax and rumor which are closely related to fake news. A hoax is considered to be a false story used to masquerade the truth, and, by the traditional definition, fake news can be seen as a form of hoax usually spread through news outlets. The term rumor refers to unsubstantiated claims that are disseminated with the lack of evidence to support them. This makes them very similar to fake news, with the main difference being that they are not necessarily false, and may turn out to be true. Rumors originate from unverified sources but may later be verified as true or false, or remain unresolved. Thereby, our definition can be seen as naturally encompassing hoaxes and false rumors.

## Nature/Characteristics

The definition of fake news is not the only thing that has changed with time. With the growth of computer-mediated communication through social media, we can see that the nature and characteristics of the problem have also evolved. Hence, we start by reviewing the literature from sociology and psychologically that explain the existence and spread of fake news at both an individual and social level.

1. Individual level: The inability of an individual to accurately discern fake from true news leads to the continued sharing and believing of false information in social media. YouGov 2017 found in a survey of 1684 British adults who were shown six individual news stories, three of which were true and three of which were fake, only 4 percent were able to identify them all correctly. The inability to discern has been attributed to cognitive abilities and ideological biases. Pennycook and Rand 2018 identified a positive correlation between propensity for analytical thinking and the ability to discern false from true information. In addition, Allcott and Gentzkow 2017 observed that people who spend more time consuming media, people with higher education, and older people had more accurate perceptions of information. The results were statistically

significant in a survey of 1208 US adults. Another study examined the impact of cognitive ability on the durability of opinions to find that individuals with lower cognitive ability adjusted their assessments after being told that the information given was incorrect, but not nearly to the same extent as those with higher cognitive ability. Besides cognitive abilities, ideological priors play an important role in information consumption. Naive realism (individuals tend to more easily believe information that is aligned with their views), confirmation bias (individuals seek out and prefer to receive information that confirms their existing views), and normative influence theory (individuals choose to share and consume socially safe options as a preference for social acceptance and affirmation) are generally regarded as important factors in the perception and sharing of fake news. The survey by Allcott and Gentzkow 2017 also found with statistical significance that people (Democrats and Republicans) are respectively, 17.2 and 14.7 percent more likely to believe ideologically aligned articles than they are to believe nonaligned articles, although the differences in magnitude across the two groups (Democrats and Republicans) are not statistically significant. These individual vulnerabilities have been exploited to successfully disseminate fake information. Higgins 2016 declared this era as an era of "post-truth" wherein objective facts are less influential in shaping public opinion than appeals to emotions and personal beliefs.

2. Social level: The nature of social media and collaborative information sharing on online platforms provides an additional dimension to fake news popularly called the echo chamber effect. The principles of naive realism, confirmation bias and normative influence theory of essentially imply the need for individuals to seek, consume and share information that is aligned with their own views and ideologies. As a consequence, individuals tend to form connections with ideologically similar individuals (social homophily), and algorithms tend to personalize recommendations (algorithmic personalization) by recommending content that suits an individual's preferences, as well as by recommending connections to similar individuals to befriend or follow. Both social homophily and algorithmic personalization lead to the formation of echo chambers and filter bubbles, wherein individuals get less exposure to conflicting viewpoints and become isolated in their own information bubble. The existence of echo chambers can improve the chances of survival and spread of fake news which can be explained by the phenomena of social credibility and frequency heuristic, where social credibility suggests that people's perception of credibility of a piece of information increases if others also perceive it as credible; and frequency heuristic refers to the increase in people's perception of credibility with multiple exposures to the same information. Gillani et al. 2018 examined a network of 1.1 M Twitter users who participated in conversations about the US 2016 presidential election between June-September 2016 and observed the existence of echo chambers and polarization of views based on the political orientation (democratic and republic) as visualized in figure that shows the follower relationships (edges) between users marked by the color of their political orientation (which is inferred from a user's profile and tweet contents as per). Quattrociocchi et al. 2016 similarly studied polarization by scientific v/s conspiracy narratives in Facebook users and observed that although both types of information were consumed similarly overall, 76.79% of all users who interacted on scientific pages and 91.53% of all users who interacted with conspiracy posts had 95% of their likes on either science or conspiracy posts. In addition, polarized users had a higher number of friends who displayed the same behaviour; and higher edge homogeneity, measuring the similarity between friends in the network, suggested that it is highly unlikely that information would propagate across the different groups.

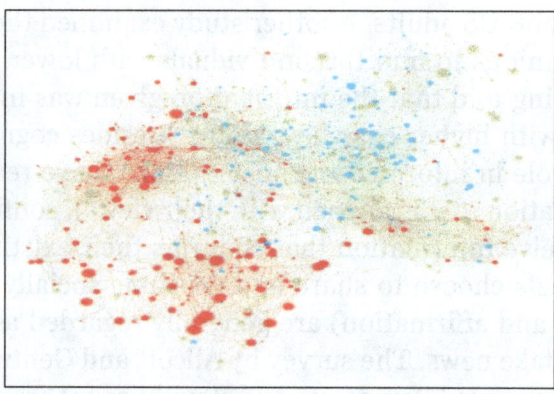

In above figure Nodes represent a sample of about 900 Twitter accounts that participated in the conversation about the US Presidential Election between June and mid-September 2016, and edges represent mutual-follower relationships between these accounts. Nodes are sized according to relative PageRank importance in the depicted network, and colored according to inferred political ideology (red: right-leaning, blue: left-leaning, white: unsure).

Fake news diffusion patterns on social media have often been studied to identify the characteristics of fake news that can help differentiate it from true news. Fake news detection works essentially rely on exploiting these differences to classify information based on its veracity. Most existing works primarily target the classification as a binary classification task (fake/true, rumor/non-rumor, hoax/non-hoax) or as a multi-class classification task (true/mostly true/half true/mostly false/false, unverified rumor/true rumor/false rumor/non-rumor). The main difference in different task settings is due to different annotation schemes or applications contexts in different datasets. Usually the datasets are collected from annotated claims on fact-checking websites such as PolitiFact, Snopes and others and therefore reflect the labeling scheme used by the particular fact-checking website/organization. In some instances, credibility scores are provided based on human annotator judgments instead of class labels. In the remainder of this topic, we examine different characteristics of fake news that are utilized for detection. We can identify three primary characteristics relevant for fake news detection, namely the source/promoters of the information, the information content, and the user responses it receives on social media.

3. Source/promoters: Zimdars 2016 maintains a list of web addresses of fake news websites; several of which are modified names of true news websites, such as "abcnews.com.co" and "washingtonsblog.com". The use of such misleading domain names are a particular characteristic of fake news sources which individuals must learn to recognize and be attentive about. However, there are two caveats to filtering information based solely on these lists. One is that not all articles from these sources are fake and the other is that the list can never be exhaustive. In particular, the use of online resources and social media make it very easy, convenient and inexpensive to create bots and register new accounts or domains. Bots are fake or compromised accounts controlled by humans or programs to introduce and promote information on social media. Subrahmanian et al. 2016 found a significant overlap between follower and followees of bot accounts that spread false information, which helps to engineer virality and credibility of posts and inflate the social status of the bot accounts. Davis et al. 2016 found that on Twitter large number of bot accounts were responsible for accelerating the speed of both true and false information roughly equally. Shu et al. 2018 randomly sampled 10,000 users who posted fake and real news on

Twitter and used the bot detection algorithm by to find that almost 22% of users involved in fake news are bots, while only around 9% of users are predicted as bot users for real news. They also investigated the temporal patterns of account activities by capturing the relationship between number of posts on Twitter at different times and days of the week for posts related to fake and true news; and observed that periods of high posting activity included odd hours when people are generally inactive, suggesting the existence of social bots. The temporal patterns observed by Shu et al. 2018 are shown in Figure below. Lastly, analyzing how source and promoters of fake news operate over the web across multiple online platforms, Zannettou et al. 2018 found that false information is more likely to spread across platforms (18% appearing on multiple platforms) compared to true information (11%), with Reddit to Twitter to 4chan being the most common direction of information flow.

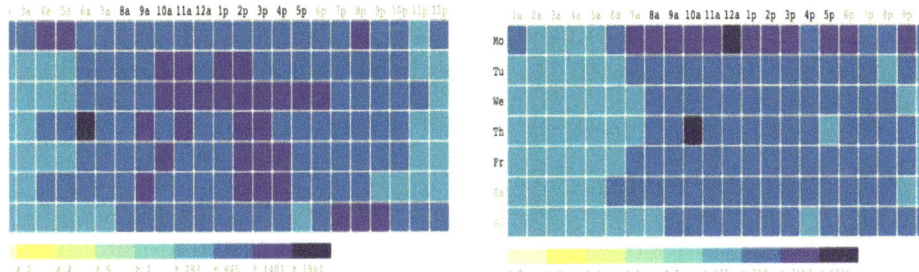

The heatmap of the day of week vs hour of tweets posted related to fake news (left) and real news (right). Darker colors indicate greater posting activity in a particular time slot.

4. Information content: The content of the information being spread is primarily what needs to be classified as true or fake. Horne and Adali 2017 identified certain characteristics that differentiate fake news contents from true news contents by studying the textual characteristics of articles from various fake news websites and contrasting them with articles from reputed journalistic websites. Their findings suggest that titles of fake news articles are longer, have more capitalized words, and use fewer stop words; and the body content of fake news articles are shorter, repetitive, have fewer nouns, and analytical and technical words. Pérez-Rosas et al. 2017 found that fake news articles contained more social words, with more verbs and temporal words suggesting that the text tends to be focused on the present and future, instead of being more objective and factual. Other textual cues include self-reference, negation statements, complaints, and generalizing items. Newman et al. 2003 analysis revealed that deceptive stories had lower cognitive complexity, fewer exclusive words, more negative emotion words, and more motion (action) words. Silverman 2015 observed that 13% of 1600 news articles had incoherent headlines and content, and used declarative headlines paired with article bodies which are skeptical about the claim in the headline.

5. User responses: User responses on social media provide auxiliary information that is extremely beneficial for fake news detection. They are known to provide stronger signals for detection than the information content, mainly because user responses and propagation patterns are harder to manipulate than the information content, and oftentimes contain obvious information about the veracity. This secondary information in the form of user engagements (likes, shares, replies or comments) contains rich information captured in the propagation structure (tree) which indicates the path of information flow, temporal information in timestamps of engagements, textual information in user comments, and user profile information by the user involved in the engagement.

Zubiaga note that it is possible to differentiate user responses by their stance, wherein the most commonly used categorization uses the following four types, namely, supporting, denying, querying and commenting (which can be neutral or unrelated). They also observe that the nature of user responses varies depending on the stages of propagation, where, in the case of rumors, it was observed that majority of the users support true rumors and a higher number deny false rumors when the entire life cycle of the rumor was considered; whereas by studying only the early reactions to rumors, it was found that users showed a tendency to support rumors independent of their veracity, which is suggestive of the fact that users have problems determining veracity in the early stages. Qian similarly found that fake news tends to receive more negative and questioning responses than true news. Another analysis of true and fake news captured the variation of sentiments in user replies, wherein it was observed that sentiment in replies to true news tended more towards neutral, in contrast to that for fake news that tended more towards negative sentiments. Friggeri also found from an analysis of user responses on Facebook, that user responses change once false information is debunked, with a 4.4 times increase in deletion probability, even in early stages of the propagation.

## Information Exchange Process

There are several different entities (individuals and organizations) that are simultaneously at play when it comes to the dissemination, moderation and consumption of fake news through social media, which makes the problem of identification and mitigation more complex and involved. We discuss each part of the information exchange process.

- Dissemination- A noticeable shift in information dissemination channels from traditional forms of journalism to online social media has been observed. In a survey of 3,000 journalists, 20%, responded that they thought that social media spelled the death of journalism. Social media sites have become the popular form of dissemination due to growing ease of access and popularity of computer-mediated communication. Fake news can have a larger impact through social media due to the large scale and reach of social media; and the ability to collaboratively share content.

- Moderation- While in traditional forms of journalism the responsibility of content creation rests with the journalist and the reporting organization, moderation in social media varies substantially. In 2017, Germany passed the NetzDG (Network Enforcement) Act5 to enforce removal of fake news within 24 hours (or up to a week depending on the complexity) by social media platforms with more than two million users. In UK, the parliament launched an investigation into how fake news is threatening modern democracy. Nevertheless, the question of distribution of responsibility remains unresolved. A recent survey by Barthel et al. 2016 determined that Americans collectively assign a fairly high and equal amount (45%) of responsibility to the government/politicians, social media platforms/search engines, and lastly, members of the public; and specifically 15% hold all three responsible, while 27% hold two and 31% hold one of three responsible.

- Consumption- Information is primarily consumed by the general public or society which is a growing body of social media users. In a 2018 survey on social media usage with 2002 US adults surveyed, established that 68% Americans use of Facebook, 73% use Youtube and between 20-40% use other social media platforms such as Twitter and Instagram, and the numbers have grown almost ten-fold since 2005. Smith and Anderson 2018 also established that 74% of the Facebook users use the site daily, with 51% using it several times a day; and a large fraction of frequent users lie in the 18-29 range. This growth in information consumption through social media adds to the risks of fake news causing wide-spread damage.

## Key Players

We now consider a more subtle aspect that usually characterizes fake news, that is, the intent to deceive. In this light, we discuss the different roles that entities (individuals and organizations) play when it comes to dealing with fake news.

- Adversary- Malicious individuals and organizations with a political or social agenda often pose as ordinary social media users using social bots or actual accounts and can act as the source as well as promoters of fake news. Such accounts are known to also indulge in group behavior wherein groups of such accounts coordinate and share the same set of fake news articles.

- Fact-checker- In an attempt to combat the growing amount of false information, various fact-checking organizations, such as Snopes and Politifact, have been initiated to expose or confirm news stories. While these organizations are based on "fact-checking journalism", that relies on human verification, more desirable automated technological solutions have been proposed by technological companies like Factmata which aim to provide fake news detection solutions to businesses and consumers and assign credibility scores to web content using artificial intelligence. Various other automated solutions in the form of plug-ins and applications such as BS-Detector and CrossCheck provide similar automated fact-checking services. An exhaustive list of fact-checking applications is provided in.

- Susceptible- Fake news affects a wide range of individuals and organizations based on the motive. We summarized different motives or intents behind the spread of fake news. For instance, reputable institutions and individuals might be susceptible to the attacks of fake news that is intended to sway public opinion about them, such as what was witnessed during the US 2016 presidential election. Other consequences can even prove to be an increased risk to the entire world. Roozenbeek and van der Linden 2018 noted that false information discrediting the seriousness of global warming can affect people's perception of climate change, posing a great risk to society and the world at large.

## Challenges

The nature of the problem presents several challenges, which we summarize as follows:

- High stakes and multiple players- The World Economic Forum (2013) has ranked the spread of false information as one of the "top risks" the world is facing today. Moreover, the involvement of multiple entities and technological platforms increases the difficulty of studying and designing computational, technological and business strategies, without compromising rapid and collaborative access to high quality information.

- Adversarial intent-Malicious intent in content design and promotion increases the complexity of the problem. The content is designed to not only make it harder for humans to identify fake news by exploiting their cognitive abilities, emotions and ideological biases, but also to make it more challenging for computational methods to detect fake news. Shu evaluated the performance of several different methods on two datasets from Politi Fact and Gossip Cop and reported a maximum detection accuracy of 69% and 79.6% respectively, even when using both article contents and social context i.e. user responses to the article on Twitter.

- Public susceptibility and lack of awareness- To raise public awareness, numerous articles and blogs have been written that provide tips on differentiating truth from falsehood. For example, award-wining journalist Laura McClure highlighted five important questions to ask yourself when trying to determine whether a news article is true or fake. In one of the questions, McClure asked the reader to consider how an article makes them feel, citing that fake news is often "designed to make you feel strong emotions". Articles such as McClure's are informative and effective for individuals; however, they do not provide a scalable and systematic solution to the problem.

- Propagation dynamics- The dynamic nature of the process of fake news propagation through social media further complicates matters. False information can easily reach and impact a large number of users in short time. Friggeri studied rumor cascades on Facebook and found that information is readily and rapidly transmitted, even when it is of dubious veracity. Fact-checking organizations like Snopes and Politifact cannot keep up with the propagation dynamics as they require human verification which inhibits a timely and cost-effective response.

- Constant change- Fast-paced developments in the world pose additional challenges to knowledge base systems which need to dynamically retrieve and update their state based on newly emerging facts. Fact-checking is ultimately essential for reliably identifying fake news. For example, while scandals are not uncommon among celebrities, when a new scandal about a celebrity comes out, without enough extra knowledge, it is very difficult to tell whether it is fake or not. Potthast note that style-based fake news detection i.e. differentiating fake and true news by an analysis of writing styles are simply alternatives used due to the unresolved challenges in automating fact-checking from knowledge bases.

## Requirements/Goals

Existing works have demonstrated significant progresses towards alleviating some of the challenges in fake news detection and mitigation. However, there is still room for improvement before the problem can be addressed in more effective ways. We suggest few requirements that are of interest in developing solutions to tackle fake news.

- Balancing aggressive and non-aggressive moderation- Identification and mitigation techniques that require very aggressive moderation by social media platforms can hurt the social media platform. Thereby, it seems necessary to design strategies that still effectively mitigate the problem of fake news, but without restricting rapid access to high quality information, and collaborative information sharing. We believe that it is also important that the moderation strategies do not further introduce more confusion and distrust into the environment. Fake news has already resulted in people becoming skeptical of even true information, which hurts the value of social media as a platform for information sharing. A survey of 1002 Us adults found that (64%) people say that fake news has caused a great deal of confusion about the basic facts of current issues and events, 24% say it has caused some confusion and 11% say not much/no confusion.

- End-to-end solutions- Reliable and timely detection of fake news should be accompanied by computational methods to intervene and prevent further spread of news that is confirmed as fake. In addition, it would be desirable to design interventions that can provide quantifiable measures of the impact of the intervention effort in terms of the exposures to fake and true news.

- Balancing timeliness v/s detection accuracy- Early detection and mitigation are critical goals of any effective system. However, the available information for detection increases as time progresses, with only the content of the article being available at the start, followed by increasing user responses as propagation continues. Most existing methods either rely on content only or on user responses only, or do not utilize responses incrementally. Detection systems must aim to utilize incrementally available information to trade-off confidence in detection accuracy v/s timeliness of the detection and mitigation effort.

- Prioritization and cost-effectiveness- The ability to optimally decide which contents to fact-check at what time, can equip the system in providing better responses by being able to quickly remove false information that can have a potentially larger and faster impact than those that might have a negligible or slower impact if allowed to propagate further in time. Also, human involvement in fact-checking increases not only the delay but also the cost of intervention, which necessitates the need for prioritization of information to manually fact-check, until reliable automated methods can be sought.

- Robustness, scalability and interpretability- The high stakes and consequences of fake news necessitate the need for reliability in detection. Mistakenly removing true information from the platform, or not detecting and removing potentially viral false information would become problematic in practice. To move from manual and semi-automated solutions to fully automated ones will not be possible without robust and also interpretable predictions. Popat emphasized transparency and interpretability in credibility assessment systems and built CredEye which verifies an input claim and provides the probability of truth and falsehood along with extracted evidence (from fact-checking or trusted news websites) with words that support the claim highlighted in green, refuting the claim highlighted in red and words overlapping with the claim provided in yellow, and the intensity of colors reflects the word's importance for the assessment (based on feature weights from the learned classifier).

- Evolution and up-to-date fact-checking- The adversarial nature of fake news necessitates that the system should be able to dynamically adapt to the changing strategies of adversarial opponents. Specifically, adversaries create new accounts and throw-away accounts to promote fake news and avoid detection, as can be seen in an instance of the US election when potentially large number of fake accounts were created to influence the election and were found to initiate coordinated attacks with specific political agendas. In addition, increased sophistication in adversarial techniques are speculated in terms of both fake content creation, as well as in strategies to promote fake content. Ruchansky observed from behaviours of suspicious users on Twitter, that these users had more similar engagement patterns towards true and fake news than on Weibo, which could demonstrate an increased sophistication in fake content promotion on Twitter.

## Six Ways to Spot Fake News

Separating fact from fiction accurately can seem daunting. But getting to the truth is always worth the effort – even if it's not what you want to hear! Use these six steps to weed out the truth from the lies:

1. Develop a critical mindset: One of the main reasons fake news is such a big issue is that it is often believable, which means it's easy to get caught out. Many fake news stories are also written to create "shock" value. This means it's essential that you keep your emotional response to such stories in check. Instead, approach what you see and hear rationally and critically. Ask yourself, "Why has this story been written? Is it to persuade me of a certain viewpoint? Is it selling me a particular product? Or is it trying to get me to click through to another website?"

2. Check the source: If you come across a story from a source that you've never heard of before, do some digging! Find out a bit more about the publisher – is it a professional and well-known news agency or is it someone's personal blog? Check the URL of the page, too. (A URL, or Uniform Resource Locator, is a web address that helps browsers to find a site on the internet.) Strange-sounding URLs that end in extensions like ".infonet" and ".offer," rather than ".com" or ".co.uk," or that contain spelling errors, may mean that the source is suspect. If the information is something that you've been told by another person, consider his reputation and professional experience. Is he known for his expertise on the matter? Or does he tend to exaggerate the truth?

3. See who else is reporting the story: Check whether the story has been picked up by other well-known news publishers. Stories from organizations like Reuters, CNN and the BBC, will have been checked and verified beforehand. If the information you have isn't from a well-known source like these, there's a chance that it could be fake. However, you need to be careful even here. People who spread fake news and "alternative facts" sometimes create web pages, newspaper mockups, or "doctored" images that look official, but aren't. So, if you see a suspicious post that looks like it's from CNN, for example, check CNN's homepage to verify that it's really there.

4. Examine the evidence: A credible news story will include plenty of facts – quotes from experts, survey data and official statistics, for example. If these are missing or the source is an unknown expert or a "friend," question it. Does the evidence prove that something definitely happened? Or, have the facts been "twisted" to back up a particular viewpoint?

5. Look for fake images: Modern editing software has made it easy for people to create fake images that look professional and real. In fact, research shows that only half of us can tell when images are fake. However, there are some warning signs you can look out for. Strange shadows on the image, for example, or jagged edges around a figure. If you still have doubts, you can use tools such as Google Reverse Image Search to check whether the image has been altered or used in the wrong context.

6. Check that it "Sounds Right": Finally, use your common sense! If a story sounds unbelievable, it probably is. Bear in mind that fake news is designed to "feed" your biases or fears. And, remember, just because a story sounds "right" and true, doesn't mean that it is. For example, it's unlikely that your favorite designer brand is giving away a million free dresses to people who turn up to its stores. Equally, just because your colleague believes that two married co-workers are having an affair, doesn't mean it's true.

## References

- Ethicscode: spj.org, Retrieved 2 August, 2019

- "Truth and the Media" (PDF). (50.1 KB) Dean, Catherine. Strathmore University Ethics Conference, 2006 (see p. 11, Harm limitation principle) Retrieved on June 9, 2009

- Government-regulation-of-media, suny-hccc-massmedia: lumenlearning.com, Retrieved 12 February, 2019

- Top-5-qualities-of-good-journalists: careeraddict.com, Retrieved 22 July, 2019

- Fake-news: mindtools.com, Retrieved 19 January, 2019

# Permissions

# Index

CPSIA information can be obtained
at www.ICGtesting.com
Printed in the USA
BVHW011557160820
586552BV00003B/129